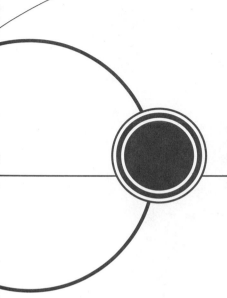

PROGRAMMING GAMES WITH
MICROSOFT® VISUAL BASIC® 6.0

Catherine Muir Dwyer and Jeanine Meyer

**COURSE
TECHNOLOGY**

THOMSON LEARNING™

Australia   Canada   Mexico   Singapore   Spain   United Kingdom   United States

COURSE TECHNOLOGY
TM
THOMSON LEARNING

Programming Games with Microsoft® Visual Basic® 6.0
by Catherine Muir Dwyer and Jeanine Meyer

Senior Product Manager:
Jennifer Muroff

Managing Editor:
Jennifer Locke

Senior Acquisitions Editor:
Christine Guivernau

Development Editor:
Amanda Brodkin

Editorial Assistant:
Janet Aras

Production Editor:
Danielle Power
Catherine DiMassa

Cover Designer:
Abigail Scholz

Compositor:
GEX Publishing Services

Manufacturing Coordinator:
Alexander Schall

Disclaimer
Course Technology reserves the right to revise this publi-cation and make changes from time to time in its content without notice.

ISBN 0-619-03561-7

⊙ PREFACE

Programming Games with Microsoft Visual Basic 6.0 gives the beginning and intermediate-level programmer the tools needed to create complete Visual Basic applications. This book's focus is on development of logic and interface design. The book can be used by itself or with a standard Visual Basic text. We have found in our teaching of programming at several levels that oftentimes, the typical exercises in textbooks do not interest students and are ineffective because they are too simplistic or too contrived. These shortcomings fail to prepare the student to do actual work. Our games prepare students by challenging their critical thinking skills as well as providing motivation and guidance in the use of general programming techniques. Using a game theme keeps students interested and motivated. The projects in this book will be useful both to students who want an introduction to programming as well as students who plan to go on to study other programming languages, systems analysis, and systems design.

APPROACH

Programming Games with Microsoft Visual Basic 6.0 provides a framework around which students create customized game applications. The book provides explanations of the interface and its required elements, player and computer actions, and logic required to create an effective game. The book also provides specific examples of code for the algorithms, event procedures, and user-defined procedures that are required in each game. *Programming Games with Microsoft Visual Basic 6.0* is not a step-by-step guide for creating cookie-cutter applications; it is up to the student to use the guidelines provided in the text to put together a working application. There is no single "right" way to program any of the games in this book.

ORGANIZATION AND COVERAGE

Software development begins with an analysis of an application's intended purpose, or functionality. Using games as the theme of this text provides familiar functionality with rules that are easily grasped. This makes the process of analysis and design a manageable one.

Visual Basic is a good programming language for beginners because it facilitates the creation of an interactive system. Although Visual Basic eases the development of interactive games, it is still quite a challenge to create *successful* applications. Creating a successful user interface is still more art than science, and requires an understanding of graphics design and the established practices of Windows based-software These subjects are covered in the development of each of the chapters' games.

Each chapter includes:

- A description of the concepts, skills, and tools covered in the chapter, including the Visual Basic features and the general programming techniques used in the game

- Background on the game or activity, with screen shots

- A Key Design Issues list of the critical tasks required to build the game, with a brief description of the logic and solutions proposed for these tasks

- A Preparing to Program section containing an explanation of the use of the Visual Basic features and programming techniques used in each game

- A Plan for the User Interface section and Form Design section, with annotated figures showing the forms used in each game

- Variables and Constants Declared in the **(General)** Section

- Algorithms for Event Procedures and Algorithms for User-Defined Procedures, including step-by-step descriptions and code examples

- Optional Enhancements, which challenge and recommend new ways users can improve their projects

- Discussion Questions, including ideas for alternative implementations and more substantial enhancements

FEATURES

Programming Games with Microsoft Visual Basic 6.0 is a superior textbook because it challenges and guides the user in the construction of projects requiring attention to logic and graphical design. It includes the following features:

- "Read This Before You Begin" section. This section is consistent with Course Technology's unequaled commitment to helping instructors introduce technology into the classroom. Technical considerations and assumptions about hardware, software, and default settings are listed in one place to help instructors save time.

- Game-based project approach. Each chapter addresses a complete programming and design challenge that is at once familiar, challenging, and fun. The user will gain skills and experiences that can be implemented for applications in business and elsewhere and prepare students for other programming environments.

- A variety of activities, challenging the student designer/programmer to create a computer version of an existing game. In many cases, this requires a balance between replicating the look and feel of a manual activity with making best use of the computer interface. The chapters include:

    - Games of luck (Rock, Paper, Scissors and a dice game we call Chance)
    - A game requiring player recall (Memory, also called Concentration)
    - An activity involving design (Mix and Match Cartoons)
    - Games of skill (guessing words in Hangman, spatial relations in Cannonball, general knowledge in Quiz, logic in Minesweeper and Tic Tac Toe)

- Presentation of features and techniques in the context of a real use. Many textbooks present features without a compelling use and avoid problems that require intricate logic. The projects here are intriguing and fun. We challenge the student to program the necessary actions of the computer.

- A pedagogical approach in which features and techniques are introduced first as solutions for critical design requirements. The "Preparing to Program" section contains explanations of each feature and technique. The reader then sees the features and techniques in use in the detailed explanations of the design of the graphical interface and the programming of the procedures.

- Introduction to professional programming techniques. The text reveals how professional programmers make decisions about data representation, definition of user-defined procedures, use of techniques such as parallel structures, and dividing an implementation into stages.

- Opportunities for users to use their creative, artistic, and programming skills to produce enhanced versions of the games. This is extremely valuable in situations where students with a variety of backgrounds take a course.

THE VISUAL BASIC ENVIRONMENT

This book was written using Microsoft Visual Basic Version 6.0 Professional Edition installed on a personal computer running Microsoft Windows 2000.

Data files for this text are found in the downloads section of www.course.com. The Data files provide a directory that contains folders for each chapter. The chapter folders contain:

- An .exe file to allow the student/reader to play each game and to see the final form of the screens.
- Image files for the following projects: Mix and Match Cartoons (Chapter 2), Chance (Chapter 3), Memory (Chapter 4), and Hangman (Chapter 5). Users are encouraged to use their own images. However, these files are available for use, if necessary.

The Solutions files contain:

- Visual Basic files: the source code and form designs for all projects.

The names of the files associated with each chapter are listed in the "Read This Before You Begin" section.

ACKNOWLEDGEMENTS

Our appreciation goes to the reviewers and members of the Course Technology team who helped guide the book's development and production. Thanks to Senior Acquisitions Editor Christine Guivernau and Senior Product Manager Jennifer Muroff for their early, encouraging support of this project.

Thanks to reviewer Peter MacIntyre for his technical feedback and to Course Technology Quality Assurance tester Nicole Ashton for her input and patience on this project.

We especially want to thank Amanda Brodkin for her valuable suggestions and efforts as our development editor. We regret her bad dreams involving hangings and being shot from a cannon while subjected to gravity and trigonometry.

Both authors would also like to acknowledge the support of the faculty and administration of Pace University, especially Susan Merritt, John Molluzzo, Ken Norz, Andrea Taylor, and Carol Wolf.

Cathy Dwyer would like to thank her husband Jim, her children Catherine and Maura, her parents Catherine and Robert Muir, and extended family for their love, support, and encouragement throughout the writing of this text.

Jeanine Meyer thanks her parents, Esther and Joseph Minkin, sister Anne Kellerman, and children, Daniel and Aviva, for their encouragement, support and company. Her children would not play a game until it had a best scores feature.

Both authors thank their students, who piloted much of this material and contributed valuable feedback.

—Cathy Dwyer and Jeanine Meyer

To the User

Terminology

In this text, we, the authors, think of you, the user/reader, as the designer and programmer of these projects. For example, we often refer to "your code." We call the person who will play the game (using your work) the player. Of course, you will also use your projects, while you are testing it and also for fun. You may also be the player for the games produced by your classmates.

Data Files

Your instructor may provide Data files to accompany this book. The Data files will be helpful for you in your creation of these projects. Each chapter of the book has its own folder, titled Ch1, Ch2, and so on. Each chapter folder includes an executable file of each project. Sample sets of image files for the projects that require images are also provided. Of course, you can also create your own versions of the image files or acquire images from other sources. Full explanations of these files can be found in the appropriate chapter. Note: Chapter 7 uses an Access database. If you are running Access 2000 and choose to create your own database, you will need to convert it to an Access 97 format to retain compatability with Visual Basic 6.0. To convert an Access 2000 database to Access 97, in your database program, open the Tools menu, then select Database Utilities, Convert Database, Prior Access Database version.

Chapter folder	File(s)	Explanation
Ch1	rps.exe	Executable form of the Rock, Paper, Scissors game
Ch2	mixed.exe	Executable form of the Mix and Match Cartoon activity
	puffy.gif top.gif happy.gif sad.gif round.gif square.gif shoes1.gif toes.gif	Eight pictures of parts of cartoon figures
Ch 3	chance.exe	Executable form of the Chance game
	die1.bmp die2.bmp die3.bmp die4.bmp die5.bmp die6.bmp	Six .bmp files of die images

Ch4	memory.exe	Executable form of the Memory game
	blank.bmp	blank image
	ethiopia.bmp ghana.bmp guinea.bmp malagass.bmp morocco.bmp namibia.bmp senegal.bmp sierleon.bmp	Eight .bmp files of country flags. These must be in the same folder as the executable file to run the game.
Ch5	hangman.exe	Executable form of the Hangman game
	blank.bmp	File of blank space
	hang1.bmp hang2.bmp hang3.bmp hang4.bmp hang5.bmp	Sequence of five images depicting the steps of the hanging
Ch6	ball.exe	Executable form of the Cannonball program
Ch7	quiz.exe	Executable form of the Quiz game
	quiz.mdb	Access 97 database with (initial) quiz questions and answers
Ch8	minesweeper.exe	Executable form of the minesweeper game
	preminesweeper.exe	Executable form of a preliminary exercise
Ch9	tictactoe.exe	Executable form of the Tic Tac Toe game
	tictactoestage1.exe	Executable form of a simpler Tic Tac Toe game
Ch10	bestscores.exe	Executable form of the Best Scores project
	best.dat	Initial database for Best Scores project

Using Your Own Computer

You can use your own computer to work on these projects. You will need the following:

- Software: Microsoft Visual Basic Version 6.0 Professional Edition, Microsoft Access 97

- Hardware: A personal computer running Windows 95, Windows 98, Windows NT 4.0, or Windows 2000

- Data files: You can get the files from your instructor or download them from the Course Technology Web site at www.course.com. The Data files are not necessary to complete the projects in the book; they are provided to show you how the completed projects should work. You can create your own image files.

Visit Our World Wide Web Site

Additional materials designed especially for you might be available for your course on the World Wide Web. Go to www.course.com. Search for this book title periodically on the Course Technology Web site for more details.

TO THE INSTRUCTOR

You must decide how much help to give your students to complete these projects. The solutions files contain the source files, that is, the Visual Basic files for all projects. You may choose to show or share some of these materials with your students.

COURSE TECHNOLOGY DATA FILES

You are granted a license to copy the Data files to any computer or computer network used by students who have purchased this book.

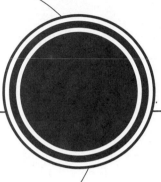

BRIEF CONTENTS

3

4

CONTENTS

6

7

CONTENTS

9

CONSTRUCTION PLAN FOR
ROCK, PAPER, SCISSORS

1

○ CONCEPTS, SKILLS, AND TOOLS

In this chapter, you will create a computer version of the childhood choosing game known as "Rock, Paper, Scissors"—a hand game used to make selections or resolve conflicts. It is usually played by two people; in this version, the game is played between the computer and a human player.

Programming this game will give you experience displaying text on a Visual Basic form and creating automatic program responses to user input entered using command buttons. These two features are common to most Visual Basic applications. You can create this game using two types of Visual Basic objects—labels and command buttons—and one decision structure, known as a Select Case statement. This version displays the player's and the computer's choices using words rather than shapes. The player clicks one of three buttons labeled "Rock," "Paper," or "Scissors" to make a choice. The computer then makes a choice, and the game's outcome appears on the screen.

You will use the following general programming concepts, skills, and tools in the Rock, Paper, Scissors construction plan:

- A form that contains the user interface
- Label controls for changing game information and for labeling that information
- Command buttons for operations of the game

The Visual Basic features used to construct this game include:
- The Click event procedure
- Select Case statements
- Randomize and Rnd functions

DESCRIPTION OF THE GAME

"Rock, Paper, Scissors" refers to the three choices a player can indicate through hand gestures. The game needs two players. The players face each other, call out "Rock, paper, scissors, shoot," then both players simultaneously make hand shapes to indicate their choice: rock (a fist), paper (a flat hand), or scissors (a V shape with two fingers). The rules for determining a win are:

- Rock breaks scissors—rock wins

- Paper covers rock—paper wins

- Scissors cut paper—scissors wins

If both players choose the same thing, the result is a tie, and typically the players keep playing until one player wins.

HOW THIS VERSION OF ROCK, PAPER, SCISSORS WORKS

The version you will program matches a human player against the computer. The player makes a selection by clicking the Rock button, Paper button, or Scissors button, and then the game generates a choice for the computer. To be fair, the game ignores the player's selection when making a choice for the computer. If the game didn't do that, it wouldn't be much of a contest. You can experiment with the game by running the **rps.exe** file, found in your Ch1 folder.

SAMPLE SCREENS

Figures 1 and 2 show an example of a possible game sequence. The player can choose Rock, Paper, or Scissors by clicking the appropriate button. In the scenario shown in Figure 1, the player chooses "Rock."

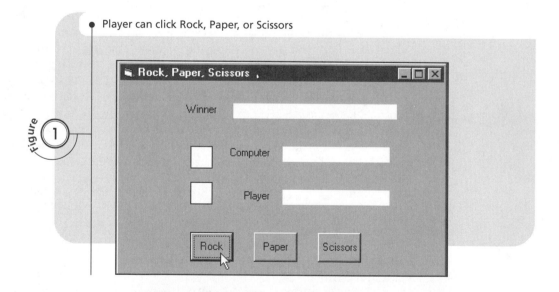

Figure 1

The game then displays the word "Rock" in the label marked "Player." Next, the game generates a choice for the computer (the exact process undertaken will be explained later). The computer chooses Scissors, and the word "Scissors" is placed in the label marked "Computer." According to the rules of the game, "Rock breaks scissors," so the player wins. The game places an X in the box next to the Player label, and the phrase "Rock breaks scissors" appears in the label marked "Winner," as shown in Figure 2.

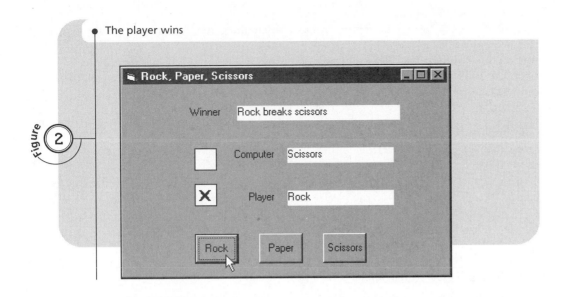

The player wins

Figure 2

CONSTRUCTION PLAN FOR ROCK, PAPER, SCISSORS

KEY DESIGN ISSUES

There are four key design tasks you—the designer and programmer—must accomplish when creating the Rock, Paper, Scissors game:

• Design the user interface to allow the player to input a choice

• Generate a choice for the computer

• Determine the winner

• Display the results

Solutions to each of these programming tasks are presented in the next section. Use these suggestions as guidelines when programming your version of Rock, Paper, Scissors.

Task: Design the user interface to allow the player to input a choice.
Logic: The player must choose between three options: Rock, Paper, or Scissors. Your design must make it clear to the player how to make that choice, and make it easy for the game to capture, or recognize, that choice. The winner is decided by comparing the player's choice to the computer's choice. When the player clicks a button, the game needs to be able to recognize the player's choice.
Solution: Put three command buttons on the screen, with captions set to "Rock," "Paper," and "Scissors." The player makes his choice by clicking one of the buttons, causing that button's Click event to be executed. In each button's Click event procedure, you will write the code to display the player's choice, generate a choice for the computer, and compare the two choices. Your code will be able to determine what choice the player made by knowing which button's Click event procedure was executed.

Task: Generate a choice for the computer.
Logic: In this version of the game, the role of the second player is handled by the computer. The computer has to make its own choice between Rock, Paper, or Scissors.
Solution: You will need to write code to generate a choice for the computer. This choice can consist of one of three possibilities—Rock, Paper, or Scissors. In addition, the choice must not have a repeatable pattern; the sequence of choices must appear random. Use the Visual Basic functions Randomize and Rnd to generate a random number, and use that number to select a choice for the computer.

Task: Determine the winner.

Logic: Once the player and the computer have chosen, the game must determine the winner by following the rules of the game.

Solution: In each button's Click event procedure, you will write the code to determine a winner. Use the Visual Basic Select Case statement to compare the player's choice with the computer's choice. Use the rules in the "Description of the Game" section to determine the winner.

Task: Display the results.

Logic: After the game has determined the winner, that information should appear on the screen.

Solution: Place two small Label objects shaped like boxes on the form: one next to the label marked "Player" and one next to the label marked "Computer." If the player wins, write code to mark the Player box with an X. If the computer wins, write code to mark the Computer box with an X.

PREPARING TO PROGRAM

You begin a Visual Basic application by selecting and placing objects on the program's main form. Most of the games in this text use only one form, although you will use multiple forms in Chapter 7.

The form for Rock, Paper, Scissors—shown in Figure 3—has eight Label objects and three Command Button objects.

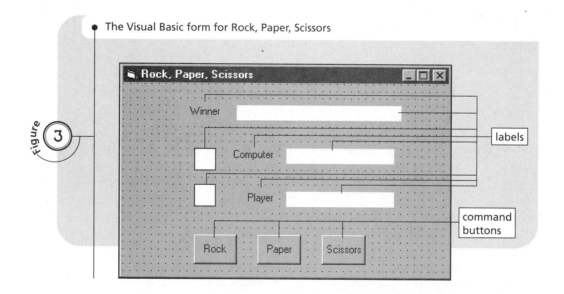

The Visual Basic form for Rock, Paper, Scissors

figure 3

To create a Label object, use the Visual Basic Label tool **A** . Use the Command Button tool ▭ to create a command button.

A **Label** is an object that can display text on a form. The text that a label displays is stored in the object's Caption property. You can give a value to the Caption property, or any other property, while you are designing the layout and placing objects on your form. You can also write Visual Basic code to change the value of a property while the game is executing (during run time).

Something to consider when designing a program is whether to limit the user's ability to change data input. Restricting user input decreases mistakes, intentional or otherwise. In general, it is better to include in your design objects that give users minimal ability to change the display. A Label object is an example of an object that restricts user input. Visual Basic does not allow the player to type text on the form and change the Caption property of a label. Because the user does not need to enter text for this game, you should use labels exclusively in Rock, Paper, Scissors.

As with any other Visual Basic object, when you place a new label on the form, Visual Basic automatically assigns it a name, such as **Label1** or **Label2**. When you create a label that will remain constant throughout the program, it is not necessary to change the name of the object at design time. This is true for the Rock, Paper, Scissors labels whose captions read "Computer," "Player," and "Winner." These are truly *labels* in the English meaning of the word. When you create an object to which your program will refer, it is a better programming practice to change the object's name in compliance with the standard naming conventions.

SETTING PROPERTIES AT DESIGN TIME

Visual Basic gives programmers two ways to set the properties of objects—at design time and by executing Visual Basic code. For objects and properties with values that remain fixed throughout the program, it makes sense to set those values at design time. For example, you can set properties such as the font for text, the form background color, or the border style of a button.

For this game, we recommend that you set the captions for the labels and command buttons at design time. The Visual Basic desktop makes this a fairly simple process. After you have laid out the form, you can set the value of an object's property by doing the following:

1. First select an object by clicking it. You can also select an object by choosing it from the list of objects on the Properties window. By selecting an object, you gain access to its properties in order to change them.

2. Once you have selected an object, you can alter its property value through the Properties window. To change the caption of the label that will display the text "Winner," select the object on the form or choose it from the list of objects on the Properties window.

3. Scroll down to the property labeled "Caption" and type the desired text (in this case, the word "Winner"). This method can be used to change other properties as well.

Figure 4 shows a suggested layout for your form and also shows how to access a Label's properties.

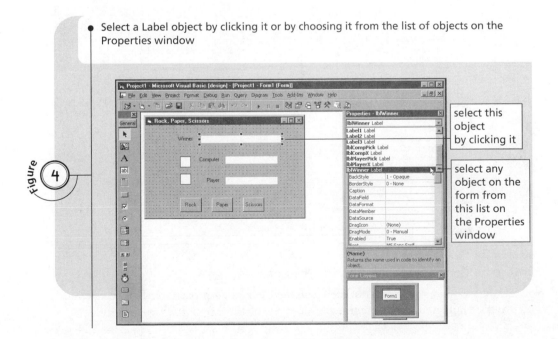

USING COMMAND BUTTONS

Command buttons are an integral part of interactive applications. They are a metaphor borrowed from the buttons that control machinery such as appliances and power tools. For example, a fan has a number of buttons, one each for changing the power level to Off, Low, Medium, or High. Each button carries out a distinct action indicated by its label.

Command buttons in software do the same thing. By clicking a command button with the mouse, the user triggers a specific action. Command buttons even look as if they have a raised surface, like a button or a switch.

Command buttons need to be clearly labeled. They must carry out a specific task. The code that executes when a command button is clicked is contained in the button's Click event procedure.

Accessing the Click Event Procedure

You will need to code three separate Click event procedures for Rock, Paper, Scissors—one for each command button. The name of the command button for rock is **cmdRock**; for paper, **cmdPaper**; and for scissors, **cmdScissors**. Visual Basic names the Click event procedure using the name of the command button. For example, **cmdRock_Click** is the name of the Click event procedure for the button **cmdRock**. It is important to understand that events belong to objects. When the player clicks **cmdRock**, the Click event happens to **cmdRock**; therefore, the **cmdRock_Click** event procedure executes. The code invoked by each button will be similar, but not exactly the same, because the choice of a command button determines the outcome of the game. It is your job to define what will happen when a command button is clicked. You must program the event procedure for each event by writing code—Visual Basic statements. You will enter this code in the Code window.

There are two ways for you to access the location in the Code window for a button's Click event procedure. The first is quite simple. Double-click the button you want to code on the form (during design, not during execution), and Visual Basic displays the corresponding Click event procedure so you, the programmer, can add code.

The second way to access a command button's Click event procedure is to select the object, then select its Click event procedure from the menu on the Code window, as shown in Figure 5.

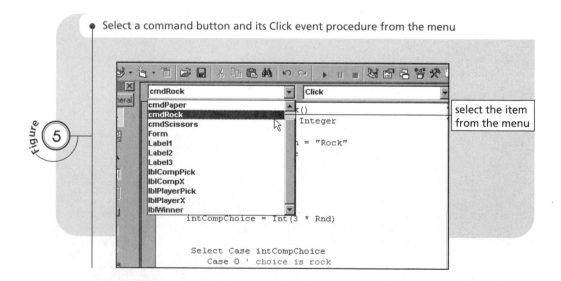

Select a command button and its Click event procedure from the menu

Figure 5

select the item from the menu

Writing the Code for the Click Event Procedure

Now we will examine the steps associated with the Click event procedure. The first step is for both players—human and computer—to choose one of three options: Rock, Paper, or

Scissors. When the player selects a button, he or she has made a choice. The computer then makes a choice, and by comparing the selections using the rules of the game, the game determines a winner.

Thus, the sequence of action in playing a game of Rock, Paper, Scissors is:

1. The player clicks a button.

2. The game changes the caption of a label to indicate the player's choice.

3. The game generates a choice for the computer.

4. The game changes a label's caption to display the computer's choice.

5. The game determines a winner based on the rules of Rock, Paper, Scissors.

6. The game changes the caption of a label to display the outcome.

Action 1 is carried out by the human player. Actions 2 through 6 are carried out by Visual Basic code. Although this analysis may seem too simplistic to even bother with, the amount of detail described here is absolutely necessary. You must specify the actions of the computer at this level of detail. Do this by coding event procedures and, for more complex projects, user-defined procedures.

Placing the Code

For this game, you will write the code for three event procedures. These event procedures are called the **cmdRock_Click** event procedure, the **cmdScissors_Click** event procedure, and the **cmdPaper_Click** event procedure. To enter the code for the **cmdRock_Click** event procedure, double-click the Rock command button. The Visual Basic desktop will set up a Code window with the first and last lines of the Click event procedure already in place, as shown in Figure 6.

Figure 6

Accessing the code window for the cmdRock_Click event procedure

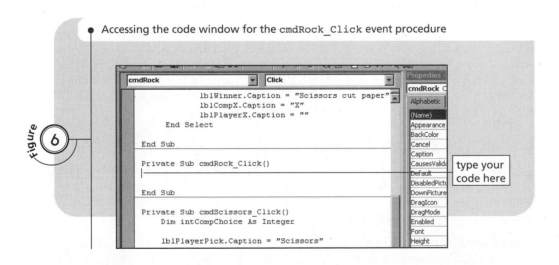

Place your code between the **Private Sub cmdRock_Click()** and **End Sub** lines, as shown in the figure.

Although you do not have to worry about typing these lines (they are generated automatically for you by Visual Basic), an explanation of some of the keywords is useful. The term **Private** means that this code will be used only by the current application. The term **Sub** means that this code is a **subroutine**.

Subroutines carry out a well-defined task—in this case, responding to a click by the player. Subroutines do not return a value, unlike functions, which do return values and can be used in expressions. The term **cmdRock** is the name of the command button, a name you (the programmer) will assign at design time (replacing the system-generated name for the button). **cmdRock_Click** is the particular event procedure that you will code. The two parentheses **( )** are placeholders for parameters, or variables that are passed in, or transferred, to a function or subroutine within the current program. The **cmdRock_Click** event has no parameters, which is why its parentheses are empty. Other event procedures and most of the routines that you will write for games in this book will include parameters.

Before you start to write code between the **Private Sub cmdRock_Click()** and **End Sub** lines, think about the sequence of action in the current Click event. If your program is executing the **cmdRock_Click** event procedure, it is only because a player has clicked the Rock button. The significance of this is that the caption on the button (Rock) is the player's choice. Although no variable is required to store the player's choice, it is still a crucial piece of information. Remember, the game compares the player's choice to the computer's choice to determine the outcome of the game. The player's choice—which is known to you (the programmer) implicitly by the fact that the game is executing the **cmdRock_Click** event procedure—therefore is one detail that determines the outcome of the game.

DISPLAYING THE PLAYER'S CHOICE

The first code you will write carries out a simple task: indicating the player's choice using the **lblPlayerPick** label. This label will always hold the player's choice no matter what it is. For example, assume that the player has clicked Rock. You will place the string "Rock" in the label's caption, because this is the Rock command button Click event procedure—if you are executing code in this event, it means the player selected the Rock button. Once again, this analysis may seem obvious, but it is necessary, because inferring conditions through indirect means is a common occurrence in programming.

The line of code that indicates that the player selected Rock is:

```
lblPlayerPick.Caption = "Rock"
```

This is an example of an assignment statement. Here the value on the right side of the expression ("**Rock**") is copied into the left side (**lblPlayerPick.Caption**). The object on the left side is on the form. When this code executes, the player's choice will appear as "Rock." Values are never copied from left to right, only from right to left. This is a standard practice for most programming languages, and is the reverse of your previous experience in reading or writing formulas in math. It will take some getting used to.

GENERATING THE COMPUTER'S CHOICE

Once labeling the player's choice is done, your code must tackle a more difficult problem—generating a choice for the computer. The player has made a move—he chose a button, and now the computer must "choose" a button. But how can a computer choose anything? It does not have any innate choice capability.

No matter what button is selected—Rock or Scissors or Paper—a choice for the computer must be generated. The player's choice should not determine the computer's choice because that wouldn't be fair. The sequence or pattern of computer choices should also vary. If the computer always chooses Paper, it would lose every game once the human player realized the computer's choice never varied.

In most games, you will need to write code that makes the computer's choice through a strategy for winning the game or a random choice. For example, in later chapters, you will learn how the computer needs to lay out the board in an unpredictable way for Minesweeper or make a move in Tic Tac Toe.

How can you include random selections in programming? The concept of randomness seems to conflict with the predictability required in programming. To create a random choice, you will need a random number. Visual Basic has a built-in random number generator that is invaluable for programming the games in this book. The underlying Visual Basic software for generating random numbers is complex, but it is a powerful and flexible tool that can provide a sequence of numbers with no discernible pattern within any range you want.

> **TIP**
>
> **The formal term for random numbers in programming is _pseudorandom numbers_, meaning similar to or like random numbers. Visual Basic uses a formula or algorithm to create random numbers. Since a formula is used, the numbers are therefore not really "random," only made to look that way.**

Now you will learn how random numbers are used to generate a choice for the computer. In this game, the computer has only three possible choices; therefore, you need code that generates a series of three possible outcomes. For reasons that will be explained later, the numbers 0, 1, and 2 will be generated, and these results will be "converted" into Rock, Paper, or Scissors. This conversion is quite simple: the number 0 becomes the choice "Rock," the number 1 is "Paper," and the number 2 is "Scissors."

Random number	Computer's choice
0	Rock
1	Paper
2	Scissors

Generating random numbers can be done using two lines of Visual Basic code. First is this line of code:

```
Randomize
```

Randomize is a procedure that sets the seed, or starting point, for the random number generator. It can be called once per game or with each request for a random number.

The second line of code uses the function Rnd, which returns a random number between 0 and 1 (it generates random fractions greater than or equal to 0 and less than 1). This game needs integer values (whole numbers), not fractions. You can make a simple calculation that converts this random fraction to one of the values you need: 0, 1, or 2. To do this conversion, follow these guidelines:

- Fractions from 0 up to, but not including 1/3, will be treated as 0.

- Fractions from 1/3 up to, but not including 2/3, will be treated as 1.

- Fractions from 2/3 up to, but not including 1, will be treated as 2.

How can you make this conversion using Visual Basic code? You could compare the fraction generated by Rnd to 1/3 and 2/3, but there is a simpler way. The Visual Basic function Int extracts the integer portion of a number that may have fractional parts. Int calculates the greatest integer less than or equal to a number. Therefore, in the case of a positive number, Int disregards the fraction and retains just the whole number. Consider the examples shown in Figure 7.

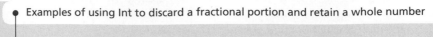

Examples of using Int to discard a fractional portion and retain a whole number

figure
7

Value	Int(value)
0	0
1	1
1.5	1
2.33333	2
23.567	23
48.666	48
5.622	5

Armed with this capability, you must expand the possible values to a range between 0 and 3. Think of it as stretching out the random choices from the 0-to-1 range that Rnd provides to 0 to 3. To do this, you multiply the number returned by Rnd by 3. Then you use the Int function to discard the fractional portion and end up with a whole number.

Therefore, after the **Randomize** line, the next line of code looks like this:

```
intCompChoice = Int(3 * Rnd)
```

This code generates a random number (either 0, 1, or 2) and stores its value in the variable **intCompChoice.intCompChoice** now contains a number that represents the computer's choice.

To summarize, the two lines of code you will need to include in each button's Click event to generate a choice for the computer are:

```
Randomize
intCompChoice = Int(3 * Rnd)
```

The statement **Randomize** sets, or starts, the random number generator. The function Rnd returns a fractional random number between 0 and 1. The result from Rnd is multiplied by 3 to generate three choices, then the function Int truncates, or throws away, the fractional portion, leaving the number 0, 1, or 2. Finally, this whole number is stored in the variable **intCompChoice**.

DETERMINING THE WINNER

Next, the game must compare the player's choice with the computer's choice. You will write code to determine the outcome of the game using the logic outlined in Figure 8.

● Logic for the rules of Rock, Paper, Scissors

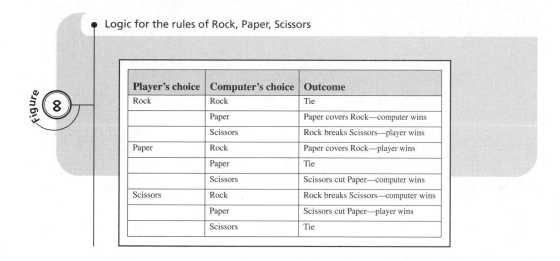

Figure 8

Player's choice	Computer's choice	Outcome
Rock	Rock	Tie
	Paper	Paper covers Rock—computer wins
	Scissors	Rock breaks Scissors—player wins
Paper	Rock	Paper covers Rock—player wins
	Paper	Tie
	Scissors	Scissors cut Paper—computer wins
Scissors	Rock	Rock breaks Scissors—computer wins
	Paper	Scissors cut Paper—player wins
	Scissors	Tie

In each Click event procedure, you will need to write code that produces three possible outcomes: a tie, the player wins, or computer wins.

For each Click event procedure, you must also compare the player's choice to the computer's choice. Since the game has three buttons, you will code three Click event procedures. They will be similar, but slightly different, reflecting the player's choice, which, of course, determines the outcome of the game.

You can write the code to compare the player's choice and the computer's choice with a Visual Basic command known as a Select Case statement. Select Case is categorized as a decision statement. It is useful when your program has to select or decide between multiple choices. The general syntax for the statement is shown in Figure 9.

● Syntax of the Select Case statement

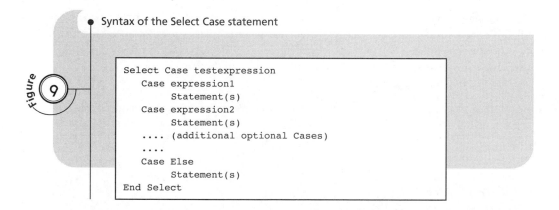

Figure 9

```
Select Case testexpression
    Case expression1
        Statement(s)
    Case expression2
        Statement(s)
    .... (additional optional Cases)
    ....
    Case Else
        Statement(s)
End Select
```

This command executes as follows: **testexpression** must be either a numeric (such as an Integer or a Single) or String expression. If the value of **testexpression** is equal to the value of any of the **Case** expressions, then the statements following the matching **Case** are executed. The most common match is a test for equality. Less common are comparisons against a range of numbers or a comparison of less than (<) or greater than (>). If none of the cases match, the **Case Else** section is executed as a default (**Case Else** is optional).

Figure 10 shows the Select Case statement for the Rock Click event procedure (**cmdRock_Click**). This code compares the player's choice of "Rock" with the computer's choice stored in **intCompChoice**.

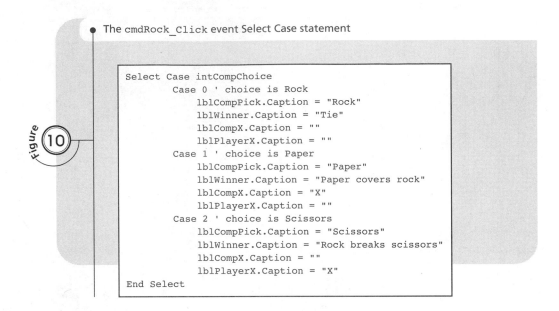

Figure 10

The cmdRock_Click event Select Case statement

```
Select Case intCompChoice
        Case 0 ' choice is Rock
                lblCompPick.Caption = "Rock"
                lblWinner.Caption = "Tie"
                lblCompX.Caption = ""
                lblPlayerX.Caption = ""
        Case 1 ' choice is Paper
                lblCompPick.Caption = "Paper"
                lblWinner.Caption = "Paper covers rock"
                lblCompX.Caption = "X"
                lblPlayerX.Caption = ""
        Case 2 ' choice is Scissors
                lblCompPick.Caption = "Scissors"
                lblWinner.Caption = "Rock breaks scissors"
                lblCompX.Caption = ""
                lblPlayerX.Caption = "X"
End Select
```

This Select Case statement implements the rules that determine a winner. You know that the player's choice is Rock, because the player selected the command button labeled Rock. **intCompChoice** is an Integer variable that holds the computer's choice. If the computer's choice is Rock, as in **Case 0**, the result is a tie. In this situation, the word "Tie" is written in **lblWinner.Caption** and the labels that mark the winner with an X are both blank (**lblCompX** and **lblPlayerX** are both empty strings).

If the computer's choice is Paper, the computer wins, so the game sets **lblWinner.Caption** to "Paper covers rock" and places an X next to the Computer label (**lblCompX.Caption**). If the computer's choice is Scissors, then the player wins, "Rock breaks scissors" appears in the **lblWinner.Caption**, and an X is placed next to the Player label (**lblPlayerX.Caption**).

You will need to write similar logic in the event procedures for the Paper command button and the Scissors command button. In each event procedure, you will use a Select Case statement to determine the winner by comparing the player's choice with the computer's choice according to the rules of the game.

Ending the Game

The player can continue to make choices as long as he or she wants. Every time the player makes a choice, the game generates a choice for the computer and determines the winner. The player can exit the game by clicking the Exit button ☒ in the upper-right corner of the game screen. In future chapters, you will learn how to implement more sophisticated exit options.

Plan for the User Interface

Although Rock, Paper, Scissors is a simple game, it introduces key game design issues as well as Visual Basic objects and commands that appear in nearly every application. Like all games, Rock, Paper, Scissors must provide a clear method for the player to make a choice. The user interface for Rock, Paper, Scissors will use command buttons to indicate the player's choice. The code in the command button Click event procedure then generates the computer's choice, and also includes the logic to determine the winner. As you develop more complex games in later chapters, you will use other event procedures to carry out the logic for your game.

The code for the Rock, Paper, Scissors interface uses labels exclusively to display text. These labels can only be altered by code by the programmer during design, not by the player during execution. In future chapters, you will add other objects—namely, text boxes—that display text and allow user input.

FORM DESIGN

This section describes all of the objects contained in the final design for Rock, Paper, Scissors, which is shown in Figure 11. Follow this plan to place all the objects needed on your form. The object names listed below are suggestions; you may rename them if desired (if you do, be sure to revise your code accordingly). Placement of objects are suggestions—you may lay out your form differently, if you wish.

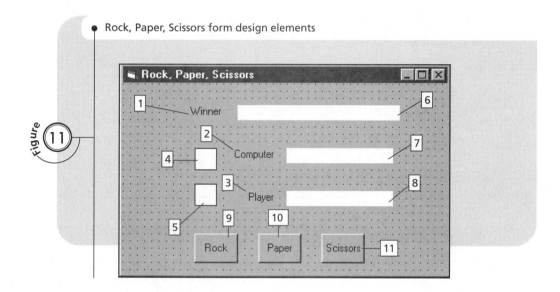

● Rock, Paper, Scissors form design elements

figure 11

Constant labels (these stay the same throughout execution)

1. **Label1**: Caption is "Winner"

2. **Label2**: Caption is "Computer"

3. **Label3**: Caption is "Player"

Variable labels (contents are updated by program to indicate game outcome)

4. **lblCompX**: Set to "X" when computer wins; otherwise, set to empty string

5. **lblPlayerX**: Set to "X" when player wins; otherwise, set to empty string

6. **lblWinner**: Announces winner or tie

7. **lblCompPick**: Displays computer's choice

8. **lblPlayerPick**: Displays player's choice

Command buttons

9. **cmdRock**: Indicates player's choice of "Rock"

10. **cmdPaper**: Indicates player's choice of "Paper"

11. **cmdScissors**: Indicates player's choice of "Scissors"

VARIABLES AND CONSTANTS DECLARED IN THE (General) SECTION

In the **General** section of your Rock, Paper, Scissors program, include the following:

Element	Explanation
`Option Explicit`	Set this option to require a declaration of all variables

There are no general constants or variables needed for this game.

ALGORITHMS FOR EVENT PROCEDURES

Write code for the following three Click event procedures:

```
Private Sub cmdScissors_Click()

Private Sub cmdRock_Click()

Private Sub cmdPaper_Click()
```

The logic for all three procedures will be very similar. You will write code to display the player's choice, create a choice for the computer, determine the winner, and display the results. The code for the **cmdScissors_Click** event is illustrated; revise this code appropriately for the **cmdRock_Click** and **cmdPaper_Click** events.

THE cmdScissors_Click() *EVENT PROCEDURE*

Include the following variable in this event procedure:

Element	Explanation
`Dim intCompChoice As Integer`	This variable stores the computer's choice. You must declare this variable separately in each Click event.

Program this Click event procedure so that it performs the following tasks:

1. Store the player's choice in the caption for the label **lblPlayerPick**. Your code will look like this:
   ```
   lblPlayerPick.Caption = "Scissors"
   ```

2. Generate the computer's choice using random numbers. Refer to the "Preparing to Program" section for an explanation of the code needed to do this. In each Click event, include the following code:
   ```
   Randomize
   intCompChoice = Int(3 * Rnd)
   ```

3. After the code in Step 2 has been executed, the value in intCompChoice is a number that represents the computer's choice. Examine the value in intCompChoice and use it to change the caption of lblCompPick to indicate the computer's choice. If intCompChoice is equal to 0, then change the caption of lblCompPick to "Rock"; if it is equal to 1, change the caption of lblCompPick to "Paper"; and if it is equal to 2, change the Caption of lblCompPick to "Scissors."

4. Compare the player's choice to the computer's choice and determine the outcome using the following logic:

   - Paper covers rock

- Scissors cut paper

- Rock breaks scissors

5. Use a Select Case statement or If Then Else loop to compare the choices. The code for the Select Case statement for the **cmdScissors_Click** event is shown in Figure 12.

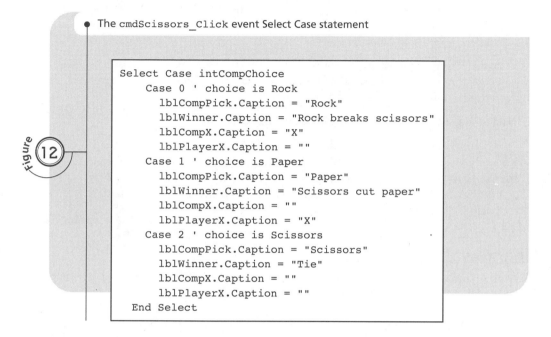

The `cmdScissors_Click` event Select Case statement

```
Select Case intCompChoice
    Case 0 ' choice is Rock
      lblCompPick.Caption = "Rock"
      lblWinner.Caption = "Rock breaks scissors"
      lblCompX.Caption = "X"
      lblPlayerX.Caption = ""
    Case 1 ' choice is Paper
      lblCompPick.Caption = "Paper"
      lblWinner.Caption = "Scissors cut paper"
      lblCompX.Caption = ""
      lblPlayerX.Caption = "X"
    Case 2 ' choice is Scissors
      lblCompPick.Caption = "Scissors"
      lblWinner.Caption = "Tie"
      lblCompX.Caption = ""
      lblPlayerX.Caption = ""
End Select
```

figure (12)

6. Indicate the winner by placing "X" in the caption of **lblCompX** (if the computer wins) or **lblPlayerX** (if the player wins) and by setting the caption in **lblWinner**. If there is a tie (both players make the same choice), indicate this by displaying "Tie" in **lblWinner** and do not place an X in either box.

THE cmdRock_Click() EVENT PROCEDURE

Include the following variable this event procedure:

Element	Explanation
`Dim intCompChoice As Integer`	This variable stores the computer's choice. You must declare this variable separately in each Click event.

The code for this event procedure is nearly identical to the code for **cmdScissors_Click**. You can copy the code from the **cmdScissors_Click** event procedure into this event procedure and then make the following changes:

- Display the player's choice as "Rock" in **lblPlayerPick.Caption**.

- In the Select Case statement, you must change the outcome to reflect the player's choice of Rock. In this event procedure, the result is a tie if the computer picks Rock, the computer wins if it selects Paper, and the player wins if he picks Scissors. You need to change the code that sets the value of **lblWinner.Caption**, **lblCompX.Caption**, and **lblPlayerX.Caption**.

THE cmdPaper_Click() EVENT PROCEDURE

Include the following variable this event procedure:

Element	Explanation
Dim intCompChoice As Integer	This variable stores the computer's choice. You must declare this variable separately in each Click event.

The code for this event procedure is nearly identical to the code for **cmdScissors_Click**. You can copy the code from the **cmdScissors_Click** event procedure into this event procedure and then make the following changes:

- Display the player's choice as "Paper" in **lblPlayerPick.Caption**.

- In the Select Case statement, you must change the outcome to reflect the player's choice of Paper. In this event procedure, the result is a tie if the computer picks Paper, the computer wins if it selects Scissors, and the player wins if he picks Rock. You need to change the code that sets the value of **lblWinner.Caption**, **lblCompX.Caption**, and **lblPlayerX.Caption**.

OPTIONAL ENHANCEMENTS

There are many ways you can customize your Rock, Paper, Scissors program. Following are some suggestions to get you started on adding original features and functionality.

1. Display images of a rock, paper, and scissors to represent the player's choice and the computer's choice.
2. Use different colors to indicate the winner and loser. For example, in addition to displaying the word "Winner," change the color of the winner's label.
3. Keep a running tally of each result; for example, keep track of how frequently the player wins, the computer wins, or a tie occurs.
4. Let the player enter his or her name on the form.

DISCUSSION QUESTIONS

1. What other action can the game perform in the case of a tie, other than a rematch?
2. In what other ways (besides the use of command buttons) can you design the user interface to allow the player to input a choice? Discuss the advantages/disadvantages of these methods.
3. Design a two-person version of Rock, Paper, Scissors. No automatic choice is generated for the computer; instead, you play against another player. You will need some technique that keeps each player's choice secret until both have made a choice. The game still has the job of determining the winner.
4. Many games include a Clear or Reset button that the player can use to start fresh. The construction plan for Rock, Paper, Scissors does not include a Clear button because it would mean that starting a new game requires two actions, not one. Discuss the advantages and disadvantages of a Clear button. How would the code for a Clear button be affected by implementing any of the enhancements listed in the previous section?
5. When you play this game, do you have the impression that the game makes its move at the same time the player does? How could you make the selections more real, in other words, how could you make the player and computer choices appear simultaneous?

MIX AND MATCH CARTOONS

◎ CONCEPTS, SKILLS, AND TOOLS

In this chapter, you will create a computer version of an activity in which cartoon figures are constructed by combining features from assortments of choices. This version of Mix and Match Cartoons combines various on-screen images of hats, faces, bodies, and shoes to create comical cartoons.

You will use the following general programming concepts, skills, and tools in the Mix and Match Cartoons construction plan:

- Producing drawings that fit together to form a figure
- Creating parallel arrays
- Handling user interactions
- Controlling user input

The Visual Basic features used to construct this game include:

- Image controls
- Control arrays of image controls
- List box controls
- The Break button and the Immediate window

◎ DESCRIPTION OF THE GAME

This Visual Basic game allows the player to create funny cartoons by combining various types of body features into one final body image. There is no winning or losing in this game; the idea is simply to have fun with the combinations. The player makes one choice from each of four categories: hats, faces, bodies, and shoes.

HOW THIS VERSION OF MIX AND MATCH CARTOONS WORKS

The player creates a cartoon by choosing body parts from list boxes on a Visual Basic form. This version of the game provides two choices for each feature category. For example, choices for hats can be "top hat" or "puffy hat." The computer displays the selection in an image control to the right of the associated list box. You must lay out the form so that each body part appears in an appropriate location on the form (in other words, the hat image must appear above the face, and so on). The player clicks the button labeled "Clear" to restart the activity. Experiment with the Mix and Match Cartoons activity by running the **mixed.exe** file located in your Ch2 folder.

SAMPLE SCREENS

As the player makes selections from the lists, the corresponding drawings appear on the form. Figure 1 shows the game screen before the player has made any selections. At this point, the form shows the lists for each of the four categories and the command button for clearing the screen.

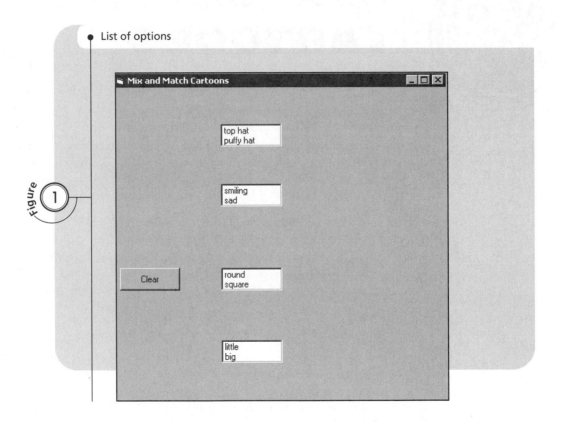

Figure 1

Figure 2 shows the form after the player has chosen a hat and shoes.

Two choices selected

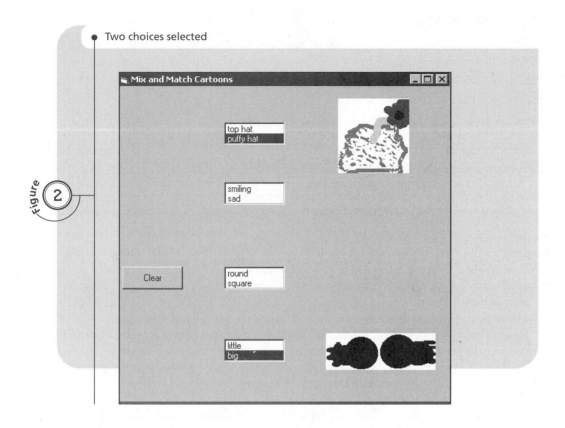

figure 2

Figure 3 shows a complete set of choices, including a hat and shoes different from the ones selected in Figure 2.

Complete mix and match cartoon figure displayed

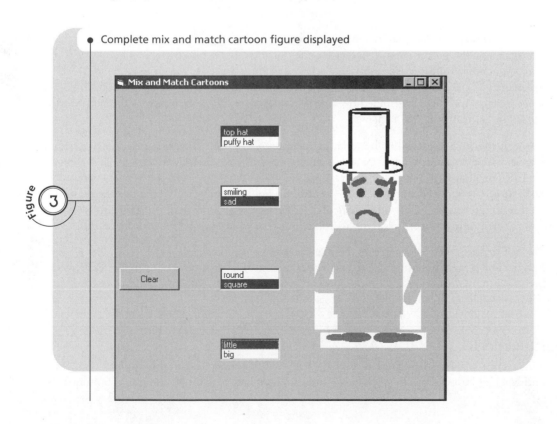

figure 3

KEY DESIGN ISSUES

There are four design tasks that you—the designer and programmer—must accomplish when creating the Mix and Match Cartoons game:

- Create a set of pictures (images) for each category that fit together to show a completed figure

- Provide a way for players to make choices in each category

- Establish an association between the names and the images

- Provide a way for the player to clear the display

Solutions to each of these programming tasks are presented in the next section. Use these suggestions as guidelines when programming your version of Mix and Match Cartoons.

Task: Create a set of pictures.
Logic: Visual Basic has two controls that hold images: the picture control and the image control. You will use arrays of image controls (which require fewer system resources than picture controls) in this chapter. You will need to give the elements of the arrays of image controls content (associate a picture with each control).
Solution: Set an image control to hold a specific image by setting its Picture property to the file name of a bit-mapped (.bmp) image file. You can use the image files supplied in the Ch2 folder, or create your own. Creation of image files is outside the scope of Visual Basic. However, you have several ways to acquire images: you can use any drawing program (for example, Microsoft Paint) to create the images, or you can find clip art or photo images online or from other computer software. You can use a software tool such as Paint Shop Pro to convert the image files to the .bmp file type. Your challenge in creating an effective game is to make the pictures fit together. For example, you want each hat in the collection of images for hats to lie on top of the face below it. There should not be any white space between the parts. It is okay for the final cartoon to look silly—at the very least, your cartoons should look better than the rough sample images shown in this book!

Task: Provide a way for players to make choices in each category.
Logic: Show the player a list of names for each of the different body parts. The player will make selections from the list.
Solution: Visual Basic supports the list box control. A list box has a list of items (in this case, body parts), which are determined by code that you will write. The names of the body parts should be indicative of the images.

Task: Establish an association between the item names and the images.
Logic: The computer has no way of knowing that what you think of as "floppy hat" refers to a particular image. You must program the game so that the names and the images correspond.
Solution: Use control arrays of image controls to hold the images. Then make the items in the list box, which should be in a particular sequence, correspond with the elements in the control arrays. Image controls have a Visible property, which can be set to True or False.

Task: Provide a way for the player to clear or reset the display.
Logic: The player should be able to restart the game with a clear display, as shown in Figure 1.
Solution: Create a command button and program its Click event procedure to set the Visible properties of all the image controls to False.

PREPARING TO PROGRAM

This section provides background on the Visual Basic features used in this application. Mix and Match Cartoons has four image controls, four list boxes, and one command button.

CREATING THE IMAGE CONTROLS

Creating image controls is done during design time. If you need to refresh your memory on how to create image controls, consult Visual Basic Help or another text.

There are two critical requirements for creating image controls for this project. First, you must have image files on your computer. Once you create an image control, you must set the Picture property of that image control to the file name of the appropriate image.

The second requirement is that you set the Visible property of each image control to False. When the player selects an image, the program code will make the appropriate images appear on the form by changing its Visible property to True.

USING A CONTROL ARRAY

For this game, you will need several image controls, sorted by body part category. Each category should correspond to a control array of image controls. Reminder: A control array is a sequence of controls, all sharing the same name, with each individual control having its own index value. When the player makes a choice from the list of body part options (see the next section), the corresponding image should appear on the game screen—in other words, the image control is made visible. You can make a control array during design time in one of two ways.

The first option is to create multiple controls, each with the same name. When you give the second control a name you have already used, Visual Basic displays a message box that asks if you intend to make a control array. Respond by clicking the Yes button and continue creating the controls.

The second way to create a control array is to set the index property of a control to 0, which signals to Visual Basic that this will be the first element of a control array (remember that indexing starts at zero). You can then continue creating the array by creating new image controls and giving them the same name as the first.

For this game, you need to make control arrays for each of the four categories of body parts.

USING LIST BOXES

The other main Visual Basic feature used by this game is the list box. You will create four list boxes at design time. However, the items in the list box—that is, the body part choices—are not specified at design time. Instead, you include code to set up these items in the Form_Load event procedure.

OTHER CONSIDERATIONS

You also will use a command button in Mix and Match Cartoons. Command buttons were covered in Chapter 1.

Finally, bear in mind that the main challenge to creating this game is the organization and management of sets of items. Your game won't be much fun if the image controls don't correspond to the list box items—if your player selects "floppy hat" and a pair of shoes appears at the top of the form, your game doesn't work.

PLAN FOR THE USER INTERFACE

As previously explained, Mix and Match Cartoons requires the creation of sets of image controls for each body part category. Use the following instructions to create control arrays and list boxes for the game's user interface.

1. Create an image control by double-clicking the **Image Control** tool in the toolbox. Scroll up in the Property list to the image control's Name property. (Recall that for Visual Basic, the Name property, which appears surrounded by

parentheses, is listed first on the Property list—all other properties appear in alphabetical order.) Change the name to **imgHats**.

2. Scroll down to the Index property and change it to **0**. Changing an item's Index property to zero establishes it as a control array.

3. Click the three dots next to the Picture property to invoke a Load Picture window. Use this window to load a picture into this image control. Use the second file image you identified for the game as this picture (for example, if you are using the pictures in your Ch2 folder, select **top.gif**).

4. Create a second image control and place it on top of the first. Load a picture using the technique described in Step 3.

5. Change the name of this second image control to **imgHats**. Note: if you omit the step of changing the index property to zero, Visual Basic will display a message box that asks if you intended to create a control array. Click **Yes**, if necessary. If you set the first image control's index to zero, the message box will not appear. In both cases, the first image will have an index value of 0 and the second image will have an index value of 1.

> **TIP**
>
> **Elements of control arrays have index values and these start with zero. The last index value is always one less than the number of elements in the control array.**

6. As a test, click the **Start** button to start this project. You should see both image controls on the form.

Use this method to create three more control arrays: one each for the faces, bodies, and shoes. Position them appropriately on the right side of the form (so that the face image controls are under the hats, and so on).

CONSTRUCTING LIST BOX CONTROLS

Next, you will create a list box for the Hats category of the Mix and Match Cartoons game program.

To place a list box control on the form, do the following:

1. Double-click the **ListBox** tool ⊞. Visual Basic places the control in a default position in the center of the form.

2. Change the name of the control to **lstHats** by clicking the **Name** property and typing in the new name. Notice that the control shows the new name.

Your form should look like Figure 4.

Placing the first list box on the form

4

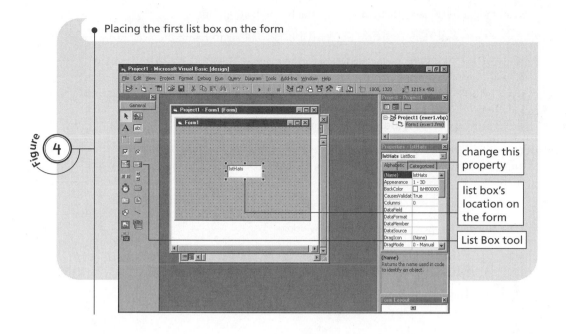

Items in the list box control are entered into the control as part of the Form_Load event procedure. You must write the code to add the hat options to your game's list box control.

Double-click anywhere on the form to open the Form_Load event procedure's Code window. Type the code shown in Figure 5 in the Form_Load Code window.

Partial code for the Form_Load event procedure

5

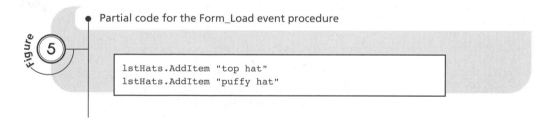

```
lstHats.AddItem "top hat"
lstHats.AddItem "puffy hat"
```

1. To see these options included in the Hat list box control, click the **Start** button ▶ to start the game. Select one of the list box items to see what happens. It should appear highlighted.

2. Click the **Stop** button ■ to return to the Design window.

3. Click the list box control to change its size on the form.

4. Make the list box control large enough so that all the items on the list are visible.

5. Restart the game. Both options should be visible, and no scroll bars should appear on the form.

This exercise is included to demonstrate how a larger list box would look.

USING THE BREAK BUTTON AND THE IMMEDIATE WINDOW

When a player makes a selection in a list box, Visual Basic sets the List Index property to the index (the position) of the selected item. Complete the following exercise to see how list boxes work and to practice using the Break button and Immediate window. These tools are important in debugging projects.

1. Start the game. Select **puffy hat** from the list of Hat options.

2. Click the **Break** button ▐▐ on the Visual Basic toolbar to pause the execution.

3. Now use the Immediate window to check the value of **lstHats.listindex**. (If you do not see an Immediate window, go to the View menu and click **Immediate Window** to make it appear.) In the Immediate window, type **print lstHats.listindex**, which instructs Visual Basic to display the current value of **lstHats.listindex** in the Immediate window.

4. You should see "1," which is the index corresponding to the selection, in the Immediate window. See Figure 6. Click the **Start** button ▶ to resume execution of the game.

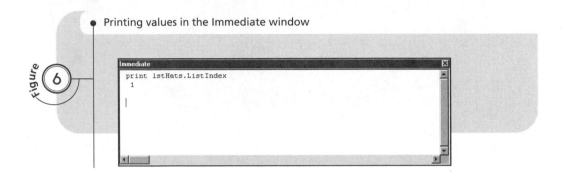

Printing values in the Immediate window

Figure 6

You can use this method to find the index value of any variable or property.

1. Next, select **top hat** from the list of Hat options. Using the method described in the previous steps, pause execution and print the **ListIndex** value. This time the printed value should be 0. Remember that indexing starts with zero.

2. End the game's execution by clicking the **End** button ■.

3. Restart the game. Do not select anything. Pause the game and retype **print lstHats.listindex** in the Debug window. This time the value -1 will appear. This is the index value if nothing has been selected on the form.

4. End execution of the game by clicking the **End** button.

PREPARING PICTURES

From this point on, the chapter assumes that you have saved on your computer two image files for each category. (You can produce more image files, if you wish. If you add images, you will need to change the code in several places to work with the new number of images. A minor adjustment to the code—namely, defining a variable or constant holding the limit for each category—allows for a distinct number of choices for each category.)

◎ FORM DESIGN

This section describes all of the objects contained on the final design for Mix and Match Cartoons, which is shown in Figure 7. Follow this plan to place all of the objects needed on your form. The object names listed below are suggestions; you may rename these objects if desired (if you do, be sure to revise your code accordingly).

Mix and Match Cartoon form design elements

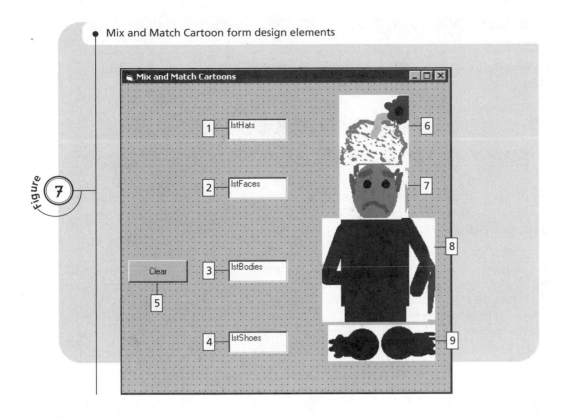

figure 7

List boxes

1. **lstHats**: Holds descriptions of hats

2. **lstFaces**: Holds descriptions of faces

3. **lstBodies**: Holds descriptions of bodies

4. **lstShoes**: Holds descriptions of shoes

Command button

5. **cmdClear**: Sets Visible property to False for all images

Control arrays of images

6. **imgHats()**: A control array of hats

7. **imgFaces()**: A control array of faces

8. **imgBodies()**: A control array of bodies

9. **imgShoes()**: A control array of (pairs of) shoes

VARIABLES AND CONSTANTS DECLARED IN THE (General) SECTION

In your Mix and Match Cartoons program, include the following statement in the (General) section:

Element	Explanation
Option Explicit	Set this option to require a declaration of all variables

There are no general constants or variables needed for this game.

IMPLEMENTATION OF THE GAME

The implementation of this project consists of creating the list box controls for each of the four categories (hats, faces, bodies and shoes) and control arrays of image controls for each of the four categories. You need to set the Picture property of each of the image controls to one of your image files. You need to write the code (using **AddItem** calls) to establish each list of options. The files for your pictures can have any name you choose, but you need to be sure that the appropriate picture appears adjacent to the phrase located in the corresponding list option box.

At times, the phrase in the list box may be identical or similar to the file name. Even if the phrase in the list box is identical to the name of a picture in an image file, you must make sure that its position in the list box corresponds with the element in the control array. As noted earlier, the game displays images based on the selection of items in the list boxes. You establish the association between items and images at design time: the order in which you place images into the image control arrays corresponds to the list box code commands.

Place the four control arrays of image controls in the appropriate images. You also need to name each list box option with a phrase describing its corresponding image, such as "floppy hat." These phrases will be the items in the corresponding list boxes. Program the Form_Load event procedure to insert the phrases in the list boxes. At design time, be sure to make the Visible property of each image False. When the player selects a list box item, the code in the list box event procedure will make the selected image Visible.

The following table shows the correspondence of image files with elements in the image control arrays. You should prepare a similar list for your images and descriptions.

Name of image file	Image control array	Index	Corresponding option
puffy.gif	imgHats	0	"puffy hat"
top.gif	imgHats	1	"top hat"
smile.gif	imgFaces	0	"smiling"
sad.gif	imgFaces	1	"sad"
round.gif	imgBodies	0	"round"
square.gif	imgBodies	1	"square"
shoesl.gif	imgShoes	0	"little"
toes.gif	imgShoes	1	"big"

Now create four list box controls. These will hold the choices for each body part category. Change the system-generated names to **lstHats**, **lstFaces**, **lstBodies**, and **lstShoes**.

Create the four control arrays, each with two image controls.

ALGORITHMS FOR EVENT PROCEDURES AND USER-DEFINED PROCEDURES

Write code for the Form_Load event procedure, the Click event procedure for the **cmdClear** button, and the Click event procedures for each of the four list boxes.

THE FORM_LOAD EVENT PROCEDURE

You need to write the code that inserts the body part options into the Form_Load event procedure. Double-click the form to open its Form_Load event Code window. Between the **Private Sub Form_Load()** and **End Sub** lines type the code shown in Figure 8.

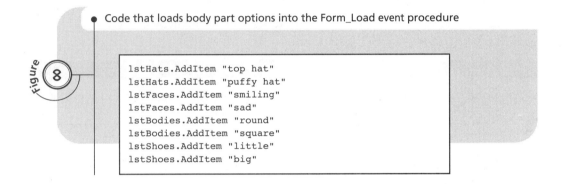

● Code that loads body part options into the Form_Load event procedure

Figure 8

```
lstHats.AddItem "top hat"
lstHats.AddItem "puffy hat"
lstFaces.AddItem "smiling"
lstFaces.AddItem "sad"
lstBodies.AddItem "round"
lstBodies.AddItem "square"
lstShoes.AddItem "little"
lstShoes.AddItem "big"
```

THE lstHats_Click EVENT PROCEDURE

Include the following local variable in the **lstHats_Click** event procedure:

Element	Explanation
Dim i as Integer	Used in the For...Next loop to iterate through the images to make each image invisible

Next, write the code that makes the selected image appear when the player selects an option. In the Hats category, the code will look like Figure 9.

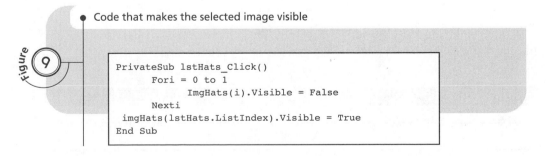

● Code that makes the selected image visible

Figure 9

```
PrivateSub lstHats_Click()
     Fori = 0 to 1
          ImgHats(i).Visible = False
     Nexti
 imgHats(lstHats.ListIndex).Visible = True
End Sub
```

All the hat images start as invisible, and then the selected one is made visible.

This code changes the **Visible** setting of the selected **ListIndex** option to True, making the selection appear on the game form.

THE lstFaces_Click EVENT PROCEDURE

Include the following local variable in the **lstFaces_Click** event procedure:

Element	Explanation
Dim i as Integer	Used in the For…Next loop to iterate through the images to make each image invisible

Copy the code from the **lstHats_Click** event procedure, changing the code to refer to **imgFaces** instead of **imgHats**. Then change **lstHats.ListIndex** to **lstFaces.ListIndex**.

THE lstBodies_Click EVENT PROCEDURE

Include the following local variable in the **lstBodies_Click** event procedure:

Element	Explanation
Dim i as Integer	Used in the For…Next loop to iterate through the images to make each image invisible

Copy the code from the **lstHats_Click** event procedure, changing the code to refer to **imgBodies** instead of **imgHats**. Then change **lstHats.ListIndex** to **lstBodies.ListIndex**.

THE lstShoes_Click EVENT PROCEDURE

Include the following local variable in the **lstShoes_Click** event procedure:

Element	Explanation
Dim i as Integer	Used in the For…Next loop to iterate through the images to make each image invisible

Copy the code from the **lstHats_Click** event procedure, changing the code to refer to **imgShoes** instead of **imgHats**. Then change **lstHats.ListIndex** to **lstShoes.ListIndex**.

THE cmdClear_Click EVENT PROCEDURE

Include the following local variable in the **cmdClear_Click** event procedure:

Element	Explanation
Dim i as Integer	Used in the For…Next loop to iterate through the images to make each image invisible

This code gives the player the option of erasing all the pictures and restarting the game.

Double-click the **cmdClear** button to open its Click event Code window. Between the **Private Sub cmdClear_Click()** and **End Sub** lines, type the code shown in Figure 10.

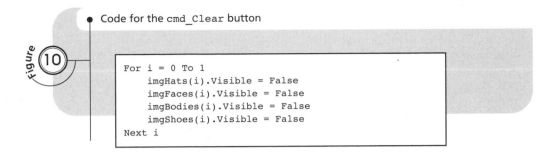

Figure 10

Code for the cmd_Clear button

```
For i = 0 To 1
    imgHats(i).Visible = False
    imgFaces(i).Visible = False
    imgBodies(i).Visible = False
    imgShoes(i).Visible = False
Next i
```

TESTING YOUR PROGRAM

Test your game by clicking the Start button ▶, making a set of image choices, and seeing if the appropriate pictures appear. Click the Clear button to erase whatever cartoons are on the screen. Click the Stop button ■ to return to the Design phase.

OPTIONAL ENHANCEMENTS

There are many ways you can customize your Mix and Match Cartoons program. Following are some suggestions to get you started on adding original features and functionality.

1. Use a different control mechanism (for example, option buttons) for indicating the player's feature selection.
2. Prepare one more picture file for each of the four categories. Make the changes in the design phase and in the programming to make the application work.
3. Add feature categories such as arms, legs, ties, and gloves, for a more detailed cartoon.
4. Make the images appear on the form so that the player can see the image before he selects it.

DISCUSSION QUESTIONS

1. It is possible to have unequal numbers of feature options; for example, you could have more hats than faces. The version of the game that you just created assumes that there are the same number of options in each category. How can you change this? (*Hint*: Declare four variables in the **(General)** section, like this:

```
Dim intHats As Integer

Dim intFaces As Integer

Dim intBodies As Integer

Dim intShoes As Integer
```

Use these values in the Clear routine in four distinct For...Next loops.)

CONSTRUCTION PLAN FOR
CHANCE

CONCEPTS, SKILLS, AND TOOLS

In this chapter, you will create a computer version of the game of Chance, a gambling game played with dice. The program simulates the rolling of dice and keeps track of whether the player wins or loses. To create an acceptable implementation of the game, the programmer must combine elements that replicate the look and feel of the traditional game while accommodating and making use of computer features.

You will use the following general programming concepts in the Chance construction plan:

- Data representation
- Creating a user interface
- Initialization
- Indexing
- Presenting feedback for user interaction
- Random events

The Visual Basic features used to construct this game include:

- For...Next statement
- Select Case statement
- Control arrays
- Image control objects
- Visibility of controls
- Message boxes
- Randomize and Rnd functions

DESCRIPTION OF THE GAME

This game simulates the rolling of dice by a single player and determines whether the player wins or loses according to the rules of a casino game known as Chance (you may also know this game by the name "Craps"). The player rolls two dice, and the spots on the dice are added together. The player wins on the first roll if the dice show a total of 7 or 11. The player loses if the total is 2, 3, or 12. If another number is thrown on the first roll—for example, a 10—that number becomes the **point**, or the goal of subsequent tosses. The player continues to roll the dice until the point or a 7 appears. Throwing a total equal to the point means the player wins; throwing a total of 7 means the player loses.

Try the game using the chance.exe file in your Ch3 folder. Get a sense of the game, especially if it is unfamiliar to you. While the program is relatively simple, you will need to construct a control array for the die faces. Control arrays were used in the Chapter 2 construction plan for Mix and Match Cartoons.

HOW THIS VERSION OF CHANCE WORKS

The game simulates the rolling of the dice using control arrays of images and program-generated pseudorandom numbers. You can implement the logic for the rules of the game (as described in the previous paragraphs) using two Select Case statements and an If statement.

SAMPLE SCREENS

Figures 1 through 5 show the game screen at various stages of play. Figure 1 shows the game screen prior to the first roll.

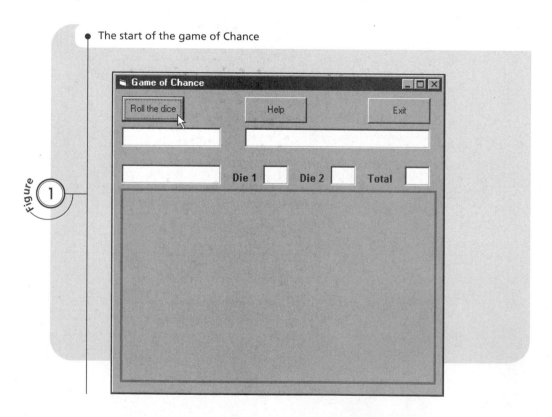

The start of the game of Chance

Figure 1

The player starts the game by rolling the dice, which is done by clicking the Roll the dice command button. If the player rolls a 7 or an 11 on the first roll, the player wins, as in Figure 2.

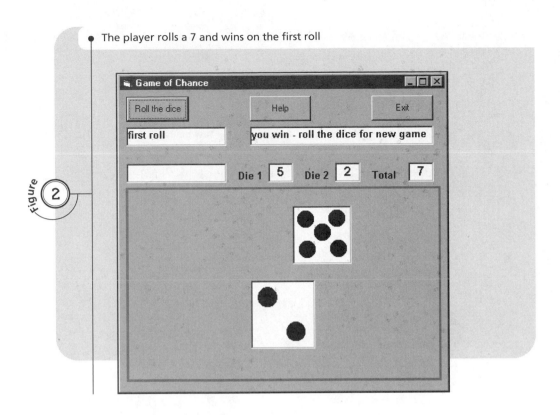

The player rolls a 7 and wins on the first roll

Figure 2

If the player rolls a 2, 3, or 12 on the first roll, he loses. If the player rolls any other number on the first roll, that number becomes the point (see Figure 3).

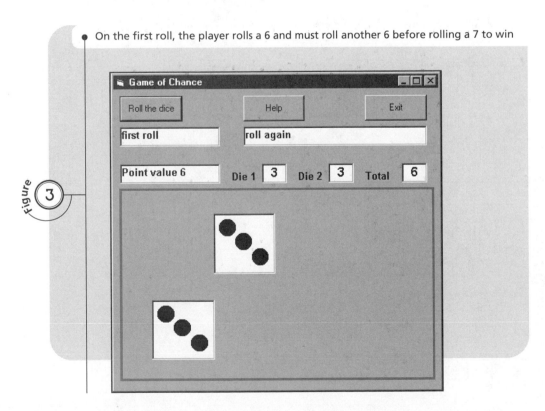

On the first roll, the player rolls a 6 and must roll another 6 before rolling a 7 to win

To win, the player must match the point value from the first roll on a follow-up roll before he rolls a 7 (see Figure 4).

The player wins by rolling a 6 on a follow-up roll

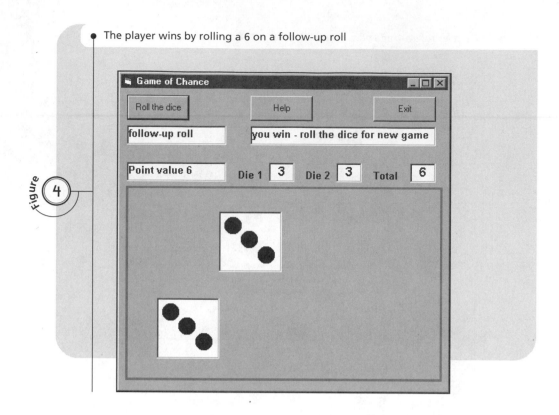

Figure 4

If the player rolls a 7 instead of the point, he loses, as in Figure 5.

The player loses by rolling a 7 on a follow-up roll

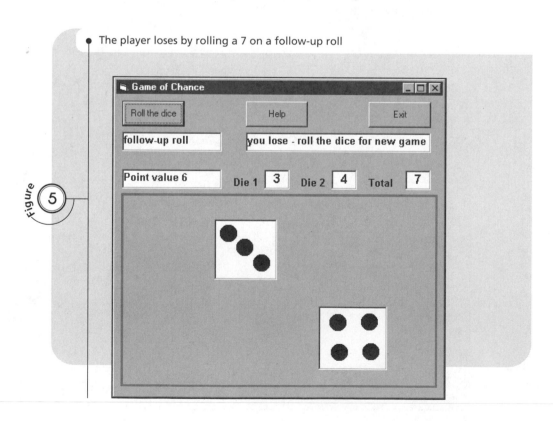

Figure 5

KEY DESIGN ISSUES

There are four key design tasks that you—the designer and programmer—must accomplish when creating the Chance game:

- Represent the dice

- Simulate rolling the dice

- Recognize whether the player is making a first roll or follow-up roll

- Determine a win or loss

Solutions to each of these programming tasks are presented in the next section. Use these suggestions as guidelines when programming your version of Chance.

Task: Represent the dice.
Logic: The game must provide a visual image of the dice.
Solution: The dice are represented with a control array of seven Image objects (indexed from 0 to 6). Each object's Index value will correspond to its die face value. The object with an Index value equal to 0 will be used for rolls of doubles; for example, two 2s, two 6s, and so on.

Task: Simulate rolling the dice.
Logic: When the player clicks the "Roll the dice" button, a seemingly random dice result must appear on the screen.
Solution: The task here is to program code to produce what appear to be random results. As you learned in Chapter 1, Visual Basic has two functions—Randomize and Rnd—that you can use to produce random numbers. For Chance, you will need to produce random numbers between 1 and 6. After your code generates these random numbers, it will make the corresponding images appear so that it will look as if dice were rolled on the screen.

Task: Recognize whether the player is making a first roll or a follow-up roll.
Logic: The game must keep track of whether the player is making an initial or a subsequent roll, because the rules for determining a win or a loss are different depending on which roll it is. For example, a 7 on a first roll is a win, but on a follow-up roll it is a loss.
Solution: Use a Boolean variable, **blnFirstRoll**, to store the status of the game; in other words, this variable will track whether the player is making a first or a follow-up roll. When play begins, **blnFirstRoll** will be set to True. After the player's first roll, it will be set to False. Whenever a game ends in a win or a loss, the game will reset the variable to True to allow the player to play another game.

Task: Determine a win or loss.
Logic: The program you produce uses the rules of the casino game to indicate wins and losses.
Solution: The logic for determining a win or a loss is implemented in the Click event procedure for the command button labeled "Roll the dice." If the player is making a first roll (determined by the value in the Boolean variable **blnFirstRoll**), then the game implements the rules for determining a win on the first roll. If the player is making a follow-up roll, then the game implements the rules for determining a win on a follow-up roll.

PREPARING TO PROGRAM

CREATING A CONTROL ARRAY

You will need to create a control array of seven Image objects. You can create the Image objects using the Image tool . You need to indicate to Visual Basic that these seven Image objects actually belong to one group called a control array. You must also associate the correct die face images (1 through 6) with the matching Image object Index values.

As you learned in Chapter 2, you can create a control array in two ways. The first method sets the Name properties of the Image objects to the same value. The second method uses the copy and paste operation. Use either method to create seven Image objects.

LOADING PICTURES INTO THE CONTROL ARRAY imgDice

Once you have created the control array, you must load it with the dice images.

To load a graphic image into an Image object:

1. Select an element of the control array **imgDice** and note its Index property from the Properties window. Figure 6 shows how to do this. (Ignore **imgDice(0)**— element 0—for the time being.)

Figure 6

Selecting a control array item

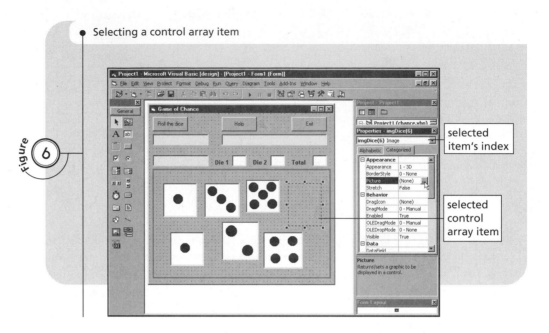

selected item's index

selected control array item

2. On the Properties window, click **Picture**.

3. From the Load Picture window, select the appropriate file (the number on the die face bitmap file must match the Index property of the selected Image object), as shown in Figure 7.

Figure 7

Visual Basic Load Picture window

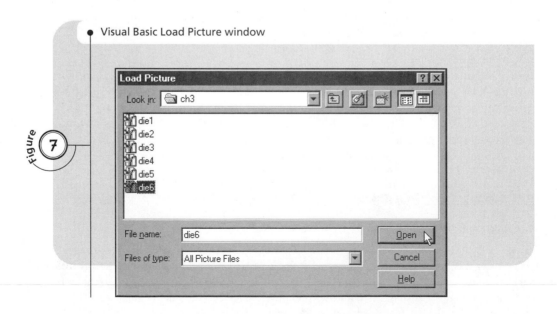

4. Click **Open** to create the association between the graphic file and the Image item.

5. Repeat this process for **imgDice(1)** through **imgDice(6)**.

Using the `imgDice(0)` Object

Recall that the `imgDice(0)` element can be used to display the die face when the player rolls doubles, that is, when the same number is produced for each die. If the Random function generates the same number for each random selection, then code in the `cmdRoll_Click` event procedure will store a copy of the die face in `imgDice(0)`.

GENERATING RANDOM ROLLS OF THE DICE

Rolling the dice is by its nature a random event. Your game needs to simulate this randomness. To do this, you will use the Randomize and Rnd functions. Randomize initializes Visual Basic's random number generator. Rnd produces a fractional value greater than or equal to zero and less than one.

Use the following formula to convert the fractional values generated by Rnd to the values 1, 2, 3, 4, 5, and 6. This code will cause the variables `intDie1` and `intDie2` to each be set to one of the values 1 through 6. Then use these values as the die values rolled by the player.

```
intDie1 = Int(1 + 6 * Rnd)
intDie2 = Int(1 + 6 * Rnd)
```

This expression that occurs in each line is evaluated as follows:

1. `intDie1` and `intDie2` are Integer variables that will store the values of each die roll.

2. Rnd returns a fraction between 0 and 1, and this fraction is multiplied by 6. This creates a number in the range of equal to or greater than 0 to less than 6.

3. Adding 1 makes the result a number in the range of equal to or greater than 1 to less than 7.

4. The Int function truncates (discards) any fractional portion. Thus, the number 1.4356783 becomes 1, the number 6.74532 becomes 6, and so forth.

Once your Visual Basic code has generated two random numbers, your code uses these numbers to display the appropriate die faces and carry out the rest of the logic for the game. If the two values are different, the code simply makes the appropriate two Image controls visible. If the two values are the same, the code must copy one image in the extra Image control and make it visible.

PLAN FOR THE USER INTERFACE

The two primary things that your Chance interface must do are provide a way for the player to roll the dice and display the status of the game (including the results of the dice roll).

DISPLAYING THE DICE ROLL

Your game should show the results of rolling the dice in two ways: images of two die faces will appear in the dice area, and the corresponding values will appear in labels on the form.

To show the dice for the game of Chance, you will need a control array of Image control objects. Each object holds a graphic image of a die face (your Ch3 data file folder contains six bitmap image files that you can use for this purpose). At most, only two of these images will be visible to the player during the game—the rest will be invisible. When a certain number is rolled by the user, the game sets the Visible property of the corresponding Image object to True. The position of the die faces on the form is fixed; that is, the 1 die always appears in the same place in the dice area, the 2 die is at another fixed position, and so on.

You might at first think you only need six images for the dice. Six will be enough for most rolls, but, as mentioned earlier, you need to allow for doubles. In this case, an extra image is needed to display the duplicate die. If the player rolls a double 3 your code will set the Picture property of the extra image equal to the Picture property of the third element of the control array. Your code will set both Visible properties to True.

You will use the Image object with an Index property equal to 0 for the double situation. Since **imgDice(0)** is automatically created when you create the other Image items (because all control arrays begin with 0), you may as well use it for this specialized job. Image items **imgDice(1)** through **imgDice(6)** correspond to the six faces of the die. No matter what die value is a double, you can always use **imgDice(0)** to display it.

TRACKING THE STATUS OF THE GAME

The user interface will use several labels to display information indicating whether the current roll (that is, the roll the player is about to make) is a first roll or a subsequent roll. Also, when appropriate, labels will indicate a win or a loss. One label indicates the point value (if the play doesn't end on the first roll), and there are also labels for the values of the dice and their sum value.

⊙ FORM DESIGN

This section describes all of the objects contained in the final design for Chance, which is shown in Figure 8. Follow this plan to place all the objects needed on your form. The object names listed below are suggestions; you may rename them if desired (if you do, be sure to revise your code accordingly). Set captions for command buttons and labels as suggested. Placement of objects are suggestions—you may lay out your form differently, if you wish.

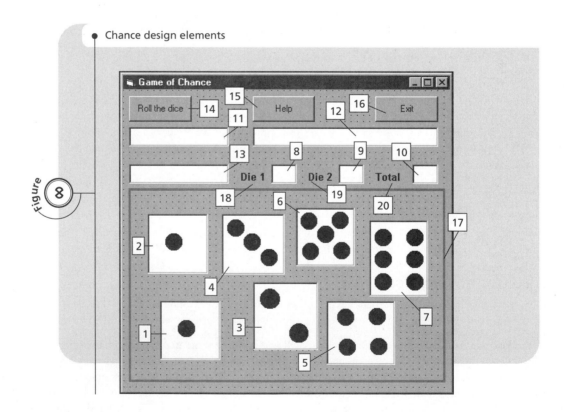

Figure 8

● Chance design elements

Control array elements

1. **imgDice(0)**: 0th element of control array of dice face images. Used in the case of doubles.

2. **imgDice(1)**: First element of control array of dice face images. Used when Randomize and Rnd generate a 1.

3. **imgDice(2)**: Second element of control array of dice face images. Used when Randomize and Rnd generate a 2.

4. **imgDice(3)**: Third element of control array of dice face images. Used when Randomize and Rnd generate a 3.

5. **imgDice(4)**: Fourth element of control array of dice face images. Used when Randomize and Rnd generate a 4.

6. **imgDice(5)**: Fifth element of control array of dice face images. Used when Randomize and Rnd generate a 5.

7. **imgDice(6)**: Sixth element of control array of dice face images. Used when Randomize and Rnd generate a 6.

Labels that display dice values

8. **lblDie1Value**: Displays the number value of first die

9. **lblDie2Value**: Displays the number value of second die

10. **lblSumDice**: Displays the number value (sum) of the two dice

Labels that display progress of game

11. **lblTurn**: Indicates whether the player is about to make a first roll or follow-up roll

12. **lblStatus**: Signals that the player has either won or lost

13. **lblPointValue**: Displays the dice value the player must match on a subsequent roll (the point) to win

Command buttons

14. **cmdRoll**: Rolls the dice for the player

15. **cmdHelp**: Displays the rules of the game of Chance (describes what determines a win and what determines a loss)

16. **cmdExit**: Exits the game

Other objects

17. **Shape1**: Rectangle shape with transparent fill for displaying the dice

18. **lblDie1**: Label with caption "Die 1"

19. **lblDie2**: Label with caption "Die 2"

20. **lblTotal**: Label with caption "Total"

VARIABLES AND CONSTANTS DECLARED IN THE (General) SECTION

In your Chance program, include the following variables and constants in the **(General)** section. These two variables define the state of the game.

Element	Explanation
Dim blnFirstRoll As Boolean	When equal to True, this variable indicates that the player is about to make a first roll. When equal to False, **blnFirstRoll** indicates that the player has already made a first roll.

Element	Explanation
`Dim intPointNum As Integer`	Stores the point (the sum of the two dice rolled by the player on a first roll; to win, the player must match this amount on a subsequent roll)

⊙ ALGORITHMS FOR EVENT PROCEDURES

THE `Form_Load()` *EVENT PROCEDURE*

The **Form_Load** event procedure occurs when this Visual Basic game is launched. For this game, you will include one line of code: set the initial value of **blnFirstRoll** to True, which initializes the game.

THE `cmdRoll_Click()` *EVENT PROCEDURE*

The **cmdRoll_Click** event procedure is triggered when the player clicks the command button labeled "Roll the dice." This event procedure contains the code to roll the dice (using the Visual Basic random number generator) and determine the outcome of the roll—win, lose, or roll again.

You will need the following variables for the **cmdRoll_Click** event procedure:

Element	Explanation
`Dim intDie1 As Integer`	Stores the value of first rolled die
`Dim intDie2 As Integer`	Stores the value of second rolled die
`Dim intTotal As Integer`	Stores the sum of the rolled dice
`Dim i As Integer`	Used in a For…Next loop to set each die image not visible

To implement the **cmdRoll_Click** event procedure:

1. Set the Visible property of each of the seven elements in **ImgDice** to False. The simplest way to do this is with a For…Next loop that goes from 0 to 6.

2. Implement a roll of the dice using the following code to load random numbers in the range from 1 through 6 in each die:

```
Randomize
intDie1 = Int(1 + 6 * Rnd)
intDie2 = Int(1 + 6 * Rnd)
```

3. Add the values of **intDie1** and **intDie2** and store the sum in **intTotal**.

4. Display the values of **intDie1**, **intDie2**, and **intTotal** on the screen by setting the Caption properties of **lblDie1Value**, **lblDie2Value**, and **lblSumDice** appropriately. You will need to use the Format function to store an Integer variable such as **intDie1**, **intDie2**, or **intTotal** in an item's Caption property. For example, this code stores the value of **intDie1** in **lblDie1Value.Caption**:
   `lblDie1Value.Caption = Format(intDie1)`
   You need similar code for **intDie2** and **intTotal**.

5. Make the two elements of **imgDice()** rolled (from **intDie1** and **intDie2**) visible (set their Visible properties to True).

If the values for both Image items are the same—that is, if the player rolled doubles—you will need to use **imgDice(0)** object to display on the second die the value of the first die. Notice that although there are six possible values for the second die (1 through 6), you only need one location to display the second copy of the double throw, no matter what its value. In the case of a double, the code shown in Figure 9 displays two dice with the same value.

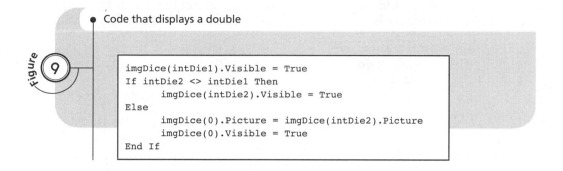

• Code that displays a double

Figure 9

```
imgDice(intDie1).Visible = True
If intDie2 <> intDie1 Then
        imgDice(intDie2).Visible = True
Else
        imgDice(0).Picture = imgDice(intDie2).Picture
        imgDice(0).Visible = True
End If
```

Finally, the game must determine the status of the player's roll. For example, did the player roll a 7 to win, or should he roll again? Remember, the rules for a win or a loss differ depending on whether it is the first roll.

The logic you need to use to determine and display status is shown in Figure 10.

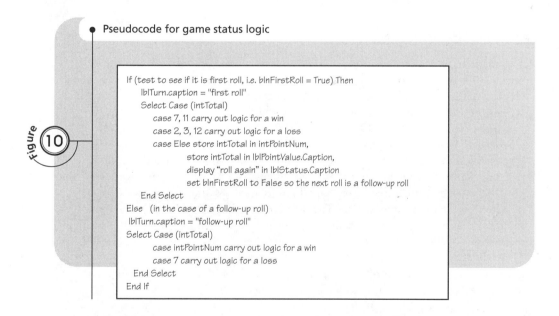

• Pseudocode for game status logic

Figure 10

```
If (test to see if it is first roll, i.e. blnFirstRoll = True) Then
    lblTurn.caption = "first roll"
    Select Case (intTotal)
        case 7, 11 carry out logic for a win
        case 2, 3, 12 carry out logic for a loss
        case Else store intTotal in intPointNum,
                store intTotal in lblPointValue.Caption,
                display "roll again" in lblStatus.Caption
                set blnFirstRoll to False so the next roll is a follow-up roll
    End Select
Else   (in the case of a follow-up roll)
 lblTurn.caption = "follow-up roll"
Select Case (intTotal)
        case intPointNum carry out logic for a win
        case 7 carry out logic for a loss
  End Select
End If
```

The Visual Basic code to carry out this logic uses an If Then Else statement that tests to determine whether the current roll is a first roll. Inside each part of the If Then Else is a nested Select Case statement that carries out the logic for determining a win or loss for either a first roll or a follow-up roll. Your code will need to follow the nested structure of the pseudocode shown in Figure 10.

THE **cmdExit_Click()** EVENT PROCEDURE

The player clicks the exit button to end the game. It has one statement:

```
End
```

THE `cmdHelp_Click()` *EVENT PROCEDURE*

A novice Chance player probably will need some assistance understanding the rules of the game. The Help button provides basic background on rules, which are as follows: "On first roll, 7 or 11 wins and 2, 3, or 12 loses. Otherwise, dice total is the point, or the target number, that you are attempting to roll. To win, you must roll the point before you roll a 7."

To program the **cmd_Help** button, declare a variable named **strRules As String**. Store the entire rules paragraph in this variable in the following manner:

```
strRules = "On first roll" _
& " 7 or 11 wins and" _
& "2, 3, or 12 loses."
...
```

and so forth until the whole paragraph is stored. Using the underscore allows you to write code longer than one line. The ampersand is the concatenation operator. An alternative way to create a long string is as follows:

```
strRules = "On first roll"
strRules = strRules & " 7 or 11 wins and"
strRules = strRules & " 2, 3, or 12 loses."
```

Finally, use the Visual Basic function MsgBox to display rules on the screen, as follows:

```
MsgBox strRules
```

OPTIONAL ENHANCEMENTS

1. The **cmdRoll_Click** event procedure could be made more modular. What sections of this button's code could you make into distinct user-defined procedures? Consult Visual Basic Help for guidance. One possibility is to extract the code that reveals the Image control objects representing the dice. There are other possibilities. Try to keep the **cmdRoll_Click** button's code on less than half a screen-length, with procedure and function names that are self-explanatory.
2. The position of the dice on the screen depends on the values of each die. Modify the program so that the location of the dice following a roll varies. (*Hint:* Look at how the extra control is used.) You can add more controls and/or you can alter positions of the dice on the screen. To make the interface appear even more natural, design your game so that the dice's borders don't necessarily line up with the rectangular borders of the form.
3. Make the dice green or some other color.
4. Dice are available with more or less than six sides. Make up a set of rules for a dice game involving such dice. Modify your Chance code accordingly.

DISCUSSION QUESTIONS

1. The approach of using one extra Image control for handling doubles is not the only way to handle doubles. Consider using two control arrays, with six elements each. How would this work?
2. Do research on dice games or other games of chance. One significant enhancement would be to implement support for so-called side bets. In casinos, other players can make bets for or against the player. Implement code that incorporates side bets into your chance program.

CONSTRUCTION PLAN FOR
MEMORY

◎ CONCEPTS, SKILLS, AND TOOLS

In this chapter, you will create a computer version of the game of Memory (also known as Concentration), a matching game played with cards.

You will use the following general programming concepts, skills, and tools in the Memory construction plan:

- Object swapping, or having objects change places in an array
- Parallel arrays, that is, sets of arrays holding corresponding items
- Coding a delay without using a Timer object (using busy wait)
- Boolean variables that control logic

The Visual Basic features used to construct this game include:

- Control visibility
- Picture Box controls that change during run time
- Message boxes
- Multiple event handling
- Select Case statement
- If Then Else statement
- User-defined subroutines and functions

⊙ DESCRIPTION OF THE GAME

Memory is played with a deck of cards containing pairs of matching images. The cards are spread out face-down and one or two players take turns making a move. A move consists of turning over two cards at a time. If the two selected cards match, the player removes both cards and keeps playing. If the cards do not match, they are turned back over, and if two people are playing, the other player takes over. Each player can see the location of the non-matching cards that were flipped by his opponent. When all the matches have been found, the player with the most cards in his discard pile wins. In the one-player situation, play can continue until the player wins by finding all the matches, or the game can be limited by the number of turns or by time.

At first, it's random luck if a player hits a match. But as more cards are turned over, the player who best remembers the location of cards has the advantage.

HOW THIS VERSION OF MEMORY WORKS

For this implementation, Memory will be a one-person game. The computer is responsible for shuffling and placing the cards, displaying cards that are selected, removing matches from the screen, and turning nonmatching cards back over. The images used in this version are the flags of eight African nations. Each flag has a matching pair, so the game will start with 16 flags face-down. Get a feel for how the game works by running the **memory.exe** file, located in your Ch4 folder.

SAMPLE SCREENS

Figure 1 shows the eight flags.

● African flags

Figure 1

Flag image	Country name	Filename
	Ethiopia	ethiopia.bmp
	Ghana	ghana.bmp
	Guinea	guinea.bmp
	Madagascar	malagass.bmp
	Morocco	morocco.bmp
	Namibia	namibia.bmp
	Senegal	senegal.bmp
	Sierra Leone	sierleon.bmp

When the game first begins (see Figure 2), the 16 flags are face down.

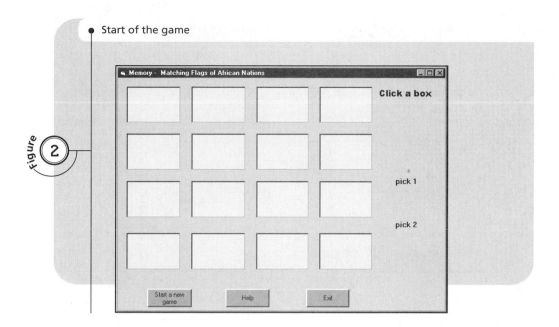

Start of the game

Figure 2

The player turns over a flag by clicking it. When the player clicks a flag, the computer displays the flag image and the name of its country. When the player turns over a second flag, the computer turns it over and displays its country name. The game then determines if the two flags match. If they do not match, the game displays the message "no match," one second elapses, and then the game turns the flags back face down. Figure 3 shows the screen that depicts two nonmatching flags.

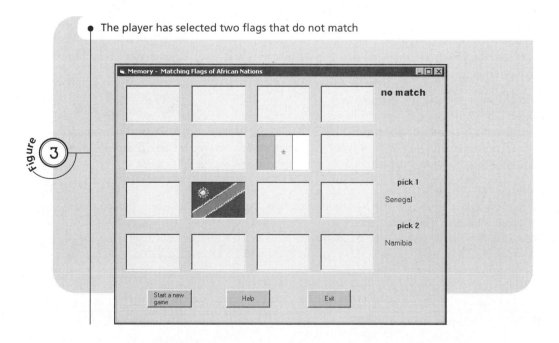

The player has selected two flags that do not match

Figure 3

If the player selects matching flags, the message "match" is displayed (see Figure 4), and the matching flags are removed from the screen as play continues. The game ends when all the flags have been matched and removed from the screen.

Player uncovers a match

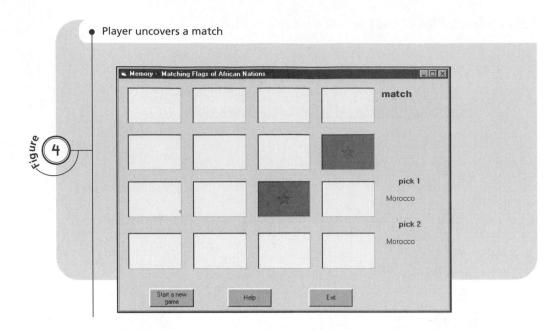

Figure 4

◎ KEY DESIGN ISSUES

There are five key design tasks that you—the designer and programmer—must accomplish when creating the Memory game:

- Display the flags on the screen

- Turn over the flags one at a time

- Shuffle the flags before play begins

- Recognize that the player has selected two flags

- Recognize a match

Solutions to each of these programming tasks are presented in the next section. Use these suggestions as guidelines when programming your version of Memory.

Task: Display the flags on the screen.
Logic: The game must display 16 flags (eight pairs) and their reverse "blank" sides.
Solution: Create a control array of Picture Box elements named **picFlag**. When play begins, each element will display a blank image by loading the file **blank.bmp**. When the player clicks a face-down flag, an image of a flag is loaded into that element.

Task: Turn over the flags one at a time.
Logic: The player must be able to see only one flag at a time. As the flag is turned face up, the game must also display its name.
Solution: Your code will use the names of the flags to load the correct image. To store the names of the flags, create a second control array named **lblFlagName** equal in size to the **picFlag** control array. This second array will remain hidden during execution of the game. The label **lblFlagName** will hold the names of the image files for the flags. When the player clicks an element of the **picFlag** control array, the image file named in the corresponding element of **lblFlagName** will be loaded into the **picFlag** control array element. This technique is called parallel arrays.

Task: Shuffle the flags before play begins.
Logic: The flags should appear in different locations each time the game is played. The computer will do the shuffling in the same way people often do the shuffling: swapping pairs of cards.

Solution: The game will shuffle the filenames of the image files for the flags rather than the flags themselves. The filenames for the flags are the key piece of information the game needs to load each flag. The layout of all eight pairs of flags occurs in the subroutine `load_names`. Then in the subroutine **swap_names**, two random numbers are generated within the range of 0 to 15 and stored in **intSwap1** and **intSwap2**. Swap the positions of the two filenames so that **intSwap1** takes the position of **intSwap2** and **intSwap2** takes the position of **intSwap1**. Repeat the swap 16 times.

Task: Recognize that the player has selected two flags.
Logic: The game performs different actions depending on whether the player is making a first selection or a second selection.
Solution: Set a Boolean variable **blnFirstTurn** equal to True during Form_Load and then reset it after every complete move. For the first player move and every subsequent one, **blnFirstTurn** is equal to True until the player selects the first card. Then, set it to False after the player has picked one flag. After the player picks a second flag, completing the move, your code should reset **blnFirstTurn** to True to allow play to continue.

Task: Recognize a match.
Logic: The game needs to perform certain actions depending on whether the player's flag selections are a match.
Solution: After the player has picked two flags, the game compares their filenames. If the filenames are equal, then the selected flags are a match. In other words, use the filenames for the calculations of the game, and then use these filenames to set the Picture properties of the Picture Box controls as needed. The filenames are hidden from the player to present an interface that resembles the real game in which there are only pictures, not names.

PREPARING TO PROGRAM

LOADING PICTURES FROM FILES

The Memory game displays images of flags. In earlier games, such as Mix and Match Cartoons and Chance, you included images in your project by loading them onto your form during design time. Since Memory uses nine images (eight flags plus one blank) it is more difficult to do this during design time. Instead, you will write code to use the Visual Basic function LoadPicture, which reads in a picture from a file during run time.

You will need nine files, one for each flag, plus an image of the blank or reverse side of the flags. You will find these files in the Ch4 folder. You should copy all nine .bmp files from the Ch4 folder into the same subdirectory as your Visual Basic project files.

When the player launches Memory, each Picture Box object displays the blank image, which is a result of using the LoadPicture function to store the picture from the file blank.bmp in each Picture object in the control array picFlags. The code to do this is:

```
For i = 0 To 15
    picFlag(i).Picture = LoadPicture("blank.bmp")
Next i
```

It is important to understand that while the player sees all blanks, the game must know where each flag is hidden. The game needs this information in order to be able to turn over the right flag and correctly determine whether the player has found a matching pair.

In order for the game to know this information, it must be coded into the program. Your game will provide the flag location data by including a second control array with the same number of elements as the first. This second control array, **lblFlagName**, will store the filename for each picture. It is never visible to the player.

When the player clicks a blank image, your code will use the filename from the corresponding **lblFlagName** element to display the correct flag. It will do this by using the contents of the Caption property to find the right filename for a flag, then use the LoadPicture function to display the flag.

When the player clicks a card, Visual Basic invokes the Click event procedure, **picFlag_Click**. Since **picFlag** is a control array, this procedure has a parameter: Index. The value of this parameter will be the specific element of the control array the player has clicked. Therefore, if the player clicks the fifth element, Index will hold the value (4). Remember: indexing starts from zero. Your code will then use this Index value to put the right picture 'into' **picFlag(Index)** and display it to the player. The code for this association is:

```
picFlag(Index).Picture = LoadPicture(lblFlagName(Index).Caption)
```

No flag is associated with a **picFlag** element until the player clicks it. Figure 5 shows the correlation between **picFlag** elements and **lblFlagName** elements.

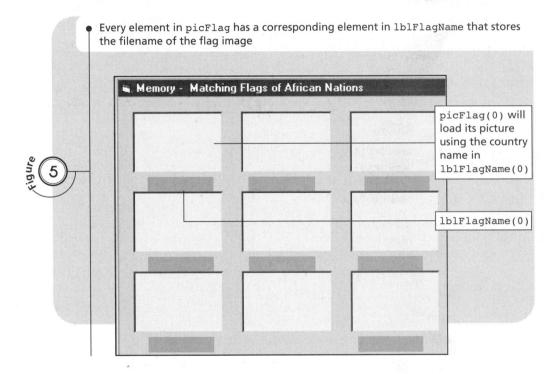

Every element in picFlag has a corresponding element in lblFlagName that stores the filename of the flag image

Figure 5

Memory - Matching Flags of African Nations

picFlag(0) will load its picture using the country name in lblFlagName(0)

lblFlagName(0)

When the player selects a flag by clicking it, the game displays the flag (the picture from **picFlag**) and its country name (the Caption property from **lblFlagName**). After the player selects a second flag and it is displayed, your code tests for a match by making a comparison between the two filenames for each flag. If these filenames match, the flags are removed from the screen by setting their Visible properties to False. If the flags do not match, then your code will redisplay the blanks. The game ends when all of the matches are found. In this basic game, there is no way for the player to lose.

SHUFFLING THE FLAGS USING SWAP

Before the game begins your code must arrange the layout of the flags. Ideally, the layout should be different each time the player starts a new game. As you can probably guess, this task involves random numbers—but the obvious solution in this case is not the best one.

At first, you might attempt to solve this problem by generating 16 pseudorandom numbers between 0 and 15, then using them to place the 16 flags. But by using this method, the most likely outcome is that you will have duplicate random numbers (it is actually highly unlikely that none of the random numbers will match). This solution also would be quite complex to implement, since it requires you to keep track of lots of information. For example, you will need to know which flags have been placed, which flags still need to be placed in a Picture Box on the form, and which spots are still free (and which have been taken).

> **TIP**
>
> The likely outcome that a group of 16 random numbers will contain duplicates is based on a mathematical idea called "permutations and combinations," which states that if you allow duplicates, then the entire set of possible random combinations is equal to 16 * 16 * 16 etc., or 16 raised to the 16th power. The number of possible combinations with no duplicates is equal to 16 * 15 * 14 * 13 * ... * 1. If you compare the results of these two formulas, you will see that the first number is much larger than the second number, so the probability is very high that you will have duplicates in the set of pseudorandom numbers that you generate.

This method would require complex logic and several data structures to keep track of the shuffling. It would also require a complex test (conditional statement) to determine when the shuffling was complete.

There is an alternative solution that works well and is quite simple to implement. When young children play cards, they are not coordinated enough to properly shuffle. Instead, they place cards face-down on a large surface and randomly mix them around. Your version of Memory will implement the computer version of this shuffling method.

First, you will only shuffle the names of the files for each flag; you don't need to shuffle the flag images, because during most of play each element displays a blank image. The flag image is loaded only when the player selects a flag. During the **Form_Load** event, all 16 filenames (eight pairs) are placed in elements 0 through 15 of the control array **lblFlagName**. This step is the equivalent of spreading out the cards. Then, your code will generate two random numbers. These numbers, stored in the variables **intSwap1** and **intSwap2**, are integer values between 0 and 15.

Next, the two elements are swapped, or change places. Performing a swap is a common task in programming. It requires a temporary storage place to allow the objects to change places without losing data. The algorithm is shown in Figure 6.

Figure 6

Pseudocode for swapping

1. Place the caption from element intSwap1 in the temporary location strName
2. Place the Caption from element intSwap2 in intSwap1
3. Place strName (remember its value comes from intSwap1) into the Caption of intSwap2

The Caption property originally from element **intSwap1** is now in **intSwap2**, and the Caption originally in **intSwap2** is now in **intSwap1**.

This shuffle is set up to swap the flags 16 times. Using random numbers, that means that most (if not all) of the flags will be moved at least once. Of course, it is possible that **intSwap1** and **intSwap2** will have the same value. In that case, neither flag will move. In the bigger picture, the final goal is to rearrange most of the flags, and this process is effective and simple to program.

USER-DEFINED SUBROUTINES AND FUNCTIONS

If you look at any of the games you have created so far, you will notice that all the code you have written is inside an event procedure. This does not include the **(General)** section, which is only used for declaring variables and constants. All the event procedures you have used so far begin with **Private Sub** and end with **End Sub**. The word **Private** indicates this code is meant for this project only, and the **Sub**… **End Sub** words act as boundaries for the event procedure.

The primary purpose of this syntax is to give your code some structure and organization. Think about how books are organized. All of the text is within a chapter, and the chapter beginnings and endings are clearly marked.

In addition to using event procedures, you have used functions and subroutines that are part of Visual Basic. You have used Randomize and Rnd to generate random numbers, and Format to display numbers in a label object. The advantage of using built-in functions and subroutines is that they are able to complete a specified task as many times as needed. For example, in the game of Chance, your code repeatedly generated two random die values whenever the player clicked the "Roll the dice" button.

As programming projects grow in size and complexity, it becomes necessary for you, the programmer, to create your own subroutines and functions. In Visual Basic, these are referred to as **user-defined subroutines** and **user-defined functions**.

The difference between a function and a subroutine is that a function returns a value while a subroutine does not. A function can be used in an expression, including standing by itself as the right-hand part of an assignment statement.

A subroutine, in contrast, does not return a value. It is invoked by the system itself when an event occurs or using the **Call** statement. Note that sometimes the terms "routine" or "procedure" are used to refer to both functions and subroutines.

Both subroutines and functions can have parameters. A parameter is a special kind of variable that is passed into a procedure. Parameters contain information vital to the performance of the task a procedure is designed to carry out. Since you are creating these procedures from scratch, you must define the number and type of parameters your procedures will need. Visual Basic constructs the event procedure headers for you.

For example, you will be writing a user-defined subroutine named **swap_names**, which will rearrange the locations of the flags before the start of a game. **swap_names** does not need to be passed any information to carry out this task. An example of a procedure that requires parameters is **test_for_match**, which compares two picks to see if they match. The procedure needs a reference to the elements the player picked, and these references are included as parameters.

For this version of Memory, you will be creating the following user-defined procedures:

Procedure
`Private Sub swap_names()`
Description
Performs the shuffling of the flags around the screen.

Example of calling code: **Call swap_names()**

Procedure

```
Private Sub delay(interval As Single)
```

Description

Pauses the game for the amount of time specified in interval.

Example of calling code: **Call delay(1)**

Procedure

```
Private Sub test_for_match(pick1 As Integer, pick2 As Integer)
```

Description

Compares two picks. If equal, the flags are removed from the game. If not equal, blanks are redisplayed.

Example of calling code: **Call test_for_match(intFirstPick,Index)**

Procedure

```
Private Sub set_up_blanks()
```

Description

Displays a blank in every Picture object.

Example of calling code: **Call set_up_blanks()**

Procedure

```
Private Function get_flag_name(Index As Integer) As String
```

Description

Index refers to the element for which a country name has been requested. By examining the Caption property of **lblFlag(Index)**, the correct country is returned.

Example of calling code: **lblPick1.Caption = get_flag_name(Index)**

It is quite simple to write your own user-defined procedures. To start writing a user-defined subroutine, scroll down to the bottom of your Code window. Find a spot outside of any existing procedures, then begin typing the procedure, starting with Private Sub. For example, for the first subroutine, you would type **Private Sub swap_names()**, then press the Enter key. Visual Basic will automatically generate the line End Sub. The code at this point will look something like this:

```
Private Sub swap_names()


End Sub
```

As in the event procedures, you place your code between the **Private Sub** and the **End Sub** keywords.

When creating a user-defined function, you begin with the words **Private Function**, and then Visual Basic generates the **End Function** code.

The syntax for returning a value for a function in Visual Basic is to assign the value to be returned to the name of the function itself. For example, you will be writing a user-defined function **get_flag_name**, which returns a String containing the name of a specific country. This code returns the name "Ethiopia":

```
get_flag_name = "Ethiopia"
```

PLAN FOR THE USER INTERFACE

The game needs to display a set of cards, or flags, face-down. It also needs a mechanism to allow the player to pick a card to turn over. The simplest way for a player to pick something from a computer screen is to click it. Therefore, you will use the Click event of each card to carry out the logic for the game.

FORM DESIGN

This section describes all of the objects contained in the final design for Memory. Follow this plan to place all of the objects needed on your form, as shown in Figure 7. The object names listed below are suggestions; you may rename these objects, if desired (if you do, be sure to revise your code accordingly).

Set captions for command buttons and labels as suggested. Placement of objects are suggestions—you may lay out your form differently, if you wish.

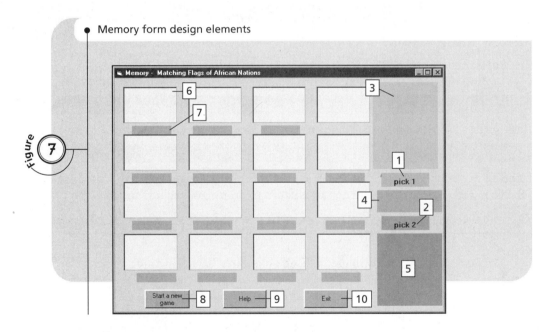

● Memory form design elements

Figure 7

Constant labels (stay the same throughout execution)

1. **Label1**: Object with caption equal to "pick 1"

2. **Label2**: Object with caption equal to "pick 2"

Variable labels (contents updated during run time)

3. **lblMsg**: Displays the messages "click a box," "match," "no match," and "game over" as the player chooses cards and plays the game to its conclusion

4. **lblPick1**: Displays the name of the country for the first flag selected by the player

5. **lblPick2**: Displays the name of the country for the second flag selected by the player

Control arrays

6. **picFlag**: Control array of 16 Picture Box objects with Index values 0 to 15.

7. **lblFlagName**: Control array of 16 Label objects (Index values 0 through 15) that remain hidden throughout the game. To make a Label object invisible during run time, set its Visible property to False. Each element in **lblFlagName** contains the name of the file for a flag image. When a player clicks a flag (an element in **picFlag**), the game uses the flag's Index value to read the corresponding information in the **lblFlagName**. The value of **lblFlagName(Index)** will be the name of the image file to be used to load the image, that is, set the Picture property, of **picFlag(Index)**.

Command buttons

8. **cmdStart**: Restarts the game with a new arrangement of flags

9. **cmdHelp**: Displays information on how to play the game

10. **cmdExit**: Ends the game

VARIABLES AND CONSTANTS DECLARED IN THE (General) SECTION

In your Memory program, use the following variables and constants in the **(General)** section:

Element	Explanation
Option Explicit	This tells Visual Basic to check to make sure all variables are declared. If you have neglected to declare a variable (didn't name it in a Dim statement) and try to run the project, Visual Basic will stop execution, highlight the variable, and display an error message.
Const conMaxMatches As Integer = 8	This constant number represents the number of matches that are available in the game. When the player obtains this many (8) matches, the game is over.
Dim blnFirstTurn As Boolean	This variable keeps track of the selection status; in other words, it determines whether the player's flag selection is the first or second flag selected in a matching attempt. If **blnFirstTurn** is equal to True, then the player needs to choose another flag before a test is made for a match. If **blnFirstTurn** is equal to False, then the player has selected two flags and the next step is for the game to test for a match.

Element	Explanation
`Dim intNumMatches As Integer`	This variable counts the number of matches found by the player. When the player obtains the maximum number of matches (stored in the constant **conMaxMatches**), the game is over.
`Dim intFirstPick As Integer`	This variable stores the Index value of the first flag picked in each attempt to find a match. When the player selects a second flag, the game compares Index values of the flags to test for a match. Flags match when their filenames, stored in the control array **lblFlagName**, are equal.

ALGORITHMS FOR EVENT PROCEDURES AND SUBROUTINES

SETTING UP THE GAME

The Form_Load Event Procedure

The **Form_Load** event is used to set up the game. Code this event precedure to perform the following tasks:

- Initialize **blnFirstTurn** to True and **intNumMatches** to 0

- Set the Caption property for **lblMsg** to "Click a box"

- Call three subroutines to complete the setup for the game: **load_names**, **set_up_blanks**, and **swap_names**

The load_names User-Defined Procedure

This subroutine is executed once at the beginning of the game. It has the effect of dealing out the flags to each element in the control array **lblFlagName**. Note that nothing is done to the **picFlag** control array of Picture controls. No flag picture is put into place until a player clicks an element of this array.

Each flag is loaded into two elements, thus establishing a pair for a match. The initial setting is always the same (the flags are always loaded into the same location on the form). After **load_names** executes, the subroutine **swap_names** does the actual work of shuffling the cards. Since **swap_names** moves the images around randomly before play begins, it does not matter that your code always puts the flags in the same place. The **swap_names** routine has the effect of shuffling the cards.

Figure 8 shows the code that loads eight pairs of flags into the **lblFlagName** control array. You can use the order shown here (it is arranged arbitrarily), or rearrange it if you like.

Visual Basic code to load flag pairs into control array

Figure 8

```
lblFlagName(0).Caption = "ethiopia.bmp"
lblFlagName(8).Caption = "ethiopia.bmp"

lblFlagName(1).Caption = "ghana.bmp"
lblFlagName(9).Caption = "ghana.bmp"

lblFlagName(2).Caption = "guinea.bmp"
lblFlagName(10).Caption = "guinea.bmp"

lblFlagName(3).Caption = "malagass.bmp"
lblFlagName(11).Caption = "malagass.bmp"

lblFlagName(4).Caption = "morocco.bmp"
lblFlagName(12).Caption = "morocco.bmp"

lblFlagName(5).Caption = "namibia.bmp"
lblFlagName(13).Caption = "namibia.bmp"

lblFlagName(6).Caption = "senegal.bmp"
lblFlagName(14).Caption = "senegal.bmp"

lblFlagName(7).Caption = "sierleon.bmp"
lblFlagName(15).Caption = "sierleon.bmp"
```

The set_up_blanks User-Defined Procedure

Using a loop, access each **picFlag** element and do the following:

- Use the **LoadPicture** function to store a blank image (**blank.bmp**) into the Picture property of each **picFlag** element (Please note: for this command to work properly, the .bmp files must reside in the same folder as your Visual Basic files. If you still encounter an error with this command, use the following syntax to direct Visual Basic to look for the file in the folder that contains your Visual Basic files: **LoadPicture(App. Path & "\blank.bmp")**.)

- Set the Visible property of each element to True

- Set the Enabled property of each element to True

The swap_names User-Defined Procedure

You will need the following local variables in the **swap_names** user-defined procedure:

Element	Explanation
Dim strName As String	A String variable that stores the Caption property of an element to enable a swap in a location between elements
Dim intSwap1 As Integer	Used by code to select an element to be part of a swap
Dim intSwap2 As Integer	Used by code to select an element to be part of a swap.
Dim i As Integer	A counting variable used to control a For…Next loop

This user-defined procedure performs the task of rearranging the locations of the flags before a game begins. As explained earlier, this logic selects two elements and has them change places. The elements that change places are the names of the picture files where the flags are stored. This information is stored in the Caption property of each element in **lblFlagName**. By repeating this swap 16 times, the flags will be sufficiently rearranged for a new game.

Insert the code from Figure 9 into this user-defined procedure.

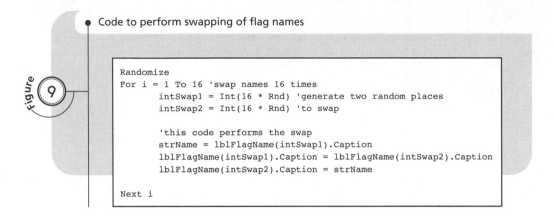

● Code to perform swapping of flag names

Figure 9

```
Randomize
For i = 1 To 16 'swap names 16 times
        intSwap1 = Int(16 * Rnd) 'generate two random places
        intSwap2 = Int(16 * Rnd) 'to swap

        'this code performs the swap
        strName = lblFlagName(intSwap1).Caption
        lblFlagName(intSwap1).Caption = lblFlagName(intSwap2).Caption
        lblFlagName(intSwap2).Caption = strName

Next i
```

RESPONDING TO PLAYER ACTIONS

The `picFlag_Click(Index As Integer)` Event Procedure

This event procedure has the following parameter:

Element	Explanation
`Index As Integer`	Index value for the element the player clicked

The **picFlag_Click** event procedure is executed when the player selects a flag to turn over. To turn over the flag, this event procedure must use the value in Index to access the file-name of the flag in the control array **lblFlagName**. The LoadPicture function displays the flag, as follows:

```
picFlag(Index).Picture = LoadPicture(lblFlagName(Index))
```

If you encounter an error and the LoadPicture command cannot locate your files, use the following syntax for this step:

```
picFlag(Index).Picture = LoadPicture(App.Path_
    & "\" & lblFlagName(Index).Caption)"
```

picFlag_Click also must set the Enabled property of the selected element to False, so that it will not respond to the Click event.

Your code must determine whether the player is making a first or second pick. The player is making a first pick if the value of the variable **blnFirstTurn** is equal to True. After the player makes his first selection, the game should reset **blnFirstTurn** to False, to indicate that one selection has been made.

You also need to store the Index of the selected flag in the variable **intFirstPick**. The program checks the content of **intFirstPick** to test the selections for a match.

Following a second pick, the program should display the correct flag, and then call the sub-routine **test_for_match**, which determines if both flags are the same.

The `test_for_match(pick1 As Integer, pick2 As Integer)` User-Defined Procedure

This user-defined procedure has the following parameters:

Element	Explanation
`pick1 As Integer`	Stores the Index property of the first element the player clicked
`pick2 As Integer`	Stores the Index property of the second element the player clicked

The **test_for_match** subroutine determines whether the player has made a match. The two parameters **pick1** and **pick2** are the Index values of the two selections to be compared. The program compares the caption of **lblFlagName(pick1)** and **lblFlagName(pick2)**. If the two captions are equal, then a match exists. Next, the program must increment **intNumMatches** by 1, and set **lblMsg.Caption** to "match." After a delay of one second (**Call delay(1)**), the game removes the matching flags from the board by setting the Enabled and Visible properties of **picFlag(pick1)** and **picFlag(pick2)** to False.

If the player's selections do not match, then the code sets **lblMsg.Caption** to "no match." After a delay of one second, the code changes the Picture properties of the two Picture Box controls to **blank.bmp**. Set the Enabled properties of **picFlag(pick1)** and **picFlag(pick2)** to True to allow the player to select them again. This has the visual effect of turning the cards back over to their blank side.

Finally, the program should determine whether the value of **intNumMatches** is equal to the value of **conMaxMatches**. If the two expressions are equal, then the game should set **lblMsg.Caption** to "Game over". If there are still flags on the form, the game should set **lblMsg.Caption** to "Click a box". Set **blnFirstTurn** to True after the test for a match, and set **lblPick1.Caption** and **lblPick2.Caption** to blank. The code to do this is:

```
lblPick1.Caption=""
lblPick2.Caption=""
```

UTILITY FUNCTIONS

The `get_flag_name(Index As Integer) As String` User-Defined Function

You need a way to extract the proper name of each country from the name of the file that contains its flag. For the purposes of this game, it is efficient to store the filename for each flag. The game uses the filename information with the function LoadPicture to display each flag. However, it might be confusing to the player to show the filename on the screen during the game—it would be more meaningful to display the proper name of the country. Therefore, **get_flag_name** "looks at" the name of the file and returns the name of the country. The string variable **strCountry** is required for this task.

A Select Case statement is the most logical way to replace the filename with the country name. The game uses the number in Index to access the flag's filename in the control array

lblFlagName. Use a Select Case statement for each country to test for the flag's filename, and store the name of the appropriate country in the variable **strCountry**.

Figure 10 shows the code that performs the Select Case operation.

figure 10

Code to display the flag's country name

```
Select Case lblFlagName(Index).Caption
    Case "ethiopia.bmp"
            strCountry= "Ethiopia"
    Case "ghana.bmp"
            strCountry= "Ghana"
    Case "guinea.bmp"
            strCountry= "Guinea"
    Case "malagass.bmp"
            strCountry= "Madagascar"
    Case "morocco.bmp"
            strCountry= "Morocco"
    Case "namibia.bmp"
            strCountry= "Namibia"
    Case "senegal.bmp"
            strCountry= "Senegal"
    Case "sierleon.bmp"
            strCountry= "Sierra Leone"
    Case Else
            strCountry= ""
End Select
```

Once the program finds a matching **Case**, the value in **strCountry** is returned using the statement **get_flag_name = strCountry**.

The **delay(interval As Single)** User-Defined Procedure

This user-defined procedure has the following parameter:

Element	Explanation
interval As Single	Indicates the amount of time for the delay

This user defined procedure requires the following local variable:

Element	Explanation
Dim sngStart As Single	Used to store starting time for delay

The **delay** subroutine pauses the game to allow the player time to memorize the flag locations before the computer turns them face-down again. The most common way in Visual Basic to create a pause is by using a Timer control object.

However, there is another method available that can be used in Visual Basic, as well as other programming languages. It is known as a "busy wait," because the program keeps itself busy by repeating a loop over and over until a certain period of time has passed. Use the code in Figure 11 to implement the busy wait.

figure

11

Code that implements the busy wait

```
sngStart = Timer    ' Set start time
    Do While Timer < SngStart  + interval
        DoEvents      ' Yield to other processes
    Loop
```

Timer is a Visual Basic function that returns the number of seconds elapsed since midnight (according to your system's clock). The parameter **interval** sets the amount of time for the delay. This loop will continue to repeat until the number returned by Timer is equal to the initial starting time (saved in **sngStart**) plus the value in **interval**.

The statement **DoEvents** allows your computer to execute other processes while executing the busy wait. For example, if you were printing a large document while playing this game, the statement **DoEvents** would allow the printing to continue during this **delay** subroutine.

COMMAND BUTTONS

The cmdStart_Click Event Procedure

The player needs to be able to restart the game to play repeatedly, if he wishes. The **cmdStart_Click** button provides the restart capability. When this button is clicked, the variable **blnFirstTurn** is set to True and **intNumMatches** is reset to 0. The instructional captions **lblMsg**, **lblPick1**, and **lblPick2** are reset to their opening values. **lblMsg.Caption** is set to "Click a box" and **lblPick1** and **lblPick2** are set to blank (""). Finally, the **cmdStart_Click** subroutine calls **set_up_blanks** and **swap_names** to complete setting up the board.

The cmdHelp_Click Event Procedure

The player accesses the rules of the game through the Help button. As in earlier chapters, insert code that constructs a string that stores the rules of the game and displays them using the MsgBox command.

The cmdExit_Click Event Procedure

The **cmdExit_Click** event procedure exits the program using the **End** statement.

OPTIONAL ENHANCEMENTS

There are many ways you can customize your Memory program. Following are some suggestions to get you started on adding original features and functionality.

1. Count and display the number of attempts a player makes to find all the matches. You can store this information in an internal variable, then use its value to display information on the form in an additional label. You can also use this number to end the game before the player has uncovered all the pairs. Define a maximum number of tries and display a message that the player has lost if that number is exceeded. Should you count every click or every two clicks? In what event would you include the code for incrementing your counter?

2. Define the end of the game by setting a fixed amount of time for play. This will require the use of a second Timer control. The player loses if all the pairs of cards have not been matched within the time limit. You can set different time limits for beginner, intermediate, and advanced players.

3. Allow the player to set levels of difficulty (beginner, intermediate, advanced) by altering the amount of time the flag is displayed before it automatically is turned face-down. Beginners get the most time, intermediates get less time, and advanced players get the least amount of time.

4. Collect sets of other images or flags and allow the user to pick from a choice of images.

5. Create or acquire the images for a regular deck of playing cards. In this case, matching is more complex. Face cards have values—namely ace, two, three, and so on—as well as suit. Two cards match if they have the same value (for example, the three of hearts and the three of diamonds are a match, but the jack of spades and seven of spades are not).

6. Add a preview button that displays all the flags for a few seconds, then turns them over. Allow the player to vary the amount of time for the preview, so he can practice with decreasing preview intervals.

DISCUSSION QUESTIONS

1. The control array `lblFlagName` remains hidden throughout the game. It stores information the game uses to load the image of each flag. Since it is used entirely by the game, it could also be represented using an internal array. How would this change in data representation change the code for the program? What are the advantages and disadvantages of each approach?

2. Memory can be a one- or two-person game. It is not evident to the computer how many people are playing. How would you plan and then implement a game in which the computer recognizes and controls two-person play? (*Hint*: You can look ahead to Chapter 7 for ideas.)

3. Computer implementations of physical games (and implementations of other human endeavors) sometimes mimic the way humans act, but other times they use strictly computer-based approaches. The method this game uses for the shuffling of cards is an example of using a typical human method. Think about other aspects of this game and other games in this text. Generally speaking, in what types of programming situations do we suggest using the human approach? When is a computer-specific solution generally preferred?

4. In the version of Memory described in this chapter, it is possible to cheat: the player has time to click and uncover more than two cards. How can you fix this loophole?

CONSTRUCTION PLAN FOR

HANGMAN

CONCEPTS, SKILLS, AND TOOLS

In this chapter, you will create a computer version of the game of Hangman. The goal of Hangman is to have a player correctly guess a computer-selected word before running out of chances.

You will use the following general programming concepts in your Hangman construction plan:

- Arrays
- Feedback to player

The Visual Basic features used to construct this game include:

- Nested If statements
- String functions
- Image controls and changing image controls during run time
- Dynamic loading of controls
- Message boxes
- Multiple events

DESCRIPTION OF THE GAME

Hangman is, typically, a two-person, paper-and-pencil game. The first player chooses a word and draws a dash to represent each letter in the chosen word. The second player guesses letters one at a time. If the second player's guessed letter is in the chosen word, the first player writes the letter in the appropriate space(s). If the guessed letter is not in the word, the first player draws the first element in a progression of drawings of a man being hanged on a gallows. The first element shows the gallows and the last element shows a stick figure with a noose around its neck. The second player wins the game by correctly guessing the word before the hanging is completed.

Before play begins, the players must agree how many incorrect guesses are allowed. (The version of the game described here permits a smaller number of attempts than would be typical.) The number of guesses corresponds to steps in the progression of drawings. For example, if the first player draws a figure consisting of six parts—two arms, two legs, a torso, and a head—plus a noose, that means the second player can make up to six incorrect guesses. If the seventh guess is wrong also, he loses. It is fairly morbid for a simple word game, but (or perhaps, consequently) it is very popular.

HOW THIS VERSION OF HANGMAN WORKS

In Hangman, many people write out the entire alphabet and cross out letters as they make guesses. This feature will be an explicit part of your implementation of Hangman.

This version of Hangman functions as a one-person game. The computer will act as the first player, picking a word and inserting correctly guessed letters into the blank spaces. The words selected come from a **word bank**: a storehouse of words held in an array variable called **strWordBank**. For purposes of initial development of the game, the number of words in **strWordBank** is very small; it is large enough, however, to test the basic concepts of the design. Experiment with the Hangman game by running the **hangman.exe** file located in your Ch5 folder.

SAMPLE SCREENS

Figures 1 through 4 present some possible results of a Hangman program. The game begins with the screen shown in Figure 1. The computer has selected a word, and the number of dashes displayed indicates that it consists of seven letters. The game displays the hanging image in a blank square, and also displays the full alphabet. Play begins when the player clicks a letter to select it.

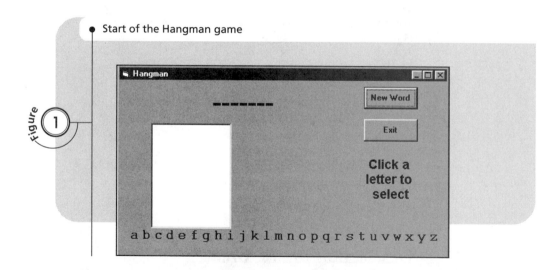

● Start of the Hangman game

Figure 1

If the player guesses correctly, the letter is placed in its correct location among the blank spaces. As the player guesses letters, they are eliminated from the alphabet. If the player guesses incorrectly, the next image in the progression appears. Figure 2 shows that the player has made both a correct guess (m) and an incorrect guess (g).

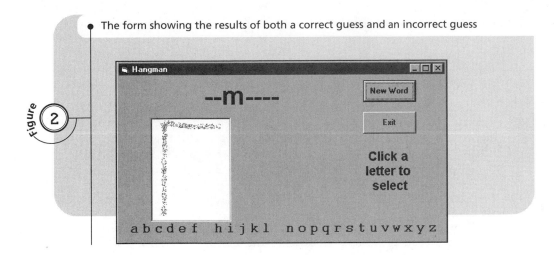

● The form showing the results of both a correct guess and an incorrect guess

Figure ②

If the player runs out of guesses before revealing the correct word, the hanging ends and the hidden word is revealed, as in Figure 3.

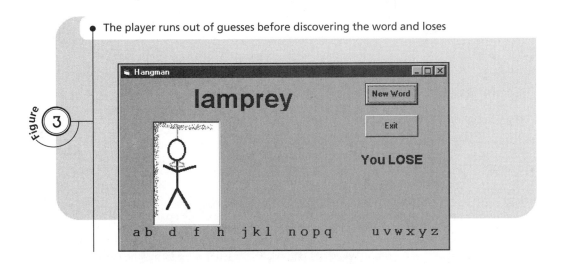

● The player runs out of guesses before discovering the word and loses

Figure ③

The player wins the game by guessing the word correctly before the hanging figure is completely drawn (see Figure 4). The player can play another round with a new word by clicking the command button labeled "New Word," or he can end the game by clicking "Exit."

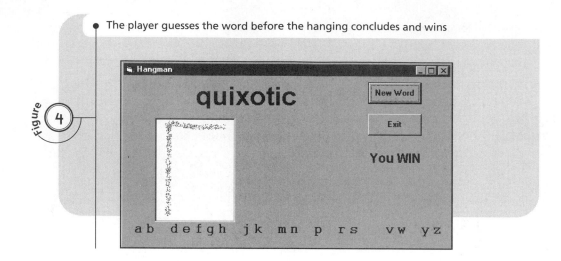

The player guesses the word before the hanging concludes and wins

figure 4

KEY DESIGN ISSUES

There are nine key design tasks that you—the designer and programmer—must accomplish when creating the Hangman game:

• Present the alphabet

• Create a bank of words from which the computer selects a word to be guessed by the player

• Display the blank letter dashes for the chosen word

• Depict the hanging progressively

• Determine that a player's letter guess is correct

• Determine that a player's word guess is correct (the player wins)

• Determine a loss

• Determine the appropriate action when the player clicks a blank space instead of a letter

• Determine the appropriate action when the player clicks a letter after losing the game

Solutions to each of these programming tasks are presented in the next section. Use these suggestions as guidelines when programming your version of Hangman.

Task: Present the alphabet.
Logic: The letters of the alphabet should appear on the opening screen of the game and should disappear from the game form as the player makes each guess.
Solution: Create a control array of Label elements named **lblAlphabet**. The first element should be created at design time and its Index property should be set to 0. During the Form_Load event procedure, create the remaining 25 **lblAlphabet** elements dynamically using the Visual Basic Load statement. To make the guessed letters disappear, you need to set the **lblAlphabet(Index).Visible** property to False. Place this code in the **lblAlphabet_Click** event procedure.

Task: Create a bank of words from which the computer selects a word to be guessed by the player.
Logic: The computer, in the role of word chooser, needs a word bank: a group of words from which to make the selection.
Solution: Create an internal array of String elements and assign words to each element. Name the array **strWordBank**. Use a constant to determine how many words will be in

the word bank. Name the constant **conNumw**. Whenever a new word is needed, the game will randomly select a word from the word bank.

Task: Display the blank letter dashes for the chosen word.
Logic: The game needs to display the same number of dashes as there are letters in the hidden word. As the player makes each choice, these dashes are replaced by the correctly guessed letters.
Solution: After the computer selects a word, your code should use the Visual Basic function Len to store the length of the hidden word. Using string concatenation, construct a string made up of the same number of dashes as there are letters in the selected word. Display this string on the screen as play begins.

Task: Depict the hanging progressively.
Logic: Each time the player guesses an incorrect letter, the hanging must progress one step. The steps are represented by images.
Solution: Use a computer drawing program (such as Microsoft Paint) to draw pictures that show the progression of the hanging (or use the files provided in the Ch5 folder). For example, the first drawing should show the gallows, the second drawing should show the gallows and the head, and so on. On the form, create a control array of Image elements and copy the pictures into this array, which should be named **imgHangman**. Make sure that the Visible properties of these elements are set to False, so that they are not visible during play. When the player guesses incorrectly, copy the first picture from **imgHangman** into **imgScene**, the blank space in which the progression of the hanging will appear. For subsequent incorrect guesses, copy the next picture from **imgHangman** into **imgScene**.

Task: Determine that a player's letter guess is correct.
Logic: If the player guesses a letter that is included in the word, that letter must appear in the series of dashes.
Solution: Have the player indicate a guess by clicking a letter of the alphabet. Testing for a match will occur in the **lblAlphabet_Click** event procedure. Inside a loop, compare the caption of the letter clicked with each letter in the hidden word. When a match is found, the matching letter should replace the appropriate dash in the hidden word's caption.

Task: Determine that a player's word guess is correct (the player wins).
Logic: If the player guesses all the letters of the word before the hanging figure is complete, the player wins. The "You WIN" message appears on the game screen.
Solution: In the **lblAlphabet_Click** event procedure, maintain a variable named **intNumPicked** that is incremented by one each time the player guesses a letter correctly. If **intNumPicked** is equal to the length of the hidden word, the player has won.

Task: Determine a loss.
Logic: If the hanging concludes before the player guesses the word, the player loses and the "You LOSE" message appears on the game screen. Since the array containing the scenes of the hanging (**imgHangman**) has a fixed number of elements—in this case, five—the player may make four incorrect letter guesses. A fifth incorrect letter guess concludes the hanging, and the game is over.
Solution: Create a variable named **intNextStep**, and use this variable to display the next picture each time the player guesses incorrectly. Increment the **intNextStep** variable by one after using it to display the next picture. The game should then test to see if the variable equals the index for the last element of **imgHangman**, which should be stored in the constant **conHung**. If the numbers are equal, the hanging has fully progressed and the player has lost.

Task: Determine the appropriate action when the player clicks a blank space instead of a letter.
Logic: Since it takes some dexterity for the player to select a letter, there will be occasions when the player unknowingly misses the letter and needs feedback from the game to know what to do.
Solution: Use the event procedure called Form_Click, which responds to a player's click if no visible letter is present at the pointer location on the form. When the Form_Click event

procedure is fired, display a message box advising the player that he has clicked a blank space and must click precisely on a letter to continue the game.

Task: Determine the appropriate action when the player clicks a letter after losing the game. **Logic**: The player may attempt to guess a letter after the hanging has concluded and he has lost the game. The game needs to recognize this situation. **Solution**: When the game determines that the player has lost, it should set a Boolean variable **blnGameOver** to True. If the player clicks a letter after a loss, the logic for this Click event procedure should test the value of **blnGameOver** and skip over the matching logic if it is True. Make sure that the procedure that initializes all of the game's internal variables, **NewGame**, has this variable set to False to allow the game to proceed normally.

PREPARING TO PROGRAM

You can use two specific programming concepts to make your Hangman game program work efficiently. Begin by learning about dynamic loading of control arrays, then learn how to implement a player's move using nested logic. The code used by Visual Basic to implement these concepts is shown within each section.

DYNAMIC LOADING OF CONTROL ARRAYS

The central graphical element of Hangman is the alphabet: a set of 26 Label objects each displaying a single letter. While you can create all 26 elements individually using the Visual Basic design tools, it is also possible to generate the alphabet dynamically by using the Visual Basic Load statement. The term **dynamic** is used in computer science to describe a process that happens as the program is running or executing.

You can create (using Load) or delete (using Unload) elements in a control array during run time. When you create an element using Load, you are copying most of the properties of the control array into the new element (the exceptions are the Index, Visible, and TabIndex properties). The Index property is passed as a parameter to the Load statement.

The positional properties of the alphabet elements—such as Left, Top, Width, and Height—are all copied from the first element. In this program, you will leave the Top, Width, and Height properties the same, which will ensure that the elements are the same size and are aligned horizontally. You will only change the Left property to allow each element to be laid out in a row across the form.

Creating the Array Elements

To dynamically create control array elements, you need to start the control array at design time. Create a single control, name it **lblAlphabet**, and set its Index property to 0, marking it as a control array at design time with one element. Set the Caption property of this first element to "a." At run time, use the statement Load to create the remaining **lblAlphabet** controls.

Figure 5, which is an image of the form at design time, shows how this technique works. It may seem strange that only one label—the letter "a"—is visible at this point, but this strategy saves effort during design time. When the program dynamically creates (loads) all but the first label using a loop, it eliminates the need for you to create and position all 26 labels individually.

Only one letter is placed on the form at design time

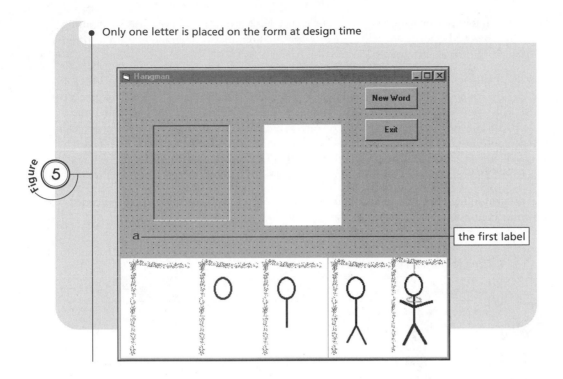

Figure 5

the first label

Once you have placed the first element, the program adds the remaining elements in Form_Load. The general algorithm for adding elements is as follows:

- Create a new alphabet element using the Load statement

- Position the new alphabet element to the right of the previous letter

- Assign the correct letter of the alphabet to the Caption property

- Make the element visible

These four steps involved in creating and setting up each element are accomplished in a For...Next loop that goes from 1 to 25 (for the last 25 letters of the alphabet). The loop starts at 1, because you already created the first element (**lblAlphabet**, with an Index value of 0) on the form. Remember: the lower bound for the Index property of control arrays is fixed at 0—you cannot change it.

Placing the Alphabet Elements

Once you have programmed the loop, you need to experiment with the distance between the elements. For this implementation, a separation of 270 twips is satisfactory; however, you may need to adjust this dimension for your system. Name the spacing constant **conLeftC**.

Twips **are units of screen measurement. There are 1440 twips in an inch.**

As discussed earlier, you load each alphabet element into the control array in the For...Next loop. Elements are positioned by setting their Left properties, which—when an element is first created—has the same value as element 0. Calculate the new value of Left by adding the starting position of the control array (represented by **lblAlphabet(i).Left**) to **i** multiplied by the constant **conLeftC**. This formula spaces each element exactly **conLeftC** twips apart.

Next, you should set the caption to the appropriate letter from the **strAlpha** string using the Visual Basic Mid function. Mid returns a specified number of characters from a string; in this case, it returns one character located at position **i + 1**.

Create a string named **strAlpha** with the value "**abcdefghijklmnopqrstuvwxyz**"; that is, the sequence of the alphabet. The letter to be returned by the Mid function is in position **i + 1** (notice that the **i**[th] control corresponds to the **i + 1** position of **strAlpha**). This situation, where references are off by one, is a common condition in programming. The displacement in this case is caused by the fact that control arrays always start with 0 and strings always start with 1. You handle this situation by using **i** to refer to the control array and **i + 1** to refer to the string. Finally, the Visible property of **strAlpha** is set to True.

The programming concepts discussed in this section can be implemented using the code shown in Figure 6.

Code for loading the alphabet

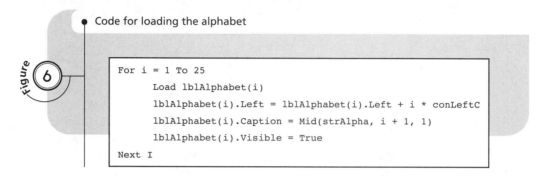

Figure 6

```
For i = 1 To 25
        Load lblAlphabet(i)
        lblAlphabet(i).Left = lblAlphabet(i).Left + i * conLeftC
        lblAlphabet(i).Caption = Mid(strAlpha, i + 1, 1)
        lblAlphabet(i).Visible = True
Next I
```

After the loop executes, your game form should look like Figure 7.

Hangman at start-up with full alphabet

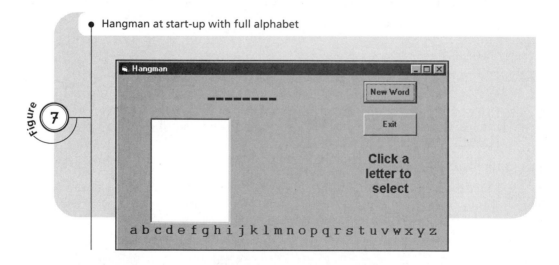

Figure 7

IMPLEMENTING A PLAYER'S MOVE USING NESTED LOGIC

In Hangman, there is only one type of move: the player chooses a letter. Your Hangman program must respond appropriately to actions by the human player. The logic the game must follow in response to a player's guess is depicted in Figure 8.

If the game is over, tell the player that play has finished.

If the letter has been guessed already, tell the player to choose another letter.

Loop through each letter of the chosen word. If the guessed letter matches, change lblHiddenPlace to include this letter in its correct position and add to the number of letters successfully picked.

If there were no matches, advance the hanging. If at the end, signal a win or a loss.

Make the guessed letter invisible.

All the logic for responding to a player's move is incorporated into the **lblAlphabet_Click (Index As Integer)** event procedure. The program uses the parameter named Index to determine which letter has been selected.

Before continuing, a brief review of the several forms of indexing used in this program will prove helpful. All control arrays and the variable arrays use origin zero; that is, index values start at 0 and go to one less than the size of the array. The position values in a string, in contrast, range from 1 to the length (Len) of the string. For example, the fourth element in the **strWordBank** is "sillygoose," yet it corresponds to index position 3 in **strWordBank**. The "y" in "sillygoose" is at string position 5. To access it, use the expression **Mid(strWordBank(3),5,1)**. Code with actual numbers seldom appears in programs; most programs use variables in their expressions.

Determining Whether the Game is Over

You do not want the player to continue clicking letters after the game is over. Declare **blnGameOver**, a Boolean variable, in the **(General)** section. Set **blnGameOver** to False in the Form_Load procedure and in **cmdNewWord_Click**. Set this variable to True whenever the player has won or lost. Then at the start of **lblAlphabet_Click**, check this variable:

```
If blnGameOver Then
    MsgBox "Game over"
```

The message box informs the player that the game is over. You should make **blnGameOver** a Boolean variable, which can be equal to True or False. Declare **blnGameOver** in the **(General)** section and not in any specific procedure. Set **blnGameOver** to False in Form_Load and to True whenever the player has won or lost a game. Reset it to False in the **cmdNewWord_Click** event procedure to allow the player to play again with a new word.

Determining Whether the Player Clicked a Blank Space

The program must determine whether the player clicked an empty space in the alphabet list (a letter of the alphabet that has already been guessed and is therefore invisible). When a control object is invisible, it no longer responds to the Click event. Instead, the event that "catches" or "traps" this condition is the Click event procedure for the form itself. Use the code shown in Figure 9 to catch the erroneous click situation.

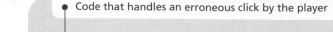

● Code that handles an erroneous click by the player

figure 9

```
Sub Form_Click()
  If blnGameOver Then
    MsgBox "Game Over"
  Else
    MsgBox "You have clicked a blank. Pick a new letter."
  End If
End Sub
```

Notice that in this procedure, it is necessary to determine once again if the game is over. You might be wondering what keeps this event procedure from being triggered when a letter is still visible and still in play. The answer is that if the mouse button is clicked over a control, that control captures all mouse events. If the control is invisible, the underlying Visual Basic form captures any mouse events that have been programmed into the game. This means that if the player clicks the form itself (and not any of the alphabet letters), the "You have clicked a blank. Pick a new letter." message appears.

Planning for these scenarios might seem like a lot of trouble, but providing feedback for each user action is a general principle in constructing user interfaces. The message boxes prevent the player from waiting for an action that will not occur.

TIP

Consider all of the player's potential actions, then decide what feedback should be supplied by the game.

Testing the Letter the Player Has Guessed

The program must check each letter of the chosen word to determine whether the guessed letter is included. This code will be included in the **lblAlphabet_Click** event procedure and will be triggered when the player clicks a letter. If the selected letter does not match any in the hidden word, the game should advance the hanging. This Click event procedure begins by setting a flag using the following code:

```
blnNoMatch = True
```

The program must produce the letter of the alphabet that matches the letter the player clicked. To do this, extract the letter from the Caption property into the variable **strLetter** of the element selected using the code:

```
strLetter = lblAlphabet(Index).Caption
```

The loop that tests for a match goes from **1**, the first position in the string representing the chosen word, to **intLength** (the length of the chosen word). Next, use the Mid function to set **strLetter** to the ith letter in the word. Remember that **strWordBank(intChoice)** references the chosen word—the loop checks each letter in the chosen word against the letter selected by the player.

The code for the start of the For...Next loop is shown below. Recall that the loop is from **1** to **intlength**, and the next line extracts the ith letter. The third parameter for Mid is **1**, because the program is comparing letters one at a time.

```
For i = 1 To intLength
    strLetter = Mid(strWordBank(intChoice), i, 1)
```

The program then compares **strLetter** and **lblAlphabet(Index).Caption** using the equality (=) operator, as follows:

```
If strLetter = lblAlphabet(Index).Caption Then
```

If the program finds a match between **strLetter** and **lblAlphabet(index).Caption**, the player has correctly guessed a letter. The program then needs to include the correctly guessed letter in the display of dashes, which is stored on the form in **lblHiddenPlace**. The program changes **lblHiddenPlace** and sets **blnNoMatch** to False, meaning there was a match. The new value that the program will give to **lblHiddenPlace** (more precisely, **lblHiddenPlace.Caption**) consists of:

- The beginning section of **lblHiddenPlace**, through the ith position, which is the left-most portion of the set of dashes and letters

- The just-discovered i^{th} letter (this is in **strLetter**)

- The right-most portion of **lblHiddenPlace**, which is the portion of the set of dashes and letters following the ith position

The code that updates **lblHiddenPlace.Caption** is:

```
lblHiddenPlace.Caption = Left(lblHiddenPlace.Caption, i - 1)_
   & strLetter & Right(lblHiddenPlace.Caption, intLength - i)
```

The Left and Right functions extract the left-most or the right-most portions of a string, respectively. The Hangman program uses these functions to build the display of the chosen word one letter at a time as the player makes each guess.

Notice that the If statement checking for a match does not have a corresponding Else. If there is no match, the program does not take any particular action within the loop, because the program will not know until after the loop is over that there were no matches. Also notice that the program does not take special action for double characters; for example, the two L's and the two O's in "sillygoose." That is, each letter is discovered (or not discovered) independently. If a letter is present in the hidden word, the code will reveal each of its occurrences.

The code in the **lblAlphabet_Click** event procedure proceeds through the whole string, looking for matches. This procedure rechecks letters in the chosen word that have already been guessed because it is simpler to check all the letters again than to check that a particular letter had already been uncovered. This approach probably differs from the approach of a human player, who might be thinking: "My new guess must be one of this smaller set of letters remaining." In programming, the most efficient way to accomplish an objective may not be the equivalent of the human method.

Determining Whether the Guess Was Correct

When the program has finished processing the For...Next loop, it determines whether the hanging is to proceed. The program should check the flag **blnNoMatch** as the condition of an If statement. If **blnNoMatch** is True (if it has not been changed to False), use the **intNextStep** counter to copy the next picture into the hanging scene. Then, your code must increment **intNextStep** by one. If **intNextStep** has reached the end—that is, if **intNextStep** equals the constant **conHung**—the program should sound a beep to signal the end of the hanging. (Since a beep is really not dramatic enough to indicate a hanging, look at Visual Basic Help to see if you can design something more appropriate.)

Summary of the **lblAlphabet_Click** Event Procedure Logic

The logic for responding to a player's move is carried out using loops and If statements nested inside one another. Nested logic can be a crucial part of a program, and always takes careful planning and testing to carry out successfully. The general structure of the **lblAlphabet_Click** event procedure follows the logic shown in Figure 10.

● Pseudocode for the `lblAlphabet` Click event procedure

Figure 10

```
If the game is over
        display message "game over"
Else
        set Visible property to False
        set blnNoMatch to True
        in a loop going from 1 to intLength
                store each letter in the hidden word one by one in strLetter
                using the Mid function compare it with the letter guessed (in lblAlphabet(Index).Caption)
                if  it is a match
                        put the guessed letter in its correct position in
                        lblHiddenPlace.Caption using the Left and Right functions
                        set blnNoMatch to False
                        add 1 to intNumPicked
                end if
        end loop
        if there is a win
                display message "You WIN"
                set blnGameOver to True
        else
                if there were no matches
                        progress the hanging
                        if there is now a loss
                                display message "You LOSE"
                                blnGameOver is True
                        end if
                end if
        end if
end if
```

The code for the **lblAlphabet_Click** event procedure will be spelled out in more specific detail in the "Algorithms for Event Procedures and Subroutines" section.

⊙ PLAN FOR THE USER INTERFACE

One of the main tasks to consider in designing the user interface is how to represent the progression of the hanging. For this Hangman implementation, you will construct a set of images at design time using a drawing program and store the drawings in a control array.

Set the Visible property of the images that make up the progression of the hanging to False—they will serve as a hidden storehouse of pictures (see Figure 5).

During play, the game should copy the appropriate picture into the "real" image control whenever a new drawing is needed, while the storehouse of images remains invisible.

It is important to note that this image storehouse feature does not replicate what people do: people make new marks on top of a drawing to make the next drawing (see the "Optional Enhancements" section to learn how to follow this approach). Most computer versions of games incorporate some changes to the basic game. Using a hidden storehouse of images is easier to program than recreating the drawing for each move. This idea is similar to how animation and moving pictures simulate movement through a progression of independent still frames.

STORING THE HIDDEN WORD

What else is needed for the game? The game needs to store the hidden word as a Label control to prevent the player from entering text into it.

1. Create a Label control and name it **lblHiddenPlace**.

2. The game will initialize the caption of **lblHiddenPlace** for each round with an appropriate number of dashes. Dashes are used rather than underscores because they appear as individual characters when there is more than one in a row. As with most games, the initialization for the game occurs at the time of loading of the form for each round.

Figure 11 shows the contents of **lblHiddenPlace** at the start of the round when the chosen word is "muon."

TIP

Yes, "muon" is a real word. Using uncommon words in your word bank will make your Hangman game more interesting and challenging.

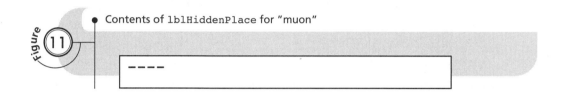

Contents of lblHiddenPlace for "muon"

figure (11)

FORM DESIGN

This section describes all of the objects contained on the final design for Hangman, which is shown in Figure 12. Follow this plan to place all the objects needed on your form. The object names listed below are suggestions; you may rename them if desired (if you do, be sure to revise your code accordingly). Set captions for command buttons and labels as suggested. Placement of objects are suggestions—you may lay out your form differnetly, if you wish.

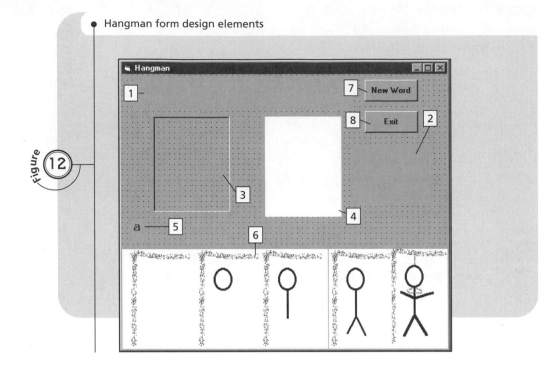

Figure 12

Hangman form design elements

Labels

1. **lblHiddenPlace**: Holds the secret word that the player will try to guess. Change font to Arial Bold, point size 29.

2. **lblMessage**: Displays messages to player. Change font to Arial Bold, point size 14.

Images

3. **imgScene**: Image control to display progressive hanging

4. **imgStorage**: Image control for storing original (blank) image in **imgScene**. Not visible during the game.

Control arrays

5. **lblAlphabet(0)**: First element of control array label holding letters of alphabet. Change its Index property to 0 to establish this as a control array. The remaining elements will be created in Form_Load.

6. **imgHangman(0-4)**: Control array of **Images** with successive pictures of hanging. Not visible during the game. Set the Picture property of these controls to hang1.bmp, hang2.bmp, and so on.

Command buttons

7. **cmdNewWord**: Command button for starting a new round (new word).

8. **cmdExit**: Command button for exiting the game.

Form Size

The form's size may be too large for you to manipulate using your mouse in the Visual Basic desktop. Click the form to select it, then open the Properties window and set the width and height as follows:

Property	Setting	Explanation
Width	7500 pixels	Form will display the entire alphabet across the player's monitor
Height	6600 pixels	Form height must stay proportional to width

Variables and Constants Declared in the (General) Section

In your Hangman program, use the following variables and constants in the **(General)** section:

Element	Explanation
`Option Explicit`	Set this option, which requires a declaration of all variables
`Const strAlpha As String = _` `    "abcdefghijklmnopqrstuvwxyz"`	A constant that holds the letters of the alphabet. The program uses this string to load a letter into each element of the **lblAlphabet** control array.
`Const conNumw As Integer = 5`	Indicates the number of words in the **strWordBank** array
`Const conHung As Integer = 5`	A constant that indicates the number of steps (pictures) in the hanging. When the player runs out of guesses (in this case, four incorrect guesses are allowed), the game is over and he has lost.
`Const conLeftC As Integer = 270`	Used to position the elements of the **lblAlphabet** control array during the dynamic loading of each element
`Dim strWordBank()As String`	An internal array that holds the collection of words from which the player attempts to guess
`Dim intChoice As Integer`	Stores a pointer or reference to the current hidden word (from the **strWordBank** array)
`Dim intLength As Integer`	A variable that stores the number of characters in the current hidden word. The program will use this variable in the logic that tests the player's letter selection for a match against the hidden word.
`Dim intNumPicked As Integer`	Keeps track of how many letters have been guessed correctly by the player

Element	Explanation
`Dim blnGameOver As Boolean`	A variable that indicates whether the game is still active. If the game is over, then the game should not perform any action as a result of the player clicking an alphabet letter.
`Dim intNextStep As Integer`	Used to reference the picture that stores the next step of the hanging

ALGORITHMS FOR EVENT PROCEDURES AND SUBROUTINES

SETTING UP THE GAME

The program executes initialization for the game in the Form_Load event procedure. Another type of initialization, which involves restarting the game by picking a new word, is carried out in **cmdNewWord_Click**.

The `Form_Load()` Event Procedure

This event procedure requires the following local variables:

Element	Explanation
`Dim i As Integer`	Used to control a For...Next loop

Program this event procedure as follows:

1. Set **imgStorage.Visible** to False.

2. Execute the code that will dynamically create the remaining elements in the control array **lblAlphabet**, as shown in Figure 13. Remember, the first (0th) element is created during design time. Use a For...Next loop to load and set the rest of the **lblAlphabet** control array, which should be positioned along the bottom of the form. Make all of the control array elements visible by setting each Visible property to True.

Code to create the alphabet

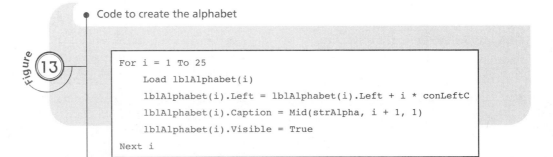

figure 13

```
For i = 1 To 25
    Load lblAlphabet(i)
    lblAlphabet(i).Left = lblAlphabet(i).Left + i * conLeftC
    lblAlphabet(i).Caption = Mid(strAlpha, i + 1, 1)
    lblAlphabet(i).Visible = True
Next i
```

USER-DEFINED PROCEDURES

The `setupwordbank()` Procedure

Program the **setupwordbank** procedure as follows:

1. Call the ReDim command on **strWordBank**, which allocates space (memory) for this array. Use a constant such as **conNumw** that represents the number of

words in **strWordBank**. For example:

```
ReDim strWordBank(conNumw)
```

2. Assign words to each element in **strWordBank**. Recall that the default lower bound (smallest index value) of arrays in Visual Basic is 0 (zero). The words used in the word bank for this implementation of Hangman are shown in Figure 14. Insert your own collection of words if you wish.

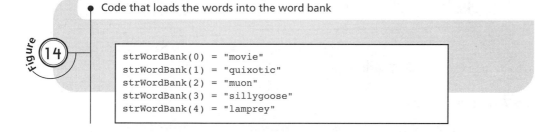

● Code that loads the words into the word bank

Figure 14

```
strWordBank(0) = "movie"
strWordBank(1) = "quixotic"
strWordBank(2) = "muon"
strWordBank(3) = "sillygoose"
strWordBank(4) = "lamprey"
```

The NewGame() Procedure

This procedure sets initial values to variables used during the play of the game. Program the **NewGame** procedure as follows:

1. Set **blnGameOver** to False.

2. Set **intNextStep** to 0.

3. Set **intNumPicked** to 0.

4. Set **lblMessage.Caption** to "Click a letter to select".

5. Place the blank image stored in **imgStorage.Picture** into **imgScene.Picture**.

The ChooseWord() Procedure

This procedure requires the following local variables:

Element	Explanation
Dim strCap As String	Holds the dashes that are displayed to the player
Dim i As Integer	Used to control a For…Next loop

Program the **ChooseWord** procedure as follows:

1. Call Randomize to initialize the random number generator

2. Use Rnd to generate a number between **0** and (**conNumw − 1**) and store the result in the variable **intChoice**. **intChoice** will act as an index for the array **strWordBank**, and will indicate the word that has been selected for the game through the following code:

```
intChoice = Int(conNumw * Rnd)
```

3. Store the length of the word selected in the variable **intLength**. The code looks like this:

```
intLength = Len(strWordBank(intChoice))
```

4. Construct a string of dashes. Assign **strCap** an initial value of **" "**, then in a For...Next loop, concatenate a dash to **strCap** (using the ampersand) for every letter in the hidden word. The code is shown in Figure 15.

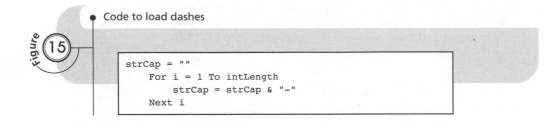

● Code to load dashes

Figure 15

```
strCap = ""
    For i = 1 To intLength
        strCap = strCap & "-"
    Next i
```

5. Store **strCap** in **lblHiddenPlace.Caption**.

PRINCIPAL EVENT PROCEDURES

The **lblAlphabet_Click(Index As Integer)** Event Procedure

Element	Explanation
Index As Integer	References the letter the player has clicked

This event procedure requires the following local variables:

Element	Explanation
Dim strLetter As String	Used to compare each letter in the hidden word with the letter the player has clicked
Dim blnNoMatch As Boolean	If false, indicates whether the player's guess matches any letters in the hidden word; if true, no match was made
Dim i As Integer	Used to control a For...Next loop

This procedure carries out the heart of the game. It compares the letter the player has selected with the letters in the hidden word. For each match, this routine increments **intNumPicked** and replaces the dash in the hidden word with the correctly guessed letter.

Program the **lblAlphabet_Click** procedure as follows:

1. Check the **blnGameOver** flag (in case the player clicks a letter after the game is over). If True, use the message box function to display the appropriate message.

2. In the Else clause of the If (if the game is not over):

   a. Set the **blnNoMatch** flag to True.

   b. Set the element of **lblAlphabet** clicked (indicated by the parameter Index) to be invisible (**lblAlphabet(Index).Visible = False**).

   c. Using a loop, compare the letter selected (contained in **lblAlphabet(Index).Caption**) with each letter in the hidden word (contained in **strWordBank(intChoice)**).

d. Use a For...Next loop to check all the letters in **strWordBank(intChoice)**. The loop should use the variable **i** to go from 1 to **intLength**. Remember to start the loop from 1, because String variables start with the first letter in the position equal to 1.

3. Within the loop, extract from the hidden word the letter needed to compare with the caption. Store the letter from position **i** of the hidden word in the variable **strLetter**. The code to do this is:

```
strLetter = Mid(strWordBank(intChoice), i, 1)
```

Use the Mid function to return a sub-string from **strWordBank(intChoice)** starting in position **i** and with a length of 1. This has the effect of looping through all the letters in the hidden word as the For...Next loop progresses through each value of **i** from 1 to **intLength**.

4. Still inside the For...Next loop, compare the letter the player selected (**lblAlphabet(Index).Caption**) with **strLetter**. If there is a match, set **blnNoMatch** to False. This will prevent the hanging from progressing to the next image. You also need to increment **intNumPicked** by one.

5. Replace the appropriate dash in the hidden word with the letter that has been selected. This task requires **string concatenation**, which is the combining of multiple strings into one string using the symbol "&". The code combines the **Left** portion of **lblHiddenPlace.Caption** from position 1 to **i − 1**, with **strLetter**, ending with the **Right** portion of **lblHiddenPlace.Caption**, as follows:

```
lblHiddenPlace.Caption = Left(lblHiddenPlace.Caption,_
i - 1) & strLetter & Right(lblHiddenPlace.Caption,_
intLength - i)
```

6. Once the For...Next loop concludes, test to see whether a match has occurred and whether the game has been won or lost. Continuing in the same Else clause, first test to determine whether **intNumPicked** is equal to **intLength**. If it is, the player has won. Change **lblMessage.Caption** to "You WIN" and set the **blnGameOver** flag to True.

7. If the player has not won the game, you need to test to see whether the hanging scene should progress and whether the player has lost on this guess. If **blnNoMatch** is True, advance the hanging by copying the next picture from **imgHangman** into **imgScene** and then incrementing **intNextStep**. Move the picture before you increment, because the **imgHangman** is a control array with a initial subscript of 0. The code to do this is:

```
imgScene.Picture = imgHangman(intNextStep).Picture
intNextStep = intNextStep + 1
```

8. If **intNextStep** is now equal to the number of steps in the hanging represented in the constant **conHung**, the game is over. Change **lblMessage.Caption** to "You LOSE". Change the **blnGameOver** flag to True. Show the player the hidden word **strWordBank(intChoice)** by displaying it in the caption of **lblHiddenPlace**.

The Form_Click() Event Procedure

This event procedure will only be triggered if the player clicks the form erroneously or clicks a **lblAlphabet** element that has its Visible property set to False.

Program the Form_Click event procedure so that it performs the following task:

1. Determines whether the game is over. If it is, use the Message Box command to tell the player that the game is over. If the game is not over, use the Message Box command to tell the player: "You clicked a blank. Click a new letter."

COMMAND BUTTONS

The cmdNewWord_Click( ) Event Procedure

As you did in earlier chapters, insert the **End** statement in this event procedure.

Element	Explanation
Dim i As Integer	Used to control a For...Next loop

This button has the effect of restarting the game if the player wishes to guess another word. The event procedure needs to reset values of internal variables and pick a new word.

Program the **cmdNewWord_Click** event procedure as follows:

1. Call the procedure **NewGame** to reset internal variables.

2. Call the procedure **ChooseWord** to pick a new word.

3. Set the Visible property of the elements in **lblAlphabet** to True using a For...Next loop.

The cmdExit_Click( ) Event Procedure

As you did in earlier chapters, insert the **End** statement in this event procedure.

⊚ OPTIONAL ENHANCEMENTS

There are many ways you can customize your Hangman program. Following are some suggestions to get you started on adding original features and functionality:

1. This implementation used a control array holding a sequence of pictures for the drawing of the hanging. Think about alternative approaches. For example, you could use graphical methods: commands that draw pixels, lines, rectangles, filled-in boxes, arcs, circles, and ellipses. Consult Visual Basic Help to learn how these work and then change your program to use these methods in place of the scene image control and the **imgHangman** control array. What are the advantages and disadvantages of this approach?

2. Allow users to select letters using the keyboard. You will need to code another event procedure that recognizes when a key has been pressed. It is also important that you carry out the same logic comparing the guess regardless of whether the player has clicked a letter or pressed a key.

3. Add categories for words using either a list box or a menu. Include a command button that gives the player hints if he is stuck.

4. Letters are represented in computers using a binary numbering system known as ASCII code. The number 97 in ASCII represents the letter "a", the number 98 represents "b", and so on. The Visual Basic function Chr returns the string associated with a particular character code. Therefore, the code **Chr(97)** returns **"a"**. Use the Chr function and a variable inside a loop to assign the correct value to each element in **lblAlphabet**.

5. Add a feature that allows additional words to be added to **strWordBank**.

6. Use the Visual Basic function InStr to determine whether a letter is contained in the hidden word. Make sure your code handles double letters (like in "sillygoose") correctly.

DISCUSSION QUESTIONS

1. In this implementation, a word is chosen randomly from a small set of words in **strWordBank**. It is possible in this implementation for the game to select the same word more than once. How could the game be changed to prevent choosing duplicate words during play?
2. Could this game be adjusted for another alphabet? Why or why not?
3. How could you construct a word bank automatically using pre-existing computerized lists of words?

CONSTRUCTION PLAN FOR
CANNONBALL

◉ CONCEPTS, SKILLS, AND TOOLS

In this chapter, you will create a program called Cannonball, a simulation of a cannon shooting at a target. The player controls the cannonball's motion by adjusting its speed and the angle of the cannon.

You will use the following general programming concepts in your Cannonball construction plan:

- Animation
- Coordinate systems to specify positions on the screen
- Processing and controlling player input

The Visual Basic features used to construct this game include:

- Shapes (lines, circles, rectangles)
- Built-in mathematical functions
- Timer control
- Mouse events (MouseDown, MouseMove, MouseUp)
- Menu commands

◉ DESCRIPTION OF THE GAME

This program simulates a cannon shooting at a target. Unlike projects you have previously programmed, Cannonball is not a full-featured game with scoring. In this chapter, you will learn programming techniques that you can use to build your own game.

In designing your version of Cannonball, you will use animation to display ballistics. **Animation** is a sequence of pictures shown in quick succession so that the human eye perceives motion. **Ballistics** is the study of objects propelled at an initial velocity and subject to the laws of gravity.

HOW CANNONBALL WORKS

This Cannonball simulation displays a simplified rendering of a cannon and a target. The cannon is drawn with a thick black line, the target is a colored rectangle, and the ground is a thick green line. The player can set the speed of the cannonball using a scroll bar; adjust the angle of the cannon by dragging the tip of the cannon with the mouse; and move the target, also using drag and drop. When the player clicks the FIRE! button, the program shows a cannonball in motion. This version does not keep score (although you can add this feature later, if you wish). Experiment with the Cannonball activity by running the `ball.eye` file located in your Ch6 folder.

SAMPLE SCREEN

Figure 1 shows the Cannonball interface.

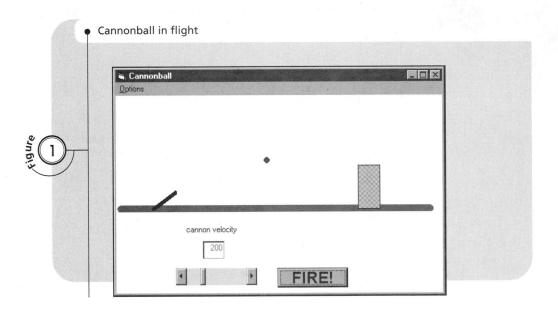

Figure 1

The flight of the cannonball is shown as an animation. Your code should show the ball moving in an arc and it also should make the target turn red when it determines that the cannonball hit the target. If the cannonball misses the target and instead hits the ground, your code will produce a beep. If the cannon is aimed too high, the cannonball will fly off the form. In this case, the program will keep checking to determine whether the ball has hit the ground and will, eventually, make a beep. The path of the cannonball's flight is determined by the angle of the cannon, its velocity (the speed and also the direction as determined by the cannon angle) as it leaves the cannon, and the position of the target.

There are five key design tasks that you—the designer and programmer—must accomplish when designing the Cannonball project:

- Represent the cannon, cannonball, target, and ground

- Display the cannonball in flight (including angle and speed of motion)

- Stop the flight of the cannonball if it hits the target or the ground

- Provide a means for the player to change the cannon's angle, increase or decrease the cannonball's speed, and move the target

- Provide a means for the player to end the game

Task: Represent the cannon, cannonball, target, and ground.
Logic: The objects in the implementation described here are simple shapes: lines, circles, and rectangles. As mentioned earlier, you may make these more elaborate.
Solution: Visual Basic provides tools for creating lines and shapes. You will use these for the cannon, cannonball, target, and ground.

Task: Display the cannonball in flight (including angle and speed of motion).
Logic: The flight pattern the ball takes is based on the initial angle of the cannon, the initial speed of the cannonball, and the effects of gravity. The game, to accurately display this path, must calculate the position of the cannonball over time. One basic method from math and physics, known as resolving the vectors, separates the horizontal and vertical components of motion. In successive time periods, your code will recalculate the ball's horizontal and vertical position and redisplay it on the form. The cannonball's speed will be measured in twips per second (recall that there are 1440 twips in an inch).
Solution: Use a Visual Basic Timer object. The Timer event procedure for a Timer control is involved at fixed intervals of time. Place the code that recalculates the cannonball position at fixed intervals in the Timer event procedure. Code the FIRE! command button to derive values from the location of the endpoint of the cannon and the speed of the cannonball and use built-in mathematical functions to recalculate the position of the cannonball. These values will be used in the Timer event.

Task: Stop the flight of the cannonball if it hits the target or the ground.
Logic: Part of the task of showing the cannonball's flight is to stop the flight at the appropriate time. In real life, the flight ends when the ball either hits the target or the ground. To produce the simulation, you must pinpoint this action explicitly by writing code to determine when the virtual cannonball has hit the virtual ground or the virtual target.
Solution: Write a function that compares the position of the cannonball with the position of the ground. If the cannonball is at the same level or below the ground, stop the flight (the situation in which the cannonball could be below the ground is explained later). Write a second function that compares the position of the cannonball with the position of the target, which encompasses a rectangular area. If the position of the cannonball overlaps the area of the target, stop the flight.

Task: Provide a means for the player to change the cannon's angle, increase or decrease the cannonball's speed, and move the target. These three factors have a direct effect on the cannonball's flight and its completion.
Logic: The standard in games is to allow direct manipulation of controls. To accomplish this in Cannonball, you should include code that allows the player to drag and drop both the target and the tip of the cannon. How to allow for adjusting the cannonball's speed is less obvious, but a good way to do this is to provide both a text box and scroll bar. You can set the scroll bar at maximum and minimum values so that the player cannot enter numbers that are too large or too small for a reasonable simulation.
Solution: Program the drag-and-drop operations using the Visual Basic MouseDown, MouseMove, and MouseUp events. Use the Visual Basic horizontal scroll control to adjust the Cannonball's speed.

Task: Provide a means for the player to end the game.

Logic: Previous games in this book have used a command button to end the game. To become familiar with another feature of Visual Basic, use a pull-down menu to end Cannonball.

Solution: Use the Visual Basic Menu Editor to set up a pull-down category with a call to a specified procedure.

PREPARING TO PROGRAM

SIMULATING THE PATH OF A CANNONBALL

The path of any projectile is predictable. If it wasn't, quarterbacks couldn't throw touchdown passes and outfielders couldn't throw out base runners. The cannonball's flight can be calculated with a formula that combines its initial speed, the angle at which it is projected, and the effects of gravity. The smaller the angle of projection, the greater its linear distance will be. You can verify this yourself with a ball. Throw it easily with a moderate arc, and the distance will be greater. Throw it as hard as you can straight up in the air, and it will hit the ground a short distance away.

There are other factors that affect the flight of the ball, namely wind speed and direction and air resistance (friction). For the purpose of this project, you may ignore these factors. This simulation will also assume the motion to be two-dimensional within the plane of the screen, as if the cannon was restricted to firing directly at the target—perhaps above or below it, but not to its left or right.

Horizontal and Vertical Components of Motion

The first step in determining the flight path of the cannonball is to calculate each location over time into horizontal and vertical components. In other words, the location of a cannonball along its flight path can be described as a combination of its height and its distance from the cannon. Traditionally, height (the vertical component) is described as Y (for the Y axis) and distance (the horizontal component) as X (for the X axis). Figure 2 illustrates these components.

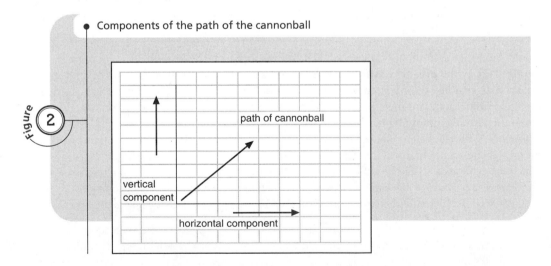

• Components of the path of the cannonball

Figure 2

path of cannonball

vertical component

horizontal component

Visual Basic has some—but not all—things in common with traditional graphics concepts. The term *coordinate* is not used in Visual Basic. However, Visual Basic does require the position of objects to be specified in two dimensions that correspond to the horizontal and vertical coordinates. For line objects, the names of the position properties are X1, Y1, X2, and Y2. These specify the endpoints of the line. For other controls, the position is specified by the Left and Top properties. See Figure 3. There is a difference relating to the vertical dimension, which will be explained later in the chapter.

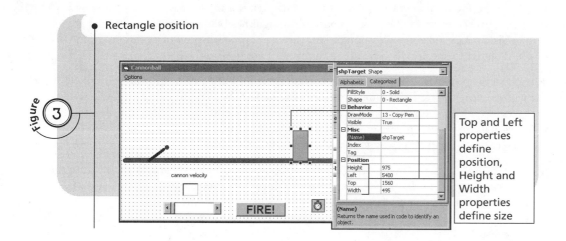

Rectangle position

Top and Left properties define position, Height and Width properties define size

You can translate the cannonball's path into its horizontal and vertical components using trigonometric functions. Use the angle of the cannon to the ground (indicated in Figure 4) to calculate these values. Call the value of the cannon angle *Theta*, because by convention, Greek letters are used to represent angles.

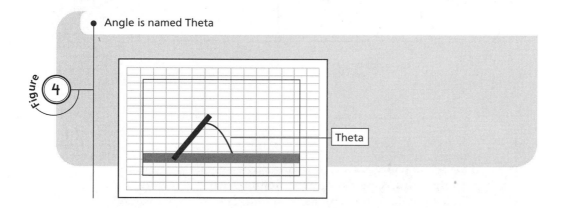

Angle is named Theta

Theta

The cannonball's horizontal and vertical components are its horizontal speed and its vertical speed, or, its speed travelling across and its speed travelling up or down. The velocity of the ball is called a **vector**, a mathematical concept for entities having magnitude and direction. The horizontal (X) and the vertical (Y) components are calculated using the following Visual Basic statements, assuming that **v** is the speed of the projectile coming out of the cannon and **Theta** is the angle of the cannon to the ground:

```
vx = v * Cos (Theta)
vy = v * Sin (Theta)
```

Refer to a trigonometry text for a further explanation of cosine, the function called by the built-in function Cos and sine, called by Sin. The horizontal velocity, **vx**, is unaffected by gravity, so using the basic equation of motion (distance = speed * time), the horizontal or x position of the cannonball is:

```
xx = vx * TT + X2
```

where **xx** is used to hold the position, **TT** is the elapsed time, and **X2** is the starting x position of the ball.

Calculations for the vertical position **yy** are more complicated, because gravity pulls on the cannonball.

It is a fact in physics that gravity affects the vertical, but not the horizontal component of motion. This is one reason that your program distinguishes between the two. Another reason is that Visual Basic (like many computer languages and programs) requires the programmer or the designer to specify the vertical and horizontal positions separately.

The effect of gravity is 1/2 times *g* (the constant denoting the force of gravity) multiplied by the elapsed time squared. This means that gravity's effects become more apparent as time progresses. Objects dropped from a great height keep accelerating until they hit the ground. Objects that are tossed up decelerate and then fall. This tendency explains the arc that is characteristic of the path of cannonballs, missiles, baseballs, and so on.

Your code also must account for a peculiarity of computer graphics that relates to calculating the vertical component. In graphs, the value of Y increases as you move up the Y axis. In standard computer graphics, the opposite is true. Figure 5 shows the difference.

Graph coordinates vs. computer screen coordinates

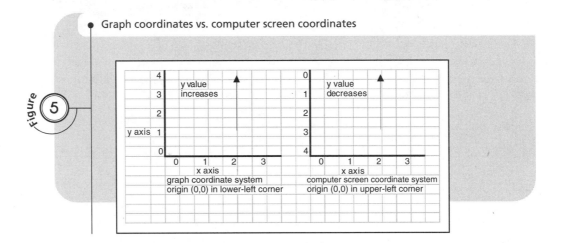

Figure 5

TIP

This incongruity is caused by the physical construction of a computer screen. Computer monitors use a technology similar to television screens. Inside the monitor is a "gun" that starts in the upper-left corner (its origin, or 0,0) and moves back and forth, drawing the screen one line at a time. When it reaches the bottom of the screen, the gun returns to the top and starts the whole process over again. Sometimes when a picture loads very slowly from a Web site, you can see this happening. The screen's origin (0,0) is in the upper-left corner, which reverses the value of the Y axis.

The reverse orientation for the Y axis affects the formula you will use for the cannonball path. To move the ball control (named **shpBall**) up the screen, you actually have to *subtract* a value. The code for **shpBall**'s vertical position is:

```
yy = .5 * g * (TT * TT) - vy * TT + Y2
```

where **.5 * g * (TT * TT)** is the effect of gravity, **- vy * TT** is the vertical speed (notice the negative sign to compensate for the computer screen reverse orientation), and **Y2** is the original vertical position.

ANIMATING THE CANNONBALL'S MOTION

Animation is achieved by displaying a series of still pictures (called frames) in a timed sequence. Each frame shows **shpBall** further along the arc of its flight path. The Visual Basic Timer control object is a very useful feature for creating simple animations. The Timer control object includes a Timer event that you can set to execute at fixed time intervals, for example, every 1/50th of a second. The calculations that determine the position of **shpBall** are executed in the Timer event.

To make the cannonball move across the screen—that is, to perform the animation—you must write code that moves the cannonball after an interval of time has elapsed. To portray this movement, your code will change the values of **shpBall**'s Top and Left properties. You can set the duration of the time between each event by setting the Interval property of the Timer object. The units for this property are thousandths of a second (or milliseconds). Keep in mind that the Timer event's Enabled property must be set to True before the Timer event can be executed.

> **TIP**
>
> **When the computer doesn't have enough time to monitor (recognize) and service (handle) all the events in an event-driven application, you can encounter problems. For example, if you set a Timer event to occur every 100 milliseconds and it takes close to (or more than) 100 milliseconds to process the event, your program may experience a slowdown, or even a system lockup. The basic project described here will work without incurring problems. However, if you create an elaborate game with multiple projectiles and targets, you may experience problems. High-performance games are implemented in efficient programming languages and use processors specially suited to games programming.**

PROGRAMMING A HIT

Although the player can see when the ball hits the ground or the target, the computer does not come with eyesight. Your program must recognize these events some other way.

The Cannonball Hits the Ground

Your programming solution will use the horizontal and vertical coordinates of the graphical elements in question. Use the following logic to indicate when **shpBall** (the Visual Basic object that represents the cannonball) hits **linGround** (the Visual Basic object that represents the ground), as shown in Figure 6.

figure 6

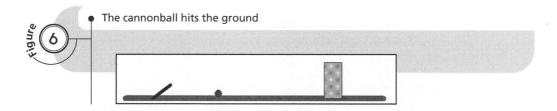

The cannonball hits the ground

Because **linGround** is a straight-line parallel to the X axis, it is only necessary to compare the Y coordinates of **linGround** and **shpBall**. **shpBall**'s new position—**YY**—is compared to **linGround.Y1**, which is stored in the variable **sngGrass** during the Form_Load event procedure. As long as **shpBall**'s **yy** value (its new position) is "above" **linGround**, the animation should continue. Remember, the reverse orientation of the Y axis reverses the meaning of "above": **yy** must be less than **sngGrass − ballrad** (compensating for the radius) to keep the animation going. The **ballrad** variable holds the radius of **shpBall**. **timFlight** is the name of the timer control used to produce the animation. The loop shown in Figure 7 carries out the code that determines whether to continue the animation.

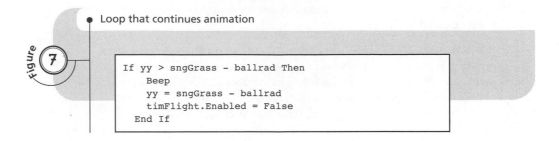

Figure 7

Loop that continues animation

```
If yy > sngGrass - ballrad Then
    Beep
    yy = sngGrass - ballrad
    timFlight.Enabled = False
End If
```

Figure 8 shows the graphical representation of the code in Figure 7.

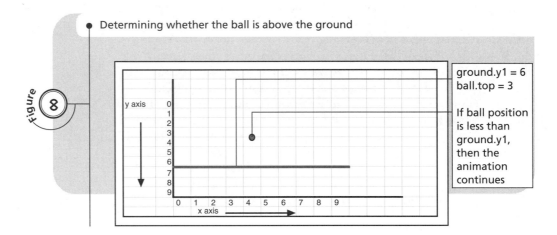

Figure 8

Determining whether the ball is above the ground

ground.y1 = 6
ball.top = 3

If ball position is less than ground.y1, then the animation continues

The use of the expression **(yy > sngGrass - ballrad)** is typical of simulations. Keep in mind that there are no physical cannonballs, grass, or targets; the only real things are your calculations. You cannot check whether the vertical coordinate, **yy**, is exactly equal to **sngGrass**, because the interval of time since the last Timer event may have taken **shpBall** below the ground. That is, your code may have produced a value for **yy** that is greater than **sngGrass**. In this case, your code must reset **yy** so that **shpBall** will (appear to) sit on top of **linGround**. This adjustment makes the simulation more realistic. Another way to describe this is that the animation occurs at discrete intervals of time, not continuously.

The Cannonball Hits the Target

Determining when **shpBall** has hit **shpTarget**, as shown in Figure 9, requires a test of both **xx** and **yy**. The player can see when **shpBall** hits **shpTarget**, but you must define the hit as a mathematical expression for the program to recognize it as such.

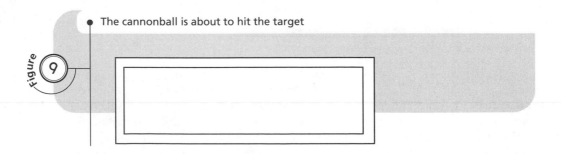

Figure 9

The cannonball is about to hit the target

shpBall hits **shpTarget** when the **xx**, **yy** position of **shpBall** is located within the boundaries of **shpTarget**. This is a complex condition—**shpBall**'s **xx** value could be within **shpTarget** while its **yy** value is outside it; or, **shpBall**'s **yy** value could be within **shpTarget** while its **xx** value is outside it, as shown in Figure 10.

Determining the position of the ball relative to the target

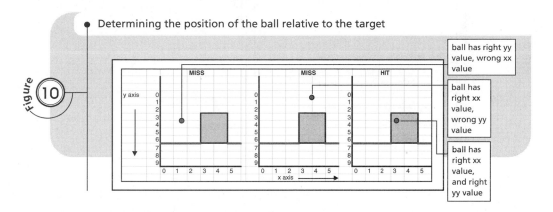

Figure 10

You must also define exactly what limits the **xx** and **yy** values can have. You know the Top and Left properties of **shpTarget**, and can calculate the bottom and right edges using the Width and Height properties. The left edge value of **shpTarget** is stored in the Left property. The right edge is equal to Left + Width. The top edge value is stored in the Top property, and the bottom edge is equal to Top + Height. These formulas compensate for the reverse orientation of the screen axis.

Hitting **shpTarget** occurs when **xx** is within the left and right edges, and **yy** is within the top and bottom edges. Place the code that determines a hit in a function that returns a Boolean value indicating whether **shpTarget** has been hit. The complex condition expression checks first to determine whether **xx**, the horizontal position, is within the horizontal range of the rectangle and if **yy**, the vertical component, is within the vertical range. The first check uses the Left and Width properties and the second check uses the Top and Height properties. A good programming tactic in cases like these is to check that parts of the expression are parallel: there should be two conditions, using two properties, for the **xx** and the same for the **yy**.

Figure 11 shows the algorithm that determines whether **shpBall** hit **shpTarget** and an example of a hit.

Pseudocode for determining whether the cannonball has hit the target

Figure 11

1. Does xx have a value between left and left + width? (Is 5 between 4 and 6? Yes.)
2. Does yy have a value between top and top + height? (Is 3 between 2 and 6? Yes.)
3. If the answer to both questions is yes, then the ball has hit the target.

Your program will implement the code for the algorithm shown in Figure 11 in a user-defined fuction named **hittarget**. The code for this function is described in greater detail in the "Algorithms for Event Procedures and User-Defined Procedures" section.

Figure 12 shows on the game screen **shpBall** hitting **shpTarget** as described in Figure 11.

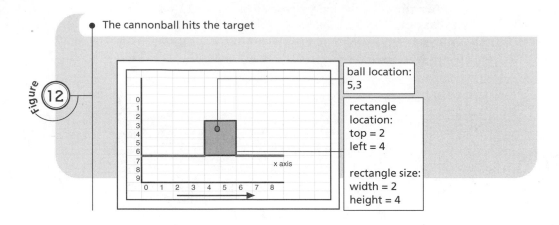

The cannonball hits the target

Figure 12

ball location:
5,3

rectangle location:
top = 2
left = 4

rectangle size:
width = 2
height = 4

Depicting the Hit

If the call to **hittarget** in the Timer event returns the value True, your code should cause your computer to beep three times (it will sound like a squawk), change the color of **shpTarget**, and turn off the animation by setting the Enabled property to False. The code that handles these changes is shown in the "Algorithms for Event Procedures and User-Defined Procedures" section later in this chapter. The "Optional Enhancements" section provides opportunities to make these features more dramatic.

> **TIP**
>
> The format for the values of colors is a hexadecimal constant. Hexadecimal numbers are numbers in base 16, so that every place in a hexadecimal number represents 0 to 15. To represent these values, hexadecimal numbers use 0 to 9 then use A to F represent 10 to 15. The hexadecimal constant that represents a color can be up to six places long. The constant for the color red, for example, is &HFF&. You can experiment or use a paint program to determine the hexadecimal values of other colors.

USE OF VARIOUS MOUSE EVENTS

Your code will let the player adjust the cannon and the target by dragging and dropping items with the mouse. Visual Basic distinguishes among several different events involving the mouse. A single left-button click—or the Click event—can be registered on many different objects, including a command button, a label, or even the form itself.

There are times when your code must distinguish between different mouse actions. For example, Visual Basic has an event procedure called Form_MouseDown, which is triggered when the player presses a mouse button while the pointer is over the form. If you have programmed the Form_MouseDown event procedure, then Visual Basic will invoke that function as soon as the player presses down on a mouse button.

The drag-and-drop process seems simple enough, but how can it be coded in Visual Basic? Drag and drop is not one event, but three. The key is to understand that although to the player this procedure is one continuous process, you will actually program it using three distinct events. You program MouseDown to start the dragging; MouseMove is called many times and is used to reset the X,Y values; and MouseUp is used to signal that dragging has stopped. The start and end of drag and drop are controlled through the use of global Boolean variables that are commonly called **flags**.

The aim of the drag-and-drop operation in the Cannonball project is to support movement of the cannon tip and the target. These tasks are handled in similar—but not identical—ways. The game compares in the MouseDown event procedure the current location of the pointer with the boundaries of **linCannon** and **shpTarget**. If the pointer is near the tip of **linCannon**, the Boolean variable **blnCannonmove** is set to True. If the pointer is within the area corresponding to **shpTarget**, then the Boolean variable **blnTargetmove** is set to True. These two Boolean variables trigger the move in the subsequent event, MouseMove. It is also possible that the pointer is not on either object. In that case, your program should ignore the click.

Moving the Cannon

First, let's examine the code used to move the end of the cannon. This code uses **closetocannon**, a function that you will write separate from any event. The function **closetocannon(xx As Single, yy As Single) As Boolean** determines whether the pointer is near the cannon's end by comparing the parameters **xx**, **yy** with the location of the end of **linCannon** (**linCannon.X2** and **linCannon.Y2**).

If **closetocannon** determines that the pointer and the end of **lincannon** are within 100 twips of each other, the function returns True; otherwise, it returns False. Notice the test is not for absolute equality, only for being in the general vicinity. Most players will probably believe that the pointer is on the tip of the cannon. Testing for equality would make it quite a challenge for the player to select an object, since the screen contains over 1400 twips per inch.

Recall that the cannon remains in a fixed location—only the angle of its barrel changes. Therefore, you only need to change the **X2**, **Y2** properties of **linCannon**. Figure 13 shows the code that moves **linCannon**.

● Code in MouseMove to move the cannon

```
If blnCannonmove Then
    linCannon.X2 = X
    linCannon.Y2 = Y
End If
```

The drag-and-drop operation concludes with the MouseUp event, which occurs when the player releases the mouse button. After MouseUp executes, the code in MouseUp resets both **blnCannonmove** and **blnTargetmove** to False to prevent additional moves. You could also test the values of **blnCannonmove** and **blnTargetmove** and only reset the one that was True, but the simplest approach is just to set them both to False. Finally, the game should refresh the screen (call **Form.Refresh**) to redraw any of the screen objects that were affected by the drag and drop.

Moving the Target

Now let's examine the code for moving the target. Assume that the MouseDown event was triggered. Within the MouseDown code, there needs to be a test to determine whether the pointer is "over" **shpTarget**; in other words, the pointer's X and Y coordinates are within the boundaries of **shpTarget**.

You already have the code to determine whether the pointer is within the **shpTarget**—it is the **hittarget** function that was described earlier. You can reuse **hittarget**, because the task here is basically the same: instead of the cannonball hitting **shpTarget**, the pointer is hitting **shpTarget**. If the pointer is over **shpTarget**, then the distances between the pointer and the Top, Left points are saved in the variables **sngDragx**, **sngDragy**.

The adjustment, or offset, values stored in variables **sngDragx** and **sngDragy** are needed to properly move **shpTarget**. The player chooses the point within the target at which to start the dragging operation. The parameters of the MouseDown event procedure indicate this position as an X,Y point on the screen. The code in Figure 14 computes this position relative to the target itself (its upper-left corner) so that the target moves smoothly as if it were being dragged by a pointer glued to the original point of contact.

figure **14**

Code in MouseDown that sets up the move of the target

```
If hittarget(X, Y) Then
    blnTargetmove = True
    sngDragx = X - shpTarget.Left
    sngDragy = Y - shpTarget.Top
Else
    blnTargetmove = False
End If
```

The change of **shpTarget**'s properties that makes it move takes place because of the MouseMove event procedure. The MouseMove event will occur many times, as long as the mouse is moving. Since the player will move the mouse for a variety of purposes, your code should ensure that **shpTarget** or **linCannon** only move if the corresponding flags, **blnTargetmove** and **blnCannonmove**, were set in a MouseDown event procedure.

The code for moving the **shpTarget** (shown in Figure 15) uses the **sngDragx** and **sngDragy** variables to ensure that the **shpTarget** is positioned correctly.

figure **15**

Code to move the target

```
If blnTargetmove Then
  shpTarget.Left = X - sngDragx
  shpTarget.Top = Y - sngDragy
End If
```

SETTING UP A MENU

Your implementation of Cannonball will use a pull-down menu to end the game. Add a new menu category called "Options" as follows: From the form Design window, click **Tools**, then click **Menu Editor**, as shown in Figure 16. Set the properties as shown in Figure 16 to establish a procedure that contains code to exit the game. Refer to the "Algorithms for Event Procedures and User-Defined Procedures" section later in the chapter for a description of the procedure **mnuExit**.

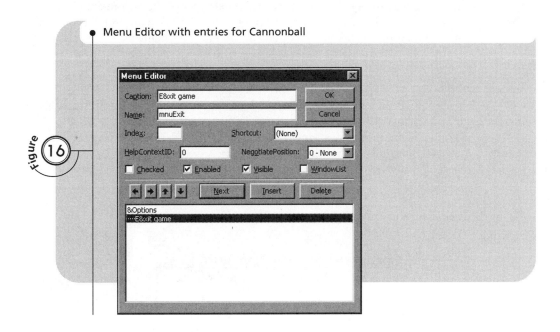

Menu Editor with entries for Cannonball

Figure 16

The settings shown in Figure 16 allow for the use of keys on the keyboard as alternatives to pull-down menu execution. If, during design time, you make the entries as indicated, with the ampersand (&) preceding the "O" in Options and the ampersand preceding the "x" in Exit, the player can hold down the Alt key and then click "O" then "x" to exit the game. Consult Visual Basic Help for more information on menus and access keys.

PLAN FOR THE USER INTERFACE

The Cannonball player can perform four actions:

- Fire the cannon

- Change the cannon angle

- Change the target position

- Change the cannonball's speed

The logical mechanism for firing the cannon is to click a command button. Changing the angle of the cannon and the position of the target have been covered already. The last topic is how to let the player adjust the cannonball's speed.

CHANGING THE CANNONBALL'S SPEED

The game should allow the player to change the cannonball's initial velocity and the cannon's angle, factors that affect how far a cannonball travels. The velocity is set using a text box (**txtSpeed**) or controlled by a scroll bar (**hsbSpeed**).

Although you could simply have the player type in the velocity with a text box, the use of a scroll bar has advantages. Text boxes in games can be problematic; player input errors can cause serious errors in interactive programs, even to the point of crashing systems. When a player enters a letter rather than a number, or enters data outside of a reasonable range, the software must catch that error, which requires extra programmer effort in anticipating and correcting mistakes.

Scroll bars allow the player to enter numeric data in a controlled way. The player cannot enter non-numeric characters, because the control's value comes from the scroll bar. Out-of-bounds values (such as a negative number or 1,000,000) are eliminated through the scroll bar's Max and Min properties. By using controlled input mechanisms such as scroll bars and list boxes, you can minimize data validation requirements and prevent many run-time errors.

FORM DESIGN

This section describes all of the objects contained on the final design for Cannonball, which is shown in Figure 17. Follow this plan to place all the objects needed on your form. The object names listed below are suggestions; you may rename them if desired (if you do, be sure to revise your code accordingly). Set the command button caption as suggested. Placement of objects are suggestions—you may lay out your form differently, if you wish.

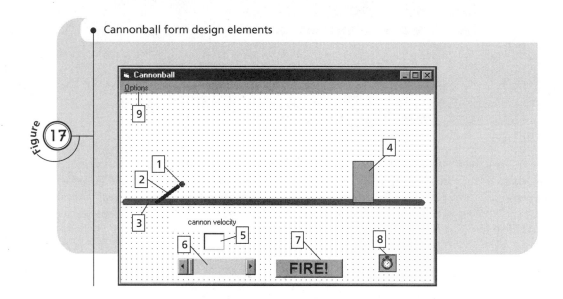

● Cannonball form design elements

Figure 17

Graphical objects

1. **shpBall**: Shape property set to 3 for circle; code in **timFlight_Timer** alters Left and Top properties (that is, moves the ball)

2. **linCannon**: Line; may be modified code in mouse events triggered by action of player (**X2** and **Y2** properties altered)

3. **linGround**: Line

4. **shpTarget**: Shape property set to 0 for rectangle; may be moved by code in mouse events triggered by player (Top and Left properties altered)

Controls modified by player, directly or indirectly

5. **txtSpeed**: Text box changed by code responding to changes to **hsbSpeed** scroll bar control

6. **hsbSpeed**: Horizontal scroll bar, directly altered by player

Command button

7. **cmdFire**: Caption is FIRE!; code starts **shpBall** movement

Timer

8. `timFlight`: Timer event supports the animation, that is, the code causes the movement of **shpBall**

Menu

9. `&Options`: Caption for drop-down menu; used to end game

VARIABLES AND CONSTANTS DECLARED IN THE `(General)` SECTION

In your Cannonball program, set the following variables and constants in the `(General)` section. The formulas used in the ballistics animation require the following constants:

Element	Explanation
`Option Explicit`	Set this option, which requires a declaration of all variables
`Const g As Single = 9.8`	The force of gravity
`Const deltat As Single = .25`	Change in time used for calculations
`Const ballrad As Integer = 50`	Radius of the cannonball
`Dim sngDragx As Single` `Dim sngDragy As Single`	Repositions **shpTarget** when it is moved by the player
`Dim vx As Single`	The initial horizontal velocity
`Dim vy As Single`	The initial vertical velocity

`Dim X1 As Single`
`Dim X2 As Single`
`Dim Y1 As Single`
`Dim Y2 As Single`
	Stores the **X1**, **X2**, **Y1**, and **Y2** properties of the **linCannon** object; used to calculate the angle of **linCannon** and place **shpBall** on top of **linCannon**

`Dim TT As Single`	Holds the elapsed time during animation
`Dim sngGrass As Single`	Vertical position of the line representing the ground
`Dim blnCannonmove As Boolean`	Flag set to True if mouse button is clicked when pointer is near the tip of **linCannon**
`Dim blnTargetmove As Boolean`	Flag set to True if mouse button is clicked when pointer is over **shpTarget**

ALGORITHMS FOR EVENT PROCEDURES AND USER-DEFINED PROCEDURES

Even though Cannonball is a small program, it benefits from an incremental development process. Coding one feature at a time and testing its implementation is a common and successful technique. You should, therefore, implement this project in three stages. In Stage 1, you will do the programming of procedures as suggested here and test the code you have written. In the subsequent stages, you will make additions to the code and perform new tests.

Stage 1: Assume a fixed speed for the cannonball (you can set the initial speed in the **txtSpeed** text box at design time) and assume that the cannon always starts at the same position (no adjustment of **linCannon**). Program movement of **shpBall** without checking for hitting **shpTarget** or **linGround**. You will need to halt the program using the Stop button ■ on the Visual Basic toolbar.

Stage 2: Add code that checks for hitting the target (**shpTarget**) or hitting the ground (**linGround**).

Stage 3: Add code for adjusting the **linCannon** angle and changing the cannonball's speed using the scroll bar.

The following table provides a general description of these three stages. Following the table are specific code examples for each procedure.

Stage	Work on these procedures	Preparation at design time	How to test the code and the anticipated program response

1	```Form_Load```
	```cmdFire_Click```
	```timFlight_Timer```
		Enter a number between 100 and 500 in the Text property of **txtSpeed**. Vary these numbers each time you run the program. Adjust the tip of the cannon higher or lower by selecting it with the mouse and moving the end point.	Click the FIRE! button. The cannonball should move in an arc. Higher speeds and higher tip of cannon will result in taller arcs. Stop the program using the Visual Basic Stop button.

2	```Form_Load```
	```timFlight_Timer```
	```hittarget```
		Same as Stage 1.	Click the FIRE! button. The cannonball should move in an arc and stop when it (appears to) hit the target or the ground.

3	```Form_Load```
	```Form_MouseDown```
	```Form_MouseMove```
	```Form_MouseUp```
	```hsbSpeed_Change```
	```hsbSpeed_Scroll```
	```closetocannon```
	```mnuExit_Click```
		No special action at design time.	Move the cannon tip with the mouse. Adjust the horizontal scroll bar. Use the pull-down menu.

STAGE 1: THE COMMAND BUTTON AND THE TIMER

To implement Stage 1, you will write code for three event procedures: the Form_Load event procedure, the Click event procedure for the **cmdFire** command button, and the Timer event procedure for the timer, **timFlight**.

Stage 1: The Form_Load Event Procedure

Include the following code to set the Interval property to 20.

```
timFlight.Interval = 20
```

Stage 1: The `cmdFire_Click` Event Procedure

Include the following local variables in this event procedure:

Element	Explanation
`Dim Theta As Double`	Represents the angle of the cannon to the ground
`Dim v As Integer`	Represents the velocity (speed) of the cannonball

This event procedure will take the value in **txtSpeed** as **shpBall**'s speed and will provide initial values to the vertical and horizontal components of the cannonball's flight, using the code described in "Preparing to Program." It will then begin the animation by setting the Enable property of the timer to True.

Following is a detailed description of the code for this event procedure:

1. Find the starting point of **shpBall** by first copying the endpoint coordinates from **linCannon** into global variables using the code shown in Figure 18.

Figure 18

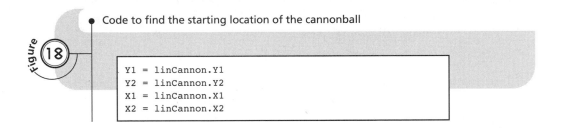

Code to find the starting location of the cannonball

```
Y1 = linCannon.Y1
Y2 = linCannon.Y2
X1 = linCannon.X1
X2 = linCannon.X2
```

2. Although the **shpBall** object looks like a circle, it is defined in Visual Basic in terms of a rectangle bounding (surrounding) a circle, positioned by its Top and Left properties and sized by its Width and Height properties. Figure 19 illustrates this concept.

Figure 19

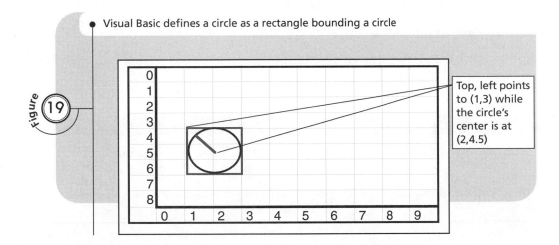

Visual Basic defines a circle as a rectangle bounding a circle

Top, left points to (1,3) while the circle's center is at (2,4.5)

3. Because the location that Top and Left refer to is not the center of the circle, you must do some adjusting. To actually place **shpBall** on top of **linCannon** (the position **X2, Y2**), make the following modification in **cmdFire_Click()**:

```
shpBall.Top = Y2 - ballrad
shpBall.Left = X2 - ballrad
```

where the radius of **shpBall** is subtracted from Top and Left. This has the effect of placing **shpBall** on the end of **linCannon**.

4. Determine the angle of **linCannon** to **linGround** using the Visual Basic Atn function, like this:

```
Theta = Atn(Abs(Y2 — Y1) / Abs (X2-X1))
```

 TIP **This function removes the negative sign for numbers less than zero.**

Note: If the player positions the cannon to fire straight up, X1 will equal X2 and the program will generate a run-time error. (See the "Optional Enhancements" section for a challenge to correct this situation.)

5. Convert the speed (entered as a text value in the **txtSpeed** text box) to numeric form using the Val function. You use this Visual Basic function to convert the string form of a number (the Text property of **txtSpeed**) into a format, such as Integer, that computers can use to do math. Use the values **vx** and **vy** to store the two vertical and horizontal components of velocity. Also, set **TT** to 0 to indicate the elapsed time. Figure 20 shows the code that performs these actions.

● Code to convert the speed to a number and store the cannonball's velocity components

Figure 20

```
V = Val(txtSpeed.Text)
vx = v * Cos(Theta)
vy = v * Sin(Theta)
TT = 0
```

6. Start the timer by setting the Enabled property, like this:

```
timFlight.Enabled = True
```

Stage 1: The `timFlight_Timer` Event Procedure

This event procedure requires the following local variables:

Element	Explanation
`Dim xx As Single`	Used to recalculate the X position of the cannonball during the animation
`Dim yy As Single`	Used to recalculate the Y position of the cannonball during the animation

Your code for the Timer event procedure incrementally moves **shpBall**. Notice that for Stage 1, the code moves the cannonball in an arc but doesn't stop. When you run your program, you will need to intervene and stop the cannonball's movement by clicking the Break button ▮▮.

Program this event procedure as follows:

1. Using the current values of **TT**, **vx**, and **vy**, compute the new horizontal and vertical positions for the cannonball, like this:

```
xx = vx * TT + X2
yy = .5 * g * (TT * TT) - vy * TT + Y2
```

2. Reposition **shpBall** based on its new horizontal and vertical coordinates:

```
shpBall.Top = yy - ballrad
shpBall.Left = xx - ballrad
```

3. Next, update the time elapsed so that the next event will use the increased value of **TT** to reposition **shpBall**:

```
TT = TT + deltat
```

The **deltat** constant represents the change in time. Try the game now by starting the program and firing the cannon. Reminder: Since you have not programmed any code to stop the animation, you must use the Break button ▌▌ to do so.

STAGE 2: DETERMINING A HIT

After you know that your code for moving the cannonball works, you are ready to make the program calculate a hit. This involves adding code to the Form_Load procedure and the Timer event procedure and writing a new user-defined procedure **hittarget**.

Stage 2: The Form_Load Event Procedure

For Stage 2 of the implementation, you need to make some additions to Form_Load to set up the checks that halt the flight of the cannonball.

Program this event procedure as follows:

1. Use the existing code that sets the **timFlight.Interval**.

2. Set the variable **sngGrass** to the vertical position of the line named **linGround**. Note: Because the ground is a horizontal line, you can use the **Y1** property or the **Y2** property, since they are the same. The code to do this is as follows:

```
sngGrass = linGround.Y2
```

3. Set **shpBall** to be invisible:

```
shpBall.Visible = False
```

Stage 2: The timFlight_Timer Event Procedure

For the second stage, you must add to this procedure code to determine whether **shpBall** hits **shpTarget** or **linGround**. Add to your previously written procedure the code in Figure 21 after the variables **sngxx** and **sngyy** are set:

Code to update the Timer

Figure 21

```
If hittarget(xx, yy) Then
    Beep
    Beep
    Beep
    shpTarget.FillColor = &HFF&
    timFlight.Enabled = False
    shpBall.Visible = False
End If
```

hittarget is a user-defined procedure that you will shortly add to this stage.

Next, write code to determine whether the cannonball has hit the ground. If your code determines that **shpBall** has fallen to ground level (its vertical component is greater than **sngGrass**), you will need to adjust the position of **shpBall** to lie on top of **linGround**, since it may have fallen below **linGround** during the animation interval. The code to do this is shown in Figure 22.

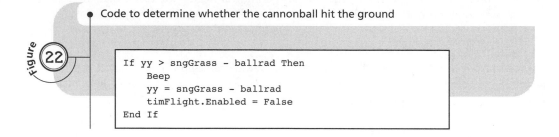

Code to determine whether the cannonball hit the ground

Figure 22

```
If yy > sngGrass - ballrad Then
    Beep
    yy = sngGrass - ballrad
    timFlight.Enabled = False
End If
```

Stage 2: The Function `hittarget(xx As Single, yy As Single) As Boolean`

This user-defined function has the following parameters:

Element	Explanation
`xx As Single`	Refers to the x location
`yy As Single`	Refers to the y location

This function has two parameters: **xx** and **yy** and returns a Boolean value. **hittarget** should determine whether the **xx**, **yy** values indicated by the parameters are within the boundaries of **shpTarget**. Program this procedure so that it follows the following logic:

1. **hittarget** must determine whether **xx** is greater than the Left property of **shpTarget** *and* less than the sum of the Left property and the Width property

and

2. **yy** is greater than the Top property of **shpTarget** *and* less than the sum of the Top property and the Height property. The code that makes these determinations is shown in Figure 23.

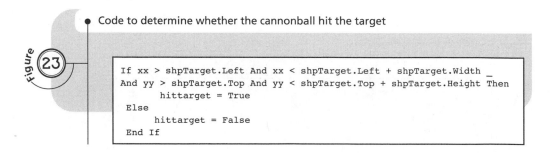

Code to determine whether the cannonball hit the target

Figure 23

```
If xx > shpTarget.Left And xx < shpTarget.Left + shpTarget.Width _
And yy > shpTarget.Top And yy < shpTarget.Top + shpTarget.Height Then
        hittarget = True
 Else
        hittarget = False
 End If
```

STAGE 3: MOVING THE CANNON AND CHANGING THE CANNONBALL SPEED

For the third stage, you need to create the code for adjusting the cannonball speed and the cannon angle.

For the speed adjustment, your code will have to adjust the properties of the horizontal scroll bar **hsbSpeed** and insert code that sets the **txtSpeed** text box to the value associated with the scroll bar in the **hsbSpeed_Change** and **hsbSpeed_Scroll** events.

In this stage, add the code that allows the player to adjust the cannon angle. The player can move **linCannon** using drag and drop. The critical event procedures you must code are Form_MouseDown, Form_MouseMove, and Form_MouseUp. The MouseDown code determines whether the pointer is near the **linCannon** endpoint (use a function you will write called **closetocannon**). If the pointer is near the cannon's end, MouseDown sets a flag that will be checked by MouseMove. MouseMove changes the X2,Y2 properties of **linCannon** to move the cannon. MouseUp stops the movement.

You also need to allow for the player to drag and drop **shpTarget**. Code in the MouseDown event procedure tests to determine whether the player has pressed the mouse button over the target. The **hittarget** procedure is used to perform this test. This is the same procedure used by your code in the Timer event to determine whether **shpBall** has hit the target. In one case, the call to **hittarget** uses the parameters from MouseDown; in the other case, the current position of **shpBall**.

Stage 3: The Form_Load Event Procedure

Include in the Form_Load event procedure all of the code you wrote and debugged in Stages 1 and 2, and add the code that controls the scroll bar, as follows:

```
txtSpeed.Text = hsbSpeed.Value
hsbSpeed.Max = 500
hsbSpeed.Min = 100
```

Stage 3: The `Form_MouseDown (Button As Integer, Shift As Integer, X As Single, Y As Single)` Event Procedure

This event procedure has the following parameters:

Element	Explanation
`X As Single`	Refers to the x location
`Y As Single`	Refers to the y location

Program this event procedure as follows:

1. Determine whether the pointer is near the **linCannon** endpoint by calling **closetocannon**, which returns True or False. If it returns True, set **blnCannonmove** to True, as shown in Figure 24.

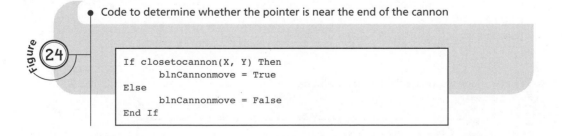

• Code to determine whether the pointer is near the end of the cannon

Figure 24

```
If closetocannon(X, Y) Then
        blnCannonmove = True
Else
        blnCannonmove = False
End If
```

2. Determine whether the pointer is on **shpTarget**. Do this by writing code to call the **hittarget** function with arguments X and Y that are part of this event procedure. These values represent the position of the pointer. The code should check the Boolean value returned by **hittarget**. If the function returns True, the code sets the

blnTargetmove flag. You also must calculate where within **shpTarget** the mouse pointer is. To do this, compute the offsets (**sngDragx** and **sngDragy**) from the top and left of **shpTarget** so that when the player drags the mouse, **shpTarget**'s coordinates change accordingly. The code to do this is shown in Figure 25.

Code to determine whether the pointer is on the target

```
If hittarget(X, Y) Then
    blnTargetmove = True
    sngDragx = X - shpTarget.Left
    sngDragy = Y - shpTarget.Top
Else
    blnTargetmove = False
End If
```

Stage 3: The `Form_MouseMove (Button As Integer, Shift As Integer, X As Single, Y As Single)` Event Procedure

This event procedure has the following parameters:

Element	Explanation
`X As Single`	Refers to the x location
`Y As Single`	Refers to the y location

Program this event procedure as follows:

1. Check the **blnCannonmove** flag. If its value is True, change the endpoint of **linCannon** to the current pointer position, using the code shown in Figure 26.

Code to update the cannon's tip position

```
If blnCannonmove Then
    linCannon.X2 = X
    linCannon.Y2 = Y
End If
```

2. Check the **blnTargetmove** flag. If it is set, change the position of **shpTarget** based on the pointer position and the offsets **sngDragx** and **sngDragy**, using the code shown in Figure 27.

Code to update the target's position

```
If blnTargetmove Then
    shpTarget.Left = X - sngDragx
    shpTarget.Top = Y - sngDragy
End If
```

Stage 3: The `Form_MouseUp (Button As Integer, Shift As Integer, X As Single, Y As Single)` **Event Procedure**

This event procedure has the following parameters:

Element	Explanation
`X As Single`	Refers to the x location
`Y As Single`	Refers to the y location

Program this event procedure as follows:

1. Reset **blnCannonmove** and **blnTargetmove** to False using the following code:

   ```
   blnTargetmove = False
   ```

   Notice that it does not matter which—if either—flag has been set.

2. Call **formCannonball.Refresh** to redraw any parts of the form that may have been disturbed. The code to do this is as follows:

   ```
   formCannonball.Refresh
   ```

   (Try the code without this command and see what happens.)

Stage 3: The `hsbSpeed_Change` **Event Procedure**

A horizontal scroll bar can be changed by the player moving the bar, clicking the directional arrow keys, or clicking between the bar and the endpoints. By including this line of code in the **hsbSpeed_Change** event procedure, you are ensuring that the procedure's code is executed no matter how the player uses the scroll bar. Insert this code in this event procedure:

```
Call hsbSpeed_Scroll
```

Stage 3: The `hsbSpeed_Scroll` **Event Procedure**

Set **txtSpeed.text** to **hsbSpeed.Value**, as follows:

```
txtSpeed.text = hsbSpeed.Value
```

You do this so that the **txtSpeed** text box holds the new speed. Your code in **cmdFire_Click** uses the text box for the cannonball's initial speed.

Stage 3: The `closetocannon(xx As Single, yy As Single) As Boolean` **User-Defined Procedure**

This user-defined procedure has the following parameters:

Element	Explanation
`xx As Single`	Refers to the x location
`yy As Single`	Refers to the y location

The code in the MouseDown procedure calls **closetocannon**. This procedure has X and Y parameters and returns the value True or False. The function allows for imprecision on the part of the player; the **xx** and **yy** locations do not have to be *exactly* at the endpoint of **linCannon** for the program to recognize that the pointer is at the end of the cannon. In the sample code for this procedure, this tolerance is written explicitly as **100**. The **closetocannon** code makes two comparisons: it compares the horizontal closeness and the vertical closeness of the pointer and the end of the cannon. This is acceptable and more efficient than computing distances, which requires calculation of squares and square roots.

Program this procedure to determine whether the absolute value of the difference between **linCannon.X2** and **xx** is less than **100** *and* the absolute value of the difference between **linCannon.Y2** and **yy** is less than **100** using the code shown in Figure 28.

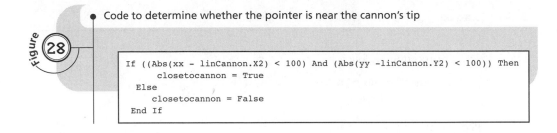

Figure 28

Code to determine whether the pointer is near the cannon's tip

```
If ((Abs(xx - linCannon.X2) < 100) And (Abs(yy -linCannon.Y2) < 100)) Then
     closetocannon = True
  Else
     closetocannon = False
  End If
```

If both conditions are true, then **closetocannon** should return True; otherwise, it should return False.

Stage 3: The mnuExit() User-Defined Procedure

At design time, you used the menu editor to set up a call to the procedure named **mnuExit**, which occurs when the player selects Exit from the pull-down menu. Program **mnuExit** using the code:

> **End**

OPTIONAL ENHANCEMENTS

There are many ways you can customize your Cannonball game. Following are some suggestions to get you started on adding original features and functionality.

1. Change the code so that adjusting the **linCannon** angle doesn't change the size of **linCannon**. Similarly, prevent the player from being able to move **shpTarget** below **linGround**. Should you put in a check to prevent the player from pointing **linCannon** away from **shpTarget**? What would happen in this case?

2. The current implementation allows the player to point **linCannon** straight up, causing a run-time error of dividing by zero. Assume that you skip the first enhancement and don't prevent the player from pointing the **linCannon** away from the **shpTarget**. Fix this error.

3. The implementation described in this chapter lets the player move **shpTarget** when the cannonball is in motion. Program your game to prevent this. Consider setting a variable in the **cmdFire_Click** routine that is checked by the MouseDown routine.

4. The sample code in this chapter includes values for speeds, gravity, and the timer interval. These values were set to give the arc of the flight a natural appearance. For another improvement in terms of reality, define the horizontal distance in terms of an appropriate unit of distance (such as meters). Find out the range of speeds of cannonballs. Adjust the **deltat** increment and the **timFlight.Interval** to simulate realistic trajectories.

5. As the game is currently coded, if you click the FIRE! button before the ball lands, the simulation starts over. Change the program to disable restarts until the current simulation is done.

6. Alter the animation to move the target and the cannonball once the player clicks the FIRE! button.

7. Instead of moving the cannonball, gradually draw a line outlining the entire arc of the ball's flight.

8. Add sound enhancements to the game (consult Visual Basic Help to learn how to handle multimedia controls). These could include the sound of the cannonball travelling, different sounds when it hits the ground or hits the target, and the sound of applause if the target is hit.

9. Add another scroll bar and supporting code to vary the **deltat** (representing the change in time used to calculate the horizontal and vertical speed) and the Interval property of the Timer control. Perform tests to determine the optimal values for **deltat** and the **Interval** property.

10. Revise the code so that when the player selects **shpTarget** (to move it), its border thickens, and its color changes. Reset to the original style once the move is completed. In addition, don't allow the player to move **shpTarget** above or below **sngGrass**.

◎ DISCUSSION QUESTIONS

1. What features and code would be required to make your current Cannonball program into a full-featured game program? Consider features such as scoring and an element that shoots back at the player. This would require a second set of controls, including a second timer. Consider including a control array of objects and timers.

2. This game is two-dimensional. The simulation of a three-dimensional event involves not just moving objects in space, but calculating (the technical term is "rendering") how the scene appears when projected on the computer screen. Research the topic of geometric modeling and explain how to incorporate a third dimension into your Cannonball program.

CONSTRUCTION PLAN FOR
QUIZ

⊚ CONCEPTS, SKILLS, AND TOOLS

In this chapter, you will create a computer game called Quiz, which is a knowledge contest for one or two players. As in a television game show, players attempt to win points by correctly answering questions. If the player answers correctly, he gains points; if he answers incorrectly, he loses points.

The structure of this game combines Visual Basic code with a database, a practice that is common in business applications. A **database** is a collection of information supported by powerful software called a **database management system** or DBMS, that can generate reports in response to queries and process changes to the information. As you have seen already, Visual Basic is a flexible tool that can quickly and easily create a user interface for an interactive program. In many business situations, professional developers use Visual Basic to create the user interface, and then use another software package, for example, a DBMS such as Microsoft Access, to manage the data for the application.

When this model is used, Visual Basic provides the **front end** of the system, where the user views information and makes requests, and the database provides the **back end**, where the data is managed and requests are processed. For this game, Visual Basic will provide the front end—the forms the players use as they play the game—and a Microsoft Access database will provide the back end.

You will use the following general programming and design concepts in the Quiz construction plan:

- Database creation and management
- Error handling
- Coding patterns for answers (model answers) using wild card characters to recognize most correct answers
- Screen design for two-person play
- Choice of events by player

The Visual Basic features used to construct this game include:

- Connecting Visual Basic to a database using the Data Object control and generations of Recordsets
- SQL (Structured Query Language)
- Like operator for detecting string patterns
- Activate event for forms
- KeyDown for use of function keys

DESCRIPTION OF THE GAME

HOW THIS VERSION OF QUIZ WORKS

Quiz can be played with one or two players. Play begins with the players choosing a topic from a list of categories. The game displays a question and its point value. As soon as the question appears, the players race to press their function keys, and the faster player types in an answer. The game compares the answer to recorded answers that are made up of models or patterns, which provide flexibility so that most correct answers will match the pattern. If the game determines that the player's answer is correct, it adds the question's point value to the player's score. If the answer is incorrect, the game subtracts the same amount from the player's score. Experiment with the Quiz game by running the **quiz.exe** file located in your Ch7 folder.

To provide you with the challenge of working with two forms in the same project, Quiz includes a feature that allows for editing, removal, or addition of questions. Ideally this question revision responsibility is handled by the host or producer of the Quiz game and not the players. This chapter refers to this character as the question editor.

SAMPLE SCREENS

The game begins with the screen shown in Figure 1.

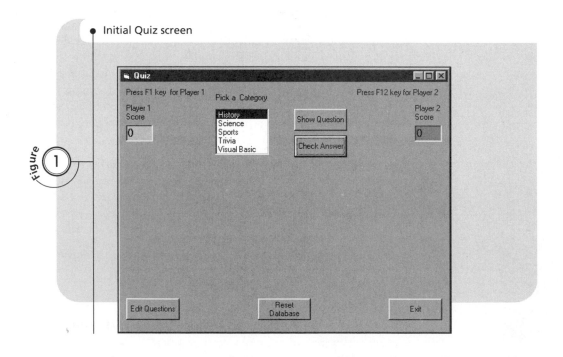

Initial Quiz screen

Figure 1

At the top of the screen are instructions for the players. The players start by agreeing to select a topic listed in the Pick a Category list box. Then, one player presses the Show Question button. As soon as the question appears (see Figure 2), Player 1 must press the F1 key for a chance to answer the question, and Player 2 must press the F12 key for a chance to answer the question. The player who presses his function key faster wins the chance to make a guess. A correct answer wins points for the player, while a wrong answer causes the player to lose points. Boxes display each player's score.

● Show Question button is clicked and players race to press their function keys

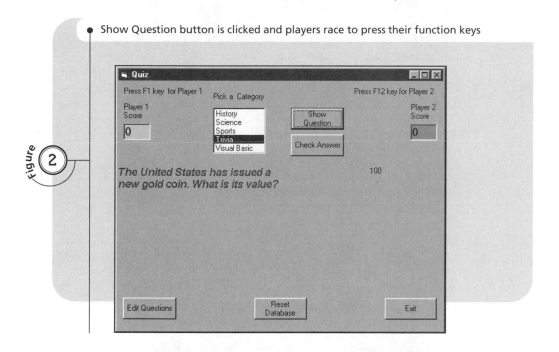

Figure 2

Since the F1 key is at the far left end of the keyboard and F12 is at the far right, two players sit side by side (Player 1 on the left and Player 2 on the right). The game detects which player pressed his key first and that player now has a chance to answer the question. As shown in Figure 3, Player 1 pressed F1 before Player 2 pressed F12, so Player 1 has a chance to answer the question. The game displays a text box where Player 1 can enter an answer. After the answer is input, Player 1 clicks the Check Answer button to compare his guess to the correct answers stored for the question.

Figure 3

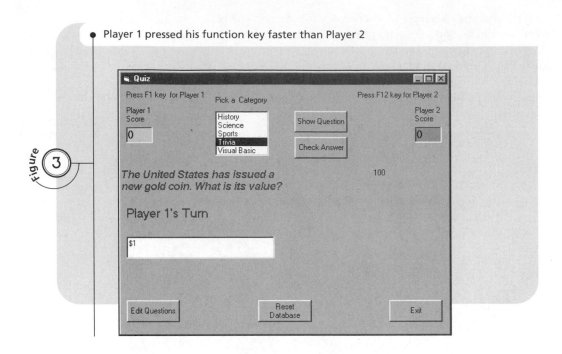

Player 1 pressed his function key faster than Player 2

Player 1's guess was correct, so the system displays "YES" for an acceptable answer and increases Player 1's score by the point value of the question, as shown in Figure 4.

Figure 4

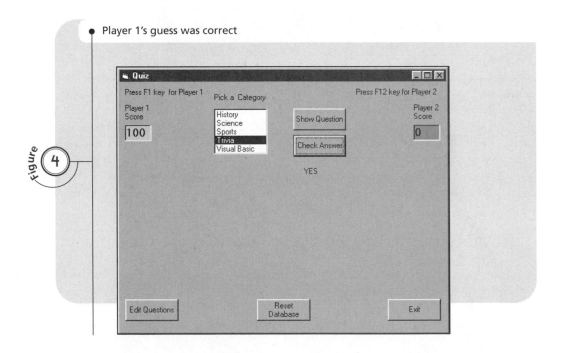

Player 1's guess was correct

The game would have accepted other answers such as "one dollar" or "a dollar." The intent of this design is to accept the same answers that a human would accept to avoid making the game appear mechanical or simplistic. After the question has been chosen, the game removes it from the list of available questions. The players can continue in this way indefinitely, picking categories and answering questions. There is nothing built into the logic of the game to control who goes next, so the players must agree who gets to pick a category for the next question. The Exit button is used to end the game.

If all the questions in a category have been asked, the game prompts the players to select another category (see Figure 5).

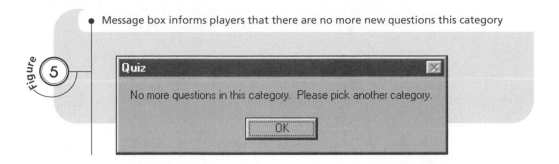

Figure 5

• Message box informs players that there are no more new questions this category

Quiz

No more questions in this category. Please pick another category.

OK

If the player clicks the Reset Database button, the game sends a request to the database to make all the questions available again. The questions exist in a database, not in the Visual Basic program, so the availability of a question is controlled in the database and not the game. If a question was asked in an earlier game, it remains unavailable until the reset operation is performed.

It is important to keep in mind that the database has an existence independent of the Visual Basic project files. This means, for example, that when the database is changed during testing, its contents will be changed even if the Visual Basic project files were not altered.

EDITING THE QUESTIONS

The second part of the game allows the question to add or update questions for Quiz. The question editor clicks the Edit Questions button, and the game displays a second form, shown in Figure 6. The form shows all the fields associated with a question: the text of the question, two models for answers, a category key, a question value, and a Used field that is automatically initialized to zero (for unused questions). It is up to the editor entering the questions to design practical model answers.

The game will use Answer 1 and Answer 2 as model answers when it tests a player's answer. The asterisks shown in the Figure 6 example represent wild card positions that can be replaced by one or more characters (or no characters). The use of wild card positions provides a pattern for an answer that allows for flexibility in the player's guess. For example, one of the questions in Quiz asks who the inventor of the polio vaccine is. The model answers in this case are *Salk* and *Sabin*. The player can enter last names, with or without first names. Of course, this means that "Salk" or "Jonas Salk" is acceptable as the answer for the question shown in Figure 6, and so is "Fred Salk."

Question editors use the scroll bar at the bottom of Figure 6 to view each question. The database contains one table with records for each question. Each record contains the text of a question, two patterns for answers, the question category, the Used field (which indicates a question's availability), and the question's point value. The Used field is set to True for unused questions and changes to False when a question is used in the game. If a question has been used (its Used field is set to False), it is no longer available.

The game allows any number of categories for the questions. As the game loads the first Quiz form, it makes a list of all categories included in the database and loads them into a list box, which the player can search when playing the game.

The button Return to Quiz allows play to continue. When the game switches to the form that allows play to resume, the Quiz form includes an updated list of question categories.

A sample Edit Questions Database form

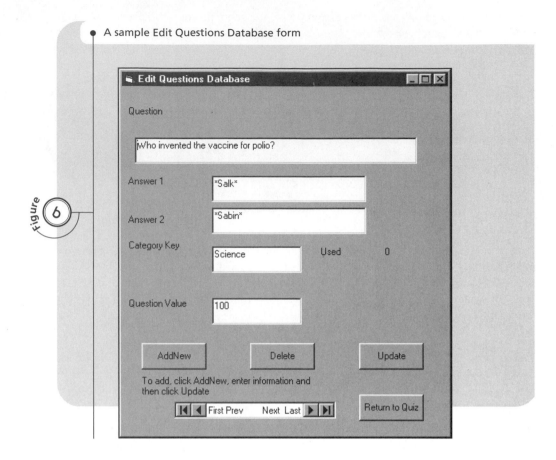

figure 6

KEY DESIGN ISSUES

There are 10 key design tasks that you—the designer and programmer—must accomplish when creating the Quiz game:

- Create a database to hold questions, categories, and potential answers

- Connect the project to the database

- Design a two-person game

- Display the available question categories

- Select a question for the player(s) to attempt to answer

- Ensure that the game asks questions only once

- Allow question editors a way to design flexible questions and answers

- Allow questions to be added, changed, or deleted

- Allow the players to move back and forth between updating the database and playing the game

- Handle error conditions generated by the DBMS

Task: Create a database to hold questions, categories, and potential answers.
Logic: Quiz is a collection of questions. Each question consists of not just the question itself, but also of an answer, category, and point value.
Solution: This is a perfect application for a database. A database consists of one or more tables. A **table** holds **records**, which are collections of facts (called **fields** or **attributes**) associated with each question.

Task: Connect the project to the database.

Logic: In this version, you will use Visual Basic to create the front end, or user interface, and another application, a DBMS, to manage the information. There must be a connection between the two to allow user requests to be serviced and information from the database retrieved. When a Visual Basic application connects to a database, the application is said to be *bound to the database*.

Solution: The built-in Visual Basic control Data Object can create a connection to a database. The Data Object is described as a **data aware control**, which means that it has properties that allow you to indicate which database you want to connect to the program. You will also connect the game to the database using a method that is independent of the form controls.

Task: Design a two-person game.

Logic: Many computer games allow more than one person to play. For practical reasons, your solution should not require the players to buy new equipment to play the game. You should design a solution for standard personal computer equipment.

Solution: The function key F1 is at the far left of the standard keyboard, and the function key F12 is at the far right. Assign the F1 key to Player 1—he will use this key to indicate that he is ready to answer a question; Player 2 will use the F12 key for the same purpose. A key press is recognized by Visual Basic as the Form_KeyDown event. Program the Form_KeyDown event procedure to recognize the key that was pressed, display a question, and allow the winning player to enter an answer.

Task: Display the available question categories.

Logic: The Quiz form contains a list box with a list of categories. Every category that is mentioned in the database needs to be part of this list and should only be listed once. For example, if the database has three questions in the Sports category, that category should only be listed once, not three times.

Solution: Use the Visual Basic database commands to create a list of all categories. You will do this using a special language for manipulating databases called Structured Query Language (SQL). Once you have used SQL to collect the categories, use Visual Basic to place each category in the list box.

Task: Select a question for the player(s) to attempt to answer.

Logic: Asking questions and attempting answers is the point of the game; therefore, the game must have some process of selecting questions.

Solution: Using special database methods and SQL, you will write code that extracts all questions in the database within the selected category. Then you can write code to select one of the questions randomly using Visual Basic's random number generator.

Task: Ensure that the game asks questions only once.

Logic: As the game is being played, every question asked should be a new question since questions that are repeated in a game would make the game very boring. Repetition is a concern—because the game is randomly asking questions, it could very quickly repeat a question if the game did not record whether it had already been asked.

Solution: When building the database, include a field that indicates whether a question has been used in the game. If the Used field is set to True (Yes), then the question is not available for the game. When the game is selecting a question for play, the code should only include questions with the Used field set to False (No).

Task: Allow question editors a way to design flexible questions and answers.

Logic: This program attempts to make the game flexible in terms of acceptable answers. Requiring answers to be exact means that some correct answers would be rejected, players would become frustrated and the computer game would seem greatly inferior to a game with human judges.

Solution: Use the string comparison Like operator so that answers can be constructed as patterns. A pattern is a model for an answer that can include wild card characters. In addition, include two answer fields in the question record. The game can then compare the player's guess to two patterns.

Task: Allow questions to be added, changed, or deleted.

Logic: When you first develop this version of Quiz, you probably will start off with just a few questions, but you will quickly want to add new questions, or make changes to existing ones.

Solution: This implementation has two forms, both of which are connected to the database. One form (`frmQuiz`) allows for playing the game, and the other form (`frmDBEdit`) allows for editing and adding of questions.

Task: Allow players to move back and forth between updating the database and playing the game.

Logic: Since the game includes the functionality of playing the game as well as maintaining the database, it must provide a way for the players to move back and forth easily between both tasks.

Solution: Going from the game form to the edit form and back is easily done using a command button and the Visual Basic statements Form_Show and Form_Hide. The design should require the category list to be regenerated once the player returns to the game form, since the editing operation may have caused a change in the categories. The Activate event is invoked as part of the initial loading of a form and also any time the form regains the focus. Include the code to generate the list of categories in the Form_Activate event procedure.

Task: Handle error conditions generated by the DBMS.

Logic: The structure of the game is such that a Visual Basic application collects data from the players, then passes it to an independent program—the database. A database can be designed with data validation requirements that all new data must meet before being added to the database. For example, most companies have a set format for information such as account numbers. If invalid data—for example, an account number in the wrong format—is passed to the database, the database normally will issue an error message and terminate. Your design must prevent a player's mistake in editing the questions from generating a nonrecoverable error.

Solution: The Visual Basic **On Error** construct allows for special error handling. Whenever the game issues a request for the database to update a record, include the **On Error** section to handle this error and continue the game's execution.

PREPARING TO PROGRAM

GENERAL DATABASE ISSUES

There are several terms you will need to be familiar with when working with databases. The type of database you will use in Quiz is called a **relational database**. A relational database stores information in tables, and tables are made up of columns and rows. Each column refers to a field, and each row refers to a record. For this implementation of Quiz, you will create a database with one table. Each record holds fields relating to one question, namely, the question itself, possible answers, the category of the question, its value, and an indication of its availability for the game.

CREATING YOUR DATABASE

The first step you need to complete is to create the database for this game, which can be done using Microsoft Access. If you need help, you can use as your database the file `quiz.mdb`, which is in your Ch7 folder; also, feel free to consult a standard textbook or online help. The code in this construction plan uses the names in the table below for elements that are part of or are connected to the database. These names are optional; however, if you change a name,

you will need to include the new name in the code you will write to manipulate the database.
Here are the items used for the game:

Element	Description	Location
quiz.mdb	Access database file created for this game	In your Ch7 folder
archive	Table that contains questions	In database **quiz.mdb**
datQuestions	Visual Basic Data Object control used to connect the Visual Basic front end to the **quiz.mdb** database	On **frmQuiz** and **frmDBEdit** forms

In your database, you will need to create records with values for the following fields:

Field Name	Data type	Description	Special instructions
question	Text	Text of question	Required field
answer1	Text	Acceptable answer using pattern with *	Required field
answer2	Text	Alternative acceptable answer using pattern with *	Not required field
category	Text	Category of question	Required field
value	Currency	Dollar value (a point value in money that mimics the format of TV game shows).	Required field; must be numeric
used	Yes/No	Used question	Required field; Boolean value

Please notice the difference between the data types for the Access database vs. the data types for Visual Basic. For example, the Text data type in Access corresponds to the String data type in Visual Basic.

Once you have created your database, you will need a mechanism to connect your Visual Basic application to the database. This sounds like a complicated task to perform, but all the complexity is handled by Visual Basic. For you—the programmer—making this connection is as simple as adding another control object to your form. To make a connection, perform the following steps using Visual Basic:

1. Create your database or use the file **quiz.mdb** from your Ch7 folder. Make sure the database and Visual Basic project files are stored in your Ch7 folder.

2. Select the **Data Object tool** from the Visual Basic toolbox and place the control on your form. Figure 7 shows the Data Object tool. Place the control as indicated in Figure 7.

3. Change the name of the new Data Object to **datQuestions**. In addition, change its Connect property to **Access**.

4. In the Form_Load event procedure of **frmQuiz**, you need to write code to assign a value to the DatabaseName property of the control **datQuestions**. (See the **frmQuiz Form_Load** event procedure in the "Algorithms for Event Procedures and User-Defined Procedures for **frmQuiz**" section for the exact code.)

Figure 7

Adding a Data Object to your form and setting the database Connect property

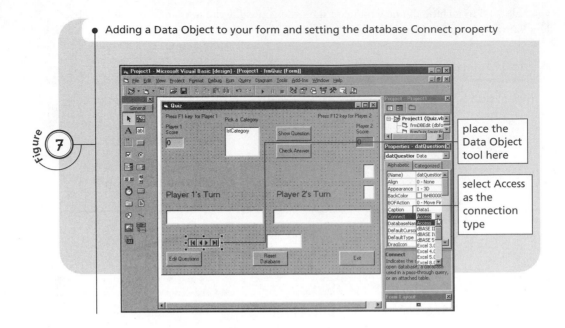

place the Data Object tool here

select Access as the connection type

DATABASE COMMANDS FOR MANIPULATING DATA

Once you have set up your database, the next step is programming the code that allows the game to select records (that is, pick a question to ask) based on some criteria. For example, the game will need access to all the questions in a certain category or at least all the available (unused) questions. The game must also have a way to select one record out of all those available, for the purpose of asking a question to play the game.

This process of selecting one or more database records is called a **query**. You will use SQL to create a query. The relevant queries for this game are:

1. Find the set of all categories cited in the questions. The term **set** means collection or grouping.

2. Find the set of all questions in a specific category that have the Used field set to False.

In addition, the game will allow the player to make these changes to the database:

- Add new questions

- Delete questions

- Change (update) questions

Precise methods are available to manipulate databases. More specifically, when you use a Data Object control to establish a connection, Visual Basic creates a **Recordset** object as the result of a query. Recordsets are ordered sequences of records in which one specific record at a time, called the **current record**, can be examined and changed. Recordsets are subsets of tables. The order of the records in a Recordset is important; much of the code described here involves the manipulation of the internal point designating the current record. Recordsets have their own sets of commands—MoveFirst, MovePrev, MoveNext, and MoveLast—which change the Visual Basic designation of the current record.

You can determine the number of records in a Recordset using its Recordcount property. The expression

```
intRc = datQuestions.Recordset.Recordcount
```

assigns the number of records in the Recordset to the variable **intRc**.

Using Visual Basic, you can also create a new record, update the current record, or delete the current record using Recordset commands. You will be adding new records (questions) to the database when the player enters information on the **frmDBEdit** form. You will include the following code to add a new record to the questions database. If **datQuestions** is the Data object connected to your database, then the command

datQuestions.Recordset.AddNew

creates a new record. The command must be followed by code that inserts data into each required field for the new record.

In this game, players add new records (questions) using the form **frmDBEdit**, which appears in Figure 8.

The Edit Questions Database form (frmDBEdit) as it is first opened

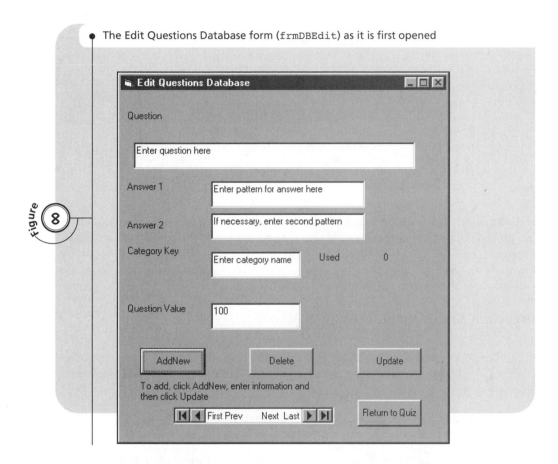

Figure 8

The player clicks the AddNew button, and the game displays input instructions in each text box. After the player has entered the required information for a new question, the player clicks the Update button and the question is added to the database. The code adds the information to the database with these instructions:

```
datQuestions.Recordset.Edit
datQuestions.Recordset.Update
```

The Edit command copies the data to a buffer and the Update method places it in the database.

DATA VALIDATION AND ERROR HANDLING

When the game attempts to update or add a record, it passes the data collected in the input fields to the DBMS, and the DBMS then updates the record after filtering it to determine whether the new data is in the correct format. For example, a numeric field cannot be used to save character or string data. If the software determines that the data being passed by your Visual Basic application is invalid, the DBMS will generate an error and the program (game) will terminate.

To avoid this situation, you must assume that the players of the game might enter invalid data. In fact, this is likely to happen, and your program should handle the situation without terminating. The game could display an error message or assign a valid default value to the field in which the player entered the incorrect data. Visual Basic's **On Error** facility gives control to the programmer. The terms "error catching" or "error trapping" are used to convey the notion that the program has a chance to provide a corrective action in response to an error instead of abruptly terminating the application.

The template for error handling is shown in Figure 9.

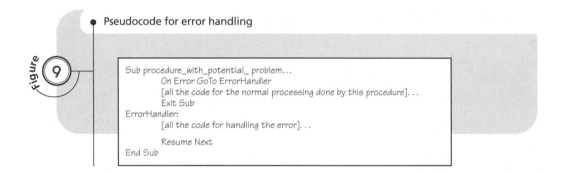

Pseudocode for error handling

Figure 9

```
Sub procedure_with_potential_ problem...
        On Error GoTo ErrorHandler
        [all the code for the normal processing done by this procedure]...
        Exit Sub
ErrorHandler:
        [all the code for handling the error]...

        Resume Next
End Sub
```

The **Exit Sub** statement acts as a filter that prevents non-erroneous data (statements) from being processed by the error handler. The **On Error** statement sets up the action if an error does occur. After the **ErrorHandler** label, the programmer enters the code for handling the error. Visual Basic Help gives information on how to do this. For the Quiz program, you can assume that the error in question relates to the data.

SELECTING A SET OF RECORDS USING SQL

You will use SQL to define subsets of the database, called, as you learned earlier, Recordsets. The following statement creates a Visual Basic Recordset that contains all the questions in the Trivia category (notice that the code extends over two lines through use of the underscore and ampersand):

```
datQuestions.RecordSource = "Select * from " _
     & "archive where category = 'trivia'"
```

This statement defines a subset of the records in the database by sending the string that specifies a SQL Select statement to the database program. Select statements are also known as queries. The asterisk (*) used in the statement indicates that you wish to select all of the fields in the archive table. The statement is interpreted by the database program as follows: Access selects records (builds a Recordset) using the SQL Select statement. The Recordset (result of the query) is made up of all of the fields (indicated by use of the asterisk) of the archive table (which was linked previously to the **datQuestions** Data Object). Only data from the records in which the Category field is trivia are included in the new Recordset.

> **TIP**
>
> **Single quotation marks are necessary here because the example is a string within a string: the string that sets up the Recordset contains the string 'trivia'. If you started the inner string with double quotation marks, Visual Basic would interpret the quotation marks as ending the string that started with Select.**

The SQL statement shown above is a simplified example—the code you will actually use (in the **cmdPick_Click** event procedure) will be more complicated for two reasons:

1. The constant 'trivia' will be replaced by a variable in your code (since the players won't always be selecting questions from the trivia category).

2. The "where" clause of the SQL statement will have an additional part, since only the records where the Used field is set to False (= 0) are to be accepted.

The result of the Select query is a Recordset with a current record. That current record is subject to the Recordset commands mentioned previously (MoveFirst and so on). The fields from the database are placed in the control objects on the form that have been linked to the appropriate fields during design time.

The SQL example shown above generated a Recordset comprising rows, which are complete records within the database. It is also possible to create a Recordset that is a subset of only the values in a column, which is a single field. This can be done independent of controls on the form—instead, you use SQL, as shown in Figure 10.

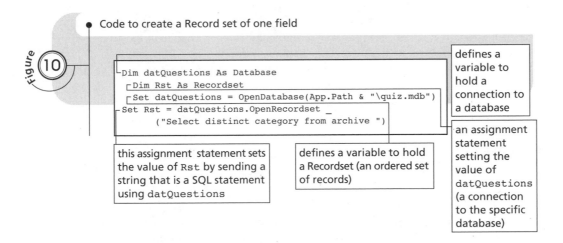

Figure 10

Code to create a Record set of one field

```
Dim datQuestions As Database
Dim Rst As Recordset
Set datQuestions = OpenDatabase(App.Path & "\quiz.mdb")
Set Rst = datQuestions.OpenRecordset _
        ("Select distinct category from archive ")
```

defines a variable to hold a connection to a database

an assignment statement setting the value of datQuestions (a connection to the specific database)

this assignment statement sets the value of Rst by sending a string that is a SQL statement using datQuestions

defines a variable to hold a Recordset (an ordered set of records)

The Visual Basic function App.Path returns the folder for the currently executing application and the & operator concatenates that folder name with the name of the database to construct a full path name. Alternatively, you can include the full pathname for the location of your database. The Visual Basic Dim statement declares **datQuestions** as a Database and **Rst** as a Recordset. The first Set statement establishes a connection to the database. The second Set statement sets **Rst** to a particular Recordset, in this case, the one defined by the SQL statement. This SQL statement is interpreted by the database program (Access) as follows: Access uses the Select statement to build a Recordset of just one field—the Category field—from the archive table. No Where condition is given, so include all of the records from the Category field. However, only include *distinct* categories (no duplicates) in the query result.

You will use this Recordset to populate the list box that displays the categories of questions. (This step will be further described in the user-defined subroutine **MakeListCategory**.) If you need help, review the material on using list boxes in Chapter 2.

CREATING FLEXIBILITY FOR CHECKING ANSWERS

This Quiz game uses patterns instead of requiring the player's answer to exactly match a stored model. For example, if a correct answer to a question was "dog" and the pattern to be matched was "d*g", then "dog", "dg", or "dawg" would match as correct answers. The asterisk wild card character (*) will match any number of characters.

The Visual Basic feature that supports pattern matching is the Like operator. You use Like instead of the equality (=) operator when making comparisons. The Like operator is used in the following format:

```
result  = string Like pattern
```

where **pattern** is a string that might include some special symbols. The most important symbol used in patterns is the asterisk (*). When part of a pattern, Visual Basic interprets the asterisk as a match for any character or characters. As the game designer, you need to decide if that is acceptable. Use Visual Basic Help to learn about other special characters that can be used in patterns.

THE ACTIVATE FORM EVENT

Any user can move back and forth between the game form and the database editing form. To provide this function, you must use code that makes each form appear and gives each form the focus, which means it is the top window on your screen. You use the Show method to give a form the focus and the Hide method to make the form disappear and lose the focus.

If the question editor does change the database by adding a new question, the game must reconstruct the category list, since this modification may mean a change in the category list. The correct place to include this reconstruction logic is the Activate event, not the Load event, which has been used in all the previous games for initialization and set-up logic. The Activate event is triggered when the form is loaded at the beginning of execution and also when a form becomes visible (shown) or when it gets the focus. Placing the logic that constructs the list of categories in this event means it will execute every time the form gets the focus.

THE KEYDOWN EVENT

As the players race to answer a question, each attempts to press his function key first—F1 or F12. The game needs to be able to determine which key was pressed first and can do so using the KeyDown event. To make sure that the **Form_KeyDown** event occurs, you will insert the **frmQuiz.SetFocus** code in the **cmdPick** routine. The **Form_KeyDown** event procedure is triggered when a player presses a key. When the KeyDown event occurs, Visual Basic invokes the KeyDown event procedure with the **KeyCode** parameter that indicates which key has been pressed. The header line for this event procedure is:

```
Private Sub Form_KeyDown(KeyCode As Integer, Shift As Integer)
```

Visual Basic contains defined constants to represent each function key. Your code can compare the value in **KeyCode** to **vbKey1** and **vbKey12** to test for F1 and F12, respectively. You will need to write this code in the KeyDown event procedure so that it checks for these two constants and does nothing if any other key is pressed.

NOTE REGARDING CHAPTER FORMAT

You will create two user interfaces—that is, two forms—for Quiz; therefore, the following sections ("Plan for the User Interface," "Form Design," "Variables and Constants Declared in the **(General)** Section," and "Algorithms for Event Procedures and User-Defined Procedures") are provided for both forms, **frmQuiz** and **frmDBEdit**. The first form, **frmQuiz**, is used when playing the game. The second form, **frmDBEdit**, allows users (called question editors) to examine and edit the contents of the database of questions.

PLAN FOR THE frmQuiz USER INTERFACE

A large number of Visual Basic objects are required for two reasons. First, connecting to a database requires many fields. Second, some duplication of functionality is required to create a game for two players. To begin, Visual Basic requires a Data Object control (**datQuestions**) that provides the physical link with the database. Then, for every field the application needs to access in the database, you need a corresponding control object. For example, the Visual Basic object **txtModel1** connects to the database field named answer1. The objects on the form that are associated with, or bound to, fields in the database are often not visible during run time. For example, you do not want to display the answer to the question while the player is entering his answer—you only want to have it available for the game to compare to the answer entered by a player.

⊚ frmQuiz FORM DESIGN

This section describes all of the objects contained in the final design for the Quiz form. Follow this plan to place all the objects needed on your form, as shown in Figure 11. The object names listed below are suggestions; you may rename them if desired (if you do, be sure to revise your code accodingly). Set the labels and captions as suggested. Placement of objects are suggestions—you may lay out your form differently, if you wish.

frmQuiz form design elements

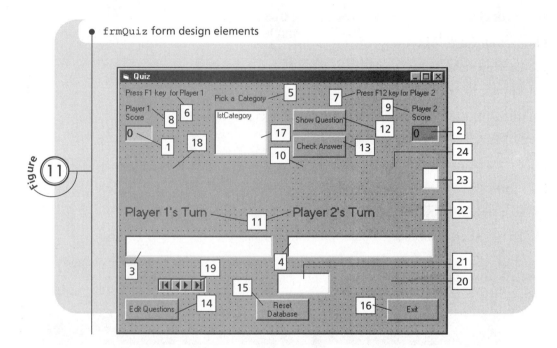

Figure 11

Controls for the players

1. **lblScore(0)**: Label control array element for Player 1

2. **lblScore(1)**: Label control array element for Player 2

3. **txtAns(0)**: Text box control array element for Player 1's answer

4. **txtAns(1)**: Text box control array element for Player 2's answer

Static labels (always visible, no properties change during run time)

5. **Label1**: Static label "Pick a Category"

6. **Label2**: Static label "Press F1 key for Player 1"

7. **Label3**: Static label "Press F12 key for Player 2"

8. **Label4**: Static label "Player 1 Score"

9. **Label5**: Static label "Player 2 Score"

Labels that display information

10. **lblResult**: Label holding result (YES for valid answer; otherwise, NO)

11. **lblPlayer**: Label control array with element for each player indicating which player will answer the question

Command buttons

12. **cmdPick**: Command button to select a question; label is "Show Question"

13. **cmdCompare**: Command button to compare player's answer with pattern texts; label is "Check Answer"

14. **cmdEditDB**: Command button to switch to edit form; label is "Edit Questions"

15. **cmdReset**: Command button to reset Used field in all settings to unused; label is "Reset Database"

16. **cmdExit**: Command button to quit game; label is "Exit"

Fields to bind to database

17. **lstCategory**: List box with categories of questions

18. **lblQuestion**: Label holding question

19. **datQuestions**: Data control linking to questions database

20. **lblUsed**: Label linked to Used switch

21. **txtCategory**: Text box for category

22. **txtModel1**: Text box for pattern for first answer

23. **txtModel2**: Text box for pattern for second answer

24. **lblQvalue**: Label holding point value of question

The following table describes which form elements are linked to fields in the database and indicates when the elements are visible as the game is played.

Visual Basic control	Function	Visible?	DataField property	DataSource property
lblScore control array	**lblScore(0)** holds score for Player 1 and **lblScore(1)** holds score for Player 2	Always	None	None
lstCategory	Holds list of all categories	Always. **lstCategory** is populated when **frmQuiz** is activated.	None (holds all the categories, not just a single category for one question)	None (holds all the categories, not just a single category for one question)
cmdPick	Picks a question from the selected category	Always	None	None

Visual Basic control	Function	Visible?	DataField property	DataSource property
cmdCompare	Checks player's answer against patterns	Always	None	None
lblQuestion	Linked to question field in database	Not visible when game begins. **lblQuestion** becomes visible after a player clicks Show Question command button.	question	**datQuestions**
lblQvalue	Point value of question linked to value field in database	Not visible when game begins. **lblQvalue** becomes visible after a player clicks Show Question command button.	value	**datQuestions**
lblPlayer control array	Label above text box where player enters an answer	Not visible when game begins. **lblPlayer** becomes visible after a player presses F1 or F12.	None	None
lblResult	Determines whether the player's answer is correct: Yes or No	Not visible when game begins. **lblResult** becomes visible after a player clicks Check Answer command button.	None	None
txtAns control array	Text box where the player enters an answer	Not visible when game begins. **txtAns** becomes visible after player presses F1 or F12.	None	None
datQuestions	Data control for linking the game to the database of questions	Never	Not applicable	Not applicable
lblUsed	Linked to Used field in database	Never	used	**datQuestions**
txtCategory	Linked to Category field	Never	category	**datQuestions**
txtModel1	Linked to first answer field	Never	answer1	**datQuestions**
txtModel2	Linked to second answer field	Never	answer2	**datQuestions**

CONSTRUCTION PLAN FOR QUIZ

Visual Basic control	Function	Visible?	DataField property	DataSource property
cmdEditDB	Command button to switch to edit form	Always	None	None
cmdExit	Command button to end game	Always	None	None
cmdReset	Command button to reset all used fields to False	Always	None	None

LINKING A VISUAL BASIC CONTROL TO A DATA SOURCE

For each Visual Basic control object that is linked to a database field, you must set the data properties as described above so they refer to the DataSource **datQuestions** and link to the correct database field. For example, to link the control object **txtModel1** to the database, follow these steps:

1. Select the object **txtModel1**, access its Properties window, and scroll down to the Data properties.

2. Set the DataField property to **answer1**.

3. Set the DataSource property to **datQuestions**.

For example, in Figure 12, the text box **txtModel1** has been selected. When you select an object, you can adjust its properties in the Properties window. Notice that the DataField property has been set to **answer1** and the DataSource property has been set to **datQuestions**. You will need to select each object on the form that is connected to a field in the database and set these two properties using the information in the previous table.

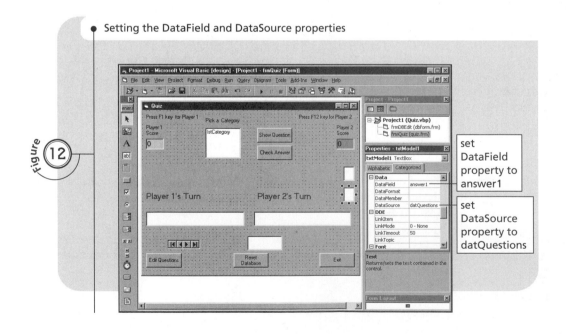

Setting the DataField and DataSource properties

Figure 12

set DataField property to answer1

set DataSource property to datQuestions

VARIABLES AND CONSTANTS DECLARED IN THE (General) SECTION FOR frmQuiz

You will need to declare the following options and variables in the (**General**) section:

Element	Explanation
`Option Explicit`	Set this option to require a declaration of all variables
`Option Compare Text`	This statement instructs Visual Basic how to compare strings. **Option Compare Text** compares strings based on a case-insensitive sort order. For example, "Salk" and "salk" are considered a match.
`Dim intPlayer As Integer`	The variable keeps track of which player is answering the question. You will write code to give it an initial value in the Activate event.
`Dim blnCatPicked As Boolean`	This variable is a flag that indicates whether a category has been picked. A player must pick a category before he attempts to answer a question. You will write code to give **blnCatPicked** an initial value in the Activate event.

ALGORITHMS FOR EVENT PROCEDURES AND USER-DEFINED PROCEDURES FOR frmQuiz

THE FORM_LOAD EVENT PROCEDURE

This event procedure does not require any local variables.

The Form_Load event procedure sets the DatabaseName property for the Data Object control to **datQuestions**, which connects the Quiz form to the database. The database file **quiz.mdb** can be found in your Ch7 folder. When you set up this application, store **quiz.mdb** in the Ch7 folder along with your Quiz Visual Basic files. Then use relative addressing to set the DatabaseName property, as follows:

```
datQuestions.DatabaseName = App.Path & "\quiz.mdb"
```

The code **App.Path** contains the name of the subdirectory that your application (**App**) resides in, and the ampersand (&) concatenates the path with the name of your Quiz program file. By using relative addressing, you can move your application from one directory to another or from one computer to another without having to change all the code references to the database.

THE MakeListCategory *USER-DEFINED SUBROUTINE*

Include the following local variables in this subroutine:

Element	Explanation
`Dim datQuestions As Database`	Used to make a connection to the database
`Dim rst As Recordset`	Contains the Recordset made up of all categories
`Dim intRc As Integer`	Contains the number of records in the Recordset
`Dim i As Integer`	Used for controlling a For...Next loop

Program the **MakeListCategory** subroutine as follows:

1. Empty **lstCategory** of any previous category entries. You need to do this because a player could delete all the questions in a category, and if you did not empty the list, an old category would still exist even though it did not have any questions. Consequently, the list is updated every time the form is displayed. Include this code to perform this task:
   lstCategory.Clear

2. Make the players' answer boxes, the question, and its value invisible. The code to do this appears in Figure 13.

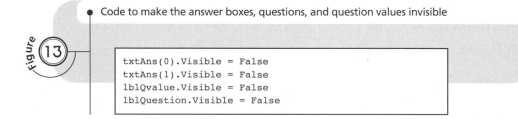

Figure 13

● Code to make the answer boxes, questions, and question values invisible

```
txtAns(0).Visible = False
txtAns(1).Visible = False
lblQvalue.Visible = False
lblQuestion.Visible = False
```

3. Make the connection between the form and the database and create a Recordset with this code:

   Set datQuestions = OpenDatabase(App.Path & "\quiz.mdb")

4. Create a new Recordset named **rst** and place in it all of the game's distinct categories using the SQL command:

   "Select distinct category from archive"

   Remember that "archive" is the name of the table in the database. The table has a record for each question. The following statement sends the SQL statement to Access and Access returns the list of distinct categories:

   Set rst = datQuestions.OpenRecordset("Select distinct_ category from archive")

5. Determine the number of categories, which equals the number of records in the Recordset named **rst**. Writing the code to determine the number of records is a two-step process. First, you have to make the last record in **rst** the current record

using the command **MoveLast**. Then you can use **RecordCount** to find out how many records are in **rst** and store that number in a variable (**intRc**). The code to do this is as follows:

```
rst.MoveLast
intRc = rst.RecordCount
```

6. The next task is to set up a loop that places each category in the list box. First, you need to reset the current record to the first record in **rst** using the command **MoveFirst**. Then, using a loop, use the command **AddItem** to store the information from **rst** in the list box. The code to do this is shown in Figure 14.

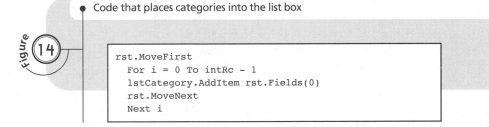

Figure 14

Code that places categories into the list box

```
rst.MoveFirst
  For i = 0 To intRc - 1
  lstCategory.AddItem rst.Fields(0)
  rst.MoveNext
  Next i
```

7. Finally, set the Index value of **lstCategory** to 0 so the first item is selected, and close the Recordset **rst**. The code to do this is as follows:

```
lstCategory.ListIndex = 0
rst.Close
```

THE cmdEditDB_Click *EVENT PROCEDURE*

This event procedure does not require any local variables. It is executed when a player wants to edit the database. You must program this event procedure to transfer the focus to the edit form, **frmEditDB**. The code to do this is:

```
frmDBEdit.Show
```

THE cmdPick_Click *EVENT PROCEDURE*

You will need the following local variables for the **cmdPick_Click** event procedure:

Element	Explanation
Dim strCat As String	Stores the category of the question
Dim intRc As Integer	Stores the record count of the Recordset
Dim intRi As Integer	Acts as an index to find a new question
Dim i As Integer	Utility variable used for managing For...Next loops

The action of the **cmdPick** button is to:

• Gather from the database all the questions within the selected category that have not been used

• Determine the count to make a random choice and pick a question

• Make the question and its point value visible to the players

- Display a message to players directing them to select another category if no questions remain

- Mark this question as used

To accomplish these actions, program the **cmdPick_Click** event procedure as follows:

1. Store a string containing the current selected category in a local variable **strCat**. Recall that the ListIndex property holds the currently selected item, so include the following code to store the selected category in **strCat**:

   strCat = lstCategory.List(lstCategory.ListIndex)

2. Create a SQL statement that selects all unused questions within the requested category and create a new Recordset. After the SQL statement is processed, a call is made to refresh the database. Note the use of the underscore (_) line continuation character and ampersand (&) concatenation operator, which are required when a long statement wraps over several lines. Use the code shown in Figure 15 to select the unused questions and connect these questions to the form controls.

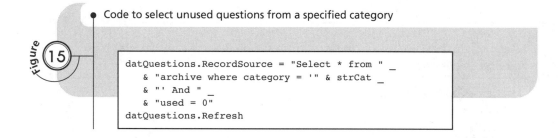

Code to select unused questions from a specified category

Figure 15

```
datQuestions.RecordSource = "Select * from " _
    & "archive where category = '" & strCat _
    & "' And " _
    & "used = 0"
datQuestions.Refresh
```

3. Use the local variable **intRc** to save the record count of the newly created Recordset. The code to do this is:

   intRc = datQuestions.Recordset.RecordCount

4. If **intRc** is greater than 0, there is at least one available question in this category. Your code will need to choose which question to ask from the set of available questions. This action should appear as a random choice. One way to do this is to scroll a random number of records from the Recordset. You do this by invoking MoveFirst to position the current record to the start of the set of records. Next, obtain a random integer (using methods you have learned in previous chapters). Then use a For...Next loop with a call to MoveNext in the body of the loop. See Figure 16. If the vlaue of **intRi** is 0, the loop does not execute at all, which is acceptable—it just means that the random choice in this case was the first record.

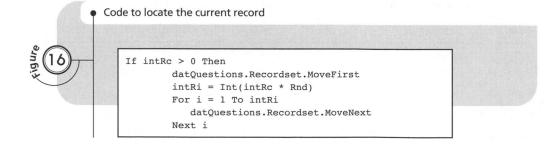

Code to locate the current record

Figure 16

```
If intRc > 0 Then
        datQuestions.Recordset.MoveFirst
        intRi = Int(intRc * Rnd)
        For i = 1 To intRi
            datQuestions.Recordset.MoveNext
        Next i
```

5. After the For...Next loop ends, the current record contains the selected question. Now all the linked fields on the Quiz form contain values from the database. You

can now make **lblQuestion** and **lblQvalue** visible so the players can see
the question, but set the question's Used field to True so that the question will not
be asked again. (Set Used to True regardless of whether the player answered the
question correctly.) Since you are making changes to a linked field, you must call
the commands **Edit** and **Update** to record the change back in the Access database. You also need to set **blnCatPicked** to True to allow the game to respond
to the player's action of pressing F1 or F12. You must also write code to make
lblResult invisible, effectively "erasing" the results from the previous question.
You must give the focus to **frmQuiz** to allow it to respond to a key press event
from either player.

The code to perform all of these actions is shown in Figure 17.

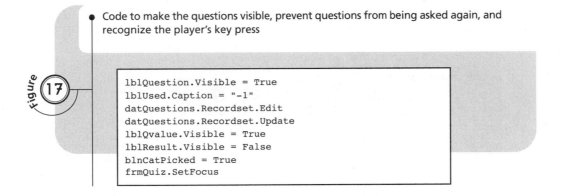

Code to make the questions visible, prevent questions from being asked again, and
recognize the player's key press

Figure 17

```
lblQuestion.Visible = True
lblUsed.Caption = "-1"
datQuestions.Recordset.Edit
datQuestions.Recordset.Update
lblQvalue.Visible = True
lblResult.Visible = False
blnCatPicked = True
frmQuiz.SetFocus
```

6. You also must allow for the possibility that there are no questions left in the category
the player selected. Remember that the local variable **intRc** contains the number of
records in the Recordset. If the number is 0, then the player must select another category. This condition is actually the false part (the Else) of the If statement at the
beginning of the **cmdPick_Click** event. The code to handle the situation in
which all the questions in a category have been asked is shown in Figure 18.

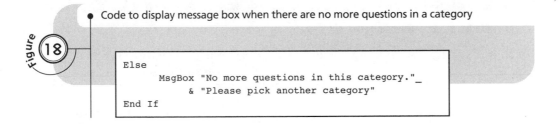

Code to display message box when there are no more questions in a category

Figure 18

```
Else
        MsgBox "No more questions in this category."_
              & "Please pick another category"
End If
```

This Else...End If clause is matched to the If...Then statement at the very beginning of this
procedure, which is:

```
If intRc > 0 Then
```

If this Else clause executes, it means the selected category has no available questions; therefore, your code must display a message instructing the player to select another category, then
click **cmdPick** again to repeat this event procedure.

THE cmdExit_Click EVENT PROCEDURE

There are no local variables needed for this event procedure, which executes when the player
wants to end the game. Insert the following code in this event procedure:

```
End
```

THE cmdRestart_Click EVENT PROCEDURE

This event procedure requires the following local variable:

Element	Explanation
`Dim datQuestions As Database`	Variable that manages the connection between your Visual Basic application and the database

This event procedure resets the Used field for all the questions so they can be asked again. Your code will make a connection to the database, then issue a SQL statement that will, for all used questions, reverse the value of the Used field from True to False so they can be included in the game. Then you must include code to close the connection to the database, as shown in Figure 19.

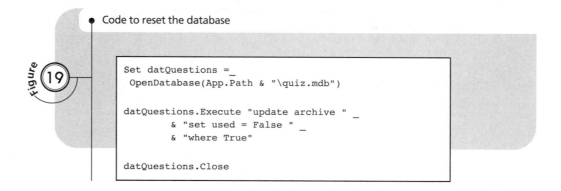

Figure 19

● Code to reset the database

```
Set datQuestions =_
 OpenDatabase(App.Path & "\quiz.mdb")

datQuestions.Execute "update archive " _
        & "set used = False " _
        & "where True"

datQuestions.Close
```

THE cmdCompare_Click EVENT PROCEDURE

This event procedure requires the following local variables:

Element	Explanation
`Dim strAns As String`	Contains the player's guess
`Dim strModel As String`	Contains a pattern from the database. The game compares the player's guess to this pattern.

This event procedure carries out the logic for comparing the player's guess with the two stored models in the database. Two local variables are used: **strAns** stores the player's answer and **strModel** stores the first model for comparison, then the second model. This event must also ensure that the player clicked the Show Question button in the proper sequence, that is, only after a question was asked and the player entered an answer. By testing the global variable **intPlayer** to see whether it has a valid value (which is set in the **Form_KeyDown** event procedure), you can ensure that a player pressed either the F1 or F12 key and made a guess.

Program the **cmdCompare_Click** event procedure to perform the following tasks:

1. Store the player's answer in **strAns**

2. Store the first model answer in **strModel**

3. Compare **strAns** and **strModel** using the Like operator

4. If the answers match, display the label "YES" and adjust the winning player's score by calling the subroutine **AdjustScore** with an argument value of 1 to indicate that the value should be added to the score.

5. If the player's guess does not match the first model, compare it with the second model. Store the second model answer in **strModel** and compare it to **strAns** using the Like operator.

6. If the player's guess matches the second model, display the label "YES" and adjust the winning player's score by calling **AdjustScore** with an argument value of 1 to indicate that the value is to be added to the player's score.

7. If neither model matches, display the label "NO" and call **AdjustScore** with an argument of -1 to indicate that the value is to be subtracted from the score of the player who entered the wrong answer.

The previous seven tasks can be accomplished in a nested If statement, as shown in Figure 20.

Code to compare the player's guess to the correct answers in the database

Figure 20

```
If intPlayer >= 0 Then
  strAns = txtAns(intPlayer).Text
  strModel = txtModel1.Text
  If strAns Like strModel Then
     lblResult.Caption = "YES"
     Call AdjustScore(1)
  Else
     strModel = txtModel2.Text
     If strAns Like strModel Then
        lblResult.Caption = "YES"
        Call AdjustScore(1)
     Else
        lblResult.Caption = "NO"
        Call AdjustScore(-1)
     End If
  End If
End If
```

After the game compares the answers, it must reset variables and make some controls invisible. Your code must make the question, its value, and the player's answer invisible. You must make the result visible. Reset **blnCatPicked** to False and **intPlayer** to -1, as shown in Figure 21.

Code to make the question, its point value, and the player's guess invisible

Figure 21

```
txtAns(intPlayer).Text = ""
txtAns(intPlayer).Visible = False
lblPlayer(intPlayer).Visible = False
blnCatPicked = False
lblQuestion  .Visible = False
lblQvalue.Visible = False
lblResult.Visible = True
intPlayer = -1
```

Complete the **cmdCompare_Click** event procedure with a final End If statement, as follows, which closes the first If statement (**If intPlayer >=0**) shown in Figure 20.

```
End If
```

THE AdjustScore(intSign As Integer) *USER-DEFINED PROCEDURE*

This procedure has the following parameter:

Element	Explanation
intSign as Integer	Contains either a +1 or a -1 to indicate whether the score should be added (+1) or subtracted (-1) from the player's score

This procedure requires the following local variable:

Element	Explanation
Dim intOscore As Integer	Used to calculate and update the player's score

The code you will write for this subroutine will use the value of the parameter **intSign** to determine whether the player's score should be increased or decreased. The code must refer to the global variable **intPlayer** to determine which player's score to change.

Player 1's score is displayed in **lblScore(0)**; Player 2's score is displayed in **lblScore(1)**. Remember, because **lblScore** is a control array, and control arrays start with an index value of 0, the index number compared to the player number is off by 1. The variable **intPlayer** stores the information identifying which player answered the question, so **lblScore(intPlayer)** is the label that contains the score of the player that will be adjusted.

You will write code to extract the current value of the player's score from **lblScore(intPlayer)** using the Visual Basic function Val, which converts a String variable to a Numeric variable. You also need to write code to extract the point value of the question so you can add or subtract it to the current player's score. The basic actions you will code are:

1. Extract the current value of the player's score from **lblScore(intPlayer)**

2. Extract the point value of the question that was asked from **lblQvalue**

3. Multiply the point value of the question by **intSign** and add it to the player's score. The result of this calculation will turn the point value into a positive number for increasing the player's score or a negative number for decreasing the player's score.

4. Store the new value of the player's score on the form

5. Make the answer entered by the player invisible

The code for the **AdjustScore** event is shown in Figure 22.

• Code to update the player's scores

```
intOscore = Val(lblScore(intPlayer).Caption)
intOscore = intOscore + sign * Val(lblQvalue.Caption)
lblScore(intPlayer).Caption = Format(intOscore, "####0")
txtAns(intPlayer).Visible = False
lblPlayer(intPlayer).Visible = False
```

THE FORM_ACTIVATE EVENT PROCEDURE

You must write code to perform the following steps for this event procedure:

1. Call the user-defined subroutine **MakeListCategory** to load all the categories from the Archive table into the list box on the form

2. Call the Visual Basic subroutine Randomize to initialize the random number generator

3. Set **blnCatPicked** to False

4. Set **intPlayer** to -1

The code for the Form_Activate event procedure is shown in Figure 23.

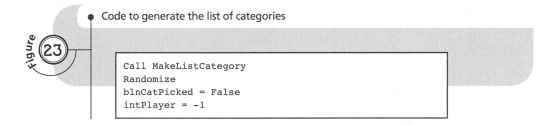

Figure 23

Code to generate the list of categories

```
Call MakeListCategory
Randomize
blnCatPicked = False
intPlayer = -1
```

THE Form_KeyDown(KeyCode As Integer, Shift As Integer) EVENT PROCEDURE

This event procedure has the following parameters:

Element	Explanation
KeyCode As Integer	Indicates what key was pressed
Shift As Integer	Indicates whether the player also pressed the shift or control key. Not used for this event procedure.

This event procedure executes whenever a player presses a key on the keyboard. Code that indicates what key was pressed is passed to this event procedure in the parameter **KeyCode**. The only keys relevant to this game are the F1 and F12 key; however, this event will execute whenever *any* key is pressed. Therefore, your logic needs to recognize when the relevant keys have been pressed, and ignore any other key presses.

First, your code tests the value of **blnCatPicked**. If **blnCatPicked** is True, it means the game has asked a question and can proceed. The next test determines whether the F1 or F12 key has been pressed. The constants **vbKeyF1** and **vbKeyF12** are defined by Visual Basic; you can use them to test for the appropriate key presses. If F1 has been pressed, you need to include code that opens the text box where Player 1 answers the question. If F12 has been pressed, include code to open the text box where Player 2 answers the question.

The code for the Form_KeyDown event procedure is shown in Figure 24.

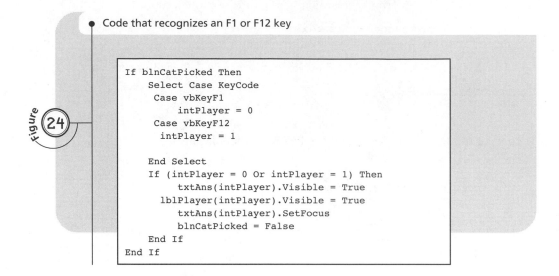

Code that recognizes an F1 or F12 key

Figure 24

```
If blnCatPicked Then
    Select Case KeyCode
    Case vbKeyF1
        intPlayer = 0
    Case vbKeyF12
      intPlayer = 1

    End Select
    If (intPlayer = 0 Or intPlayer = 1) Then
        txtAns(intPlayer).Visible = True
      lblPlayer(intPlayer).Visible = True
        txtAns(intPlayer).SetFocus
        blnCatPicked = False
    End If
End If
```

You have now coded all the events for the quiz form, **frmQuiz**. Next, you will learn about the **frmDBEdit** elements.

PLAN FOR THE frmDBEdit USER INTERFACE

This form allows users (question editors) to make changes to the database. **frmDBEdit** has fields for the question editor to enter new questions and model answers. It has buttons to allow the player to add, delete, or update (edit) a question, and a button to return to the game.

frmDBEdit FORM DESIGN

This section describes all of the objects contained on the final design for the Quiz game's Edit Questions Database form. Follow this plan to place all the objects needed on your form, as shown in Figure 25. The object names listed below are suggestions; you may rename them if desired (if you do, be sure to revise your code accordingly). Set the command button and label captions as suggested. Placement of objects are suggestions—you may lay out your form differently, if you wish.

frmDBEdit form design elements

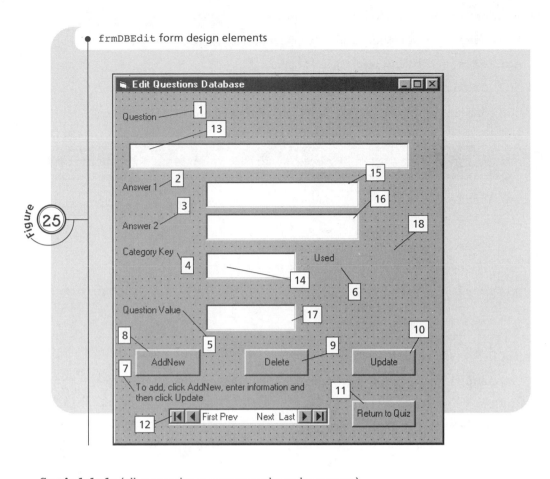

Figure 25

Static labels (all properties are constant throughout game)

1. **Label1**: Label "Question"

2. **Label2**: Label "Answer 1"

3. **Label3**: Label "Answer 2"

4. **Label4**: Label "Category Key"

5. **Label5**: Label "Question Value"

6. **Label6**: Label "Used"

7. **Label7**: Label describes how to add a new question, "To add, click AddNew, enter information, and then click Update"

Command buttons

8. **cmdAdd**: For adding a new question

9. **cmdDel**: For deleting a question from database

10. **cmdUpdate**: For updating a question

11. **cmdReturn**: For returning to the Quiz form

Fields that bind to the database

12. **datQuestions**: Data Object control that links this form to the database

13. **txtQuestion**: Text box for question text

14. **txtCategory**: Text box for category name

15. **txtAnswer1**: Text box for first model answer (pattern)

16. **txtAnswer2**: Text box for optional second model answer (pattern)

17. **txtValue**: Text box for point value of question

18. **lblUsed**: Label for used or not used designation (initialized to 0)

The following table describes the link between control objects and fields in the database.

Visual Basic control	Function	Visible?	DataField property	DataSource property
datQuestions	Data Object control for linking Quiz form to database of questions	Always	Not applicable	Not applicable
txtQuestion	Text box for entering a new question or editing an existing question	Always	question	datQuestions
txtAnswer1	Text box for first model answer	Always	answer1	datQuestions
txtAnswer2	Text box for second model answer	Always	answer2	datQuestions
txtValue	Point value of the question	Always	value	datQuestions
lblUsed	A flag that indicates whether this question has been used yet; initialized to 0 (False)	Always	used	datQuestions

VARIABLES AND CONSTANTS DECLARED IN THE (General) SECTION FOR frmDBEdit

There are no variables required for the (**General**) section of the form. Include the statement **Option Explicit** to force type declarations for variables.

ALGORITHMS FOR EVENT PROCEDURES FOR frmDBEdit

This form will manage the database by allowing players to add, delete, or update (edit) questions. To add a record, the player (question editor) must click the AddNew button, enter the new question and related fields, then click the Update button to apply the new data.

You will write code for the Form_Load event procedure and the Form_Activate event procedure to set up a connection with the database and reset the database's current record to the first record whenever this form is accessed. You will also need to write Click event procedures for each of the four command buttons on this form. When the form is loaded, it is bound to the questions database, so the values of the current record will be displayed on the form.

THE FORM_ACTIVATE EVENT PROCEDURE

This event occurs whenever this form regains the focus. In order to ensure the database has been reset to its first record, issue this command:

```
datQuestions.Refresh
```

THE FORM_LOAD EVENT PROCEDURE

In this event procedure, use the following code to set up the connection to the database for this form:

```
datQuestions.DatabaseName = App.Path & "\quiz.mdb"
datQuestions.RecordSource = "archive"
```

THE cmdAdd_Click EVENT PROCEDURE

For this procedure, you will write code to add a new record to the database. You first need to call **AddNew**, a method that does the initial setup for a new record. Then you need to place instructions in the new record's text boxes and set default values in the Used and Value fields.

The player can alter these default values if he wishes. Finally, call the **Update** database command to apply the default values, then bookmark this new record so that when the player makes changes and clicks the Update button, those changes are applied to this record. The **Update** and **Bookmark** commands are necessary because adding a record is implemented in two parts: setting up a new record and then placing values into this new record. The code for the **cmdAdd_Click** event is shown in Figure 26.

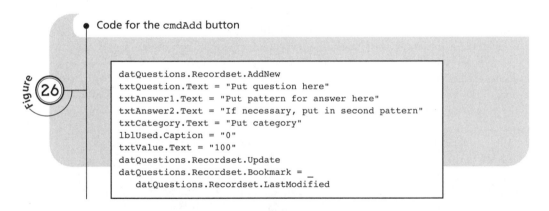

Code for the cmdAdd button

Figure 26

```
datQuestions.Recordset.AddNew
txtQuestion.Text = "Put question here"
txtAnswer1.Text = "Put pattern for answer here"
txtAnswer2.Text = "If necessary, put in second pattern"
txtCategory.Text = "Put category"
lblUsed.Caption = "0"
txtValue.Text = "100"
datQuestions.Recordset.Update
datQuestions.Recordset.Bookmark = _
    datQuestions.Recordset.LastModified
```

THE cmdReturn_Click EVENT PROCEDURE

This event procedure does not require any local variables. It closes the Edit Questions Database. Place the following code in the event procedure:

```
frmDBEdit.Hide
```

THE cmdDel_Click EVENT PROCEDURE

This event procedure does not require any local variables. It updates the database by deleting a record. First, call the **Delete** command. Remember that Recordsets have an implicit pointer that points to the current record. You do not want this pointer to point to a deleted record, because this would cause an error condition that might terminate your program. Therefore, you must include in your code a call to the **MovePrevious** command. The code for the **cmdDel_Click** event procedure is:

```
datQuestions.Recordset.Delete
datQuestions.Recordset.MovePrevious
```

THE cmdUpdate_Click EVENT PROCEDURE

This event procedure does not require any local variables. It executes when the player wants to change some information in the database. Since it is possible that the player could make an error when entering data, use the Visual Basic error handler syntax (which you learned about earlier in this chapter) to catch and handle errors. For normal processing, update the database. The code for the **cmdUpdate_Click** event procedure is shown in Figure 27.

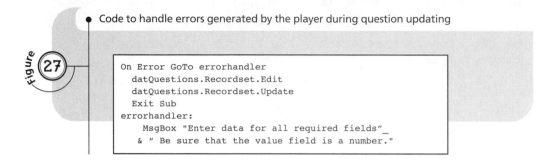

Code to handle errors generated by the player during question updating

Figure 27

```
On Error GoTo errorhandler
  datQuestions.Recordset.Edit
  datQuestions.Recordset.Update
  Exit Sub
errorhandler:
   MsgBox "Enter data for all required fields"_
   & " Be sure that the value field is a number."
```

OPTIONAL ENHANCEMENTS

There are many ways you can customize your Quiz program. Following are some suggestions to get you started on adding original features and functionality.

1. Instead of complicating the game with added features, create a simpler game with multiple choice or true/false answers.
2. Build a self-test/drill program on a topic of your choice.
3. Your implementation of the Quiz game uses a message box to handle a player's failure to enter required data. Instead, consider programming the error handler to automatically enter default values—this could happen in some situations, but not necessarily in all situations. For example, if the player neglected to specify a category, the game could automatically set the category as "General." In the case of an empty answer or non-numeric data in the value field, the code could automatically enter "100" as the default point value. On the other hand, a missing question or a missing first answer field is not acceptable. Finish the design and programming for a default approach and include feedback to the user on what is happening.
4. Design a finish point for the game, or multiple finishes. This could involve a fixed number of turns, one player reaching a certain point total, or one player falling below a certain point total.
5. Modify the Quiz game so that it uses a combination of players taking turns and racing to answer questions. Watch a TV game show such as "Jeopardy" or "Who Wants to Be a Millionaire?" to learn how it works. Decide whether a player who has correctly answered a question gets another question, or whether the players race again. How do they agree on a category? Can the players switch categories mid-play?
6. In the current version of Quiz, questions that have been asked are set to Used in the database, a value that persists even after you have closed the game. Use the Form_Terminate event, which occurs as the Visual Basic application is ending, to reset all the questions in the database from True (used) to False (unused).
7. In the current version of Quiz, a question is marked as Used when it is asked—regardless of whether the player's answer is correct. Change the program so that questions are only marked as used when they are answered correctly.
8. If a player attempts to answer a question and gets it wrong, let the other player attempt an answer. Award double points when the second player answers correctly.
9. If a category exists in the database but all its questions have been asked in the current game, remove it from the list of categories displayed to the players.

1. In this game, a database is used to store information that is used to play the game. In other games, such as Hangman or Memory, such data has been stored as variables and objects that are part of the Visual Basic program. What factors determine whether you should use an external database or internal variables to manage the data for a new project?

2. What advantages and disadvantages does the use of patterns and the Like operator bring to database searching? What other applications could it be useful for?

3. What other information could be stored in a database that relates to this game? How could additional tables be normalized (look up "normalized") and related to each other to optimize their use?

4. As it is currently programmed, there is nothing in the game that prevents players from accessing the database of questions—potentially giving them the answers to the questions. What programming methods could you use to maintain the connection between the game and the database while keeping players from seeing the contents of the database?

CONSTRUCTION PLAN FOR
MINESWEEPER

CONCEPTS, SKILLS, AND TOOLS

In this chapter, you will program a simplified version of Minesweeper, the popular computer game. This version includes logic to respond to left and right mouse clicks and maintaining a timer. The game must also keep track of a two-dimensional minefield, the locations of hidden mines, and the marks made by the player on the minefield while playing the game.

You will use the following general programming concepts, skills, and tools in the Minesweeper construction plan:

• Creation of a data structure to represent data in two dimensions (rows and columns)
• Translation between one- and two-dimensional representations of the minefield
• Recursion

The following Visual Basic features used to construct this game include:

• Control arrays
• MouseDown and MouseUp events
• A Timer control to display elapsed time

DESCRIPTION OF THE GAME

This chapter implements a simplified version of the popular computer game Minesweeper. It is a one-person game, with the player playing against the computer. The playing board is a grid made up of a fixed number of rows and columns. Each location on the grid is called a cell.

HOW THIS VERSION OF MINESWEEPER WORKS

As play begins, the computer randomly hides mines in cells throughout the grid. The number of mines in the minefield varies with each game. The player must chart the minefield, that is, determine the position of each mine. The player moves by uncovering a cell, flagging a mine, or using a shortcut to complete the uncovering of surrounding cells when the mines have been marked.

The player can uncover a cell by positioning the pointer over a cell and clicking the left mouse button. If the player uncovers (examines) a cell that is empty (doesn't contain a mine), the computer calculates and displays the number of mines in the neighboring cells. If your code determines that the number of neighboring mines is zero, it will then uncover all the neighboring cells. This is done as a convenience for the player, because if a cell has no neighboring mines, the player could immediately uncover each neighboring cells with impunity. If the cell does contain a mine, uncovering it ends the game. The computer then uncovers the remaining cells, flagging those with mines and correcting any cells the player may have mistakenly flagged.

The player flags often a cell as containing a mine by positioning the pointer over the cell and clicking the right mouse button; however, the game does not immediately indicate whether the player's move is correct. The player can deduce which cells contain mines by analyzing the information provided by uncovering cells. The shortcut move—done by holding down the right mouse button and clicking the left—uncovers all cells surrounding a cell that has been examined and has all surrounding mines flagged.

A clock keeps track of elapsed time. Any player can experience bad luck, but, for the most part, skilled players will win (or at least go further than unskilled players). This version of Minesweeper corresponds to the beginner level of the standard game.

SAMPLE SCREENS

Figure 1 shows the game board at the start of the game: there are 64 cells with 12 mines present; no cells are marked. Note: the elapsed time to be shown in the box at bottom of the screen does not begin incrementing until the player clicks a cell.

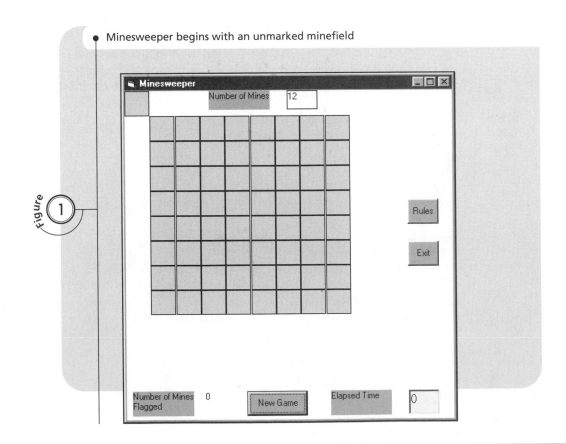

Figure 1

Minesweeper begins with an unmarked minefield

Figure 2 shows the game in progress with two cells flagged as containing mines and 41 cells uncovered. The player can deduce that the cell immediately to the right of the flagged cell must *not* contain a mine, because it is adjacent (diagonally above and to the right) to a cell that has exactly one neighbor with a mine and that mine has already been flagged. This, of course, assumes that the flagging is correct. This kind of reasoning is the basis for a successful Minesweeper strategy.

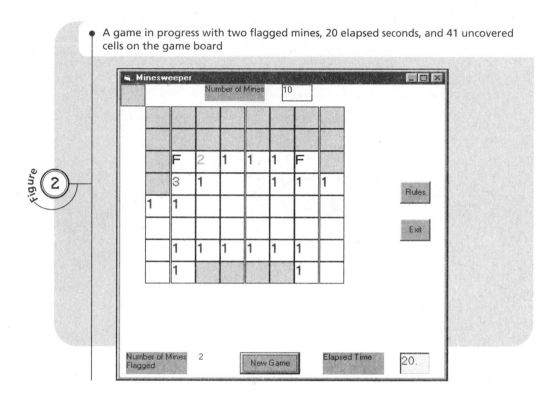

● A game in progress with two flagged mines, 20 elapsed seconds, and 41 uncovered cells on the game board

Figure **2**

Figure 3 shows a game ending in a loss.

Before reading further in the chapter, you should play the game to get a feel for how it works. You can find the minesweeper.exe file in your Ch8 folder. You should be aware of an important distinction between playing the game and programming it: While the player must master a strategy to win the game, there are no logical deductions or game strategies incorporated in the computer's side of the game. The game only keeps track of what has been uncovered and what has been flagged by the player. Minesweeper is a classic example of an interactive, event-driven project.

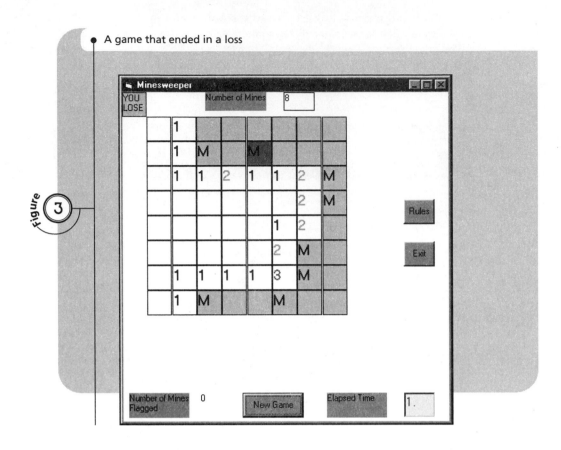

A game that ended in a loss

figure 3

KEY DESIGN ISSUES

There are 11 key design issues that you—the designer and programmer—must accomplish when creating your Minesweeper game:

- Create a display for the minefield

- Randomly lay mines throughout the minefield

- Keep a record of the mine locations

- Compare the cell the player has marked with the actual placement of mines

- Keep track of the cells the player has marked

- When a cell is uncovered by the player, calculate and display the number of mines in neighboring cells

- Keep track of elapsed time

- Respond to the player's left and right mouse button clicks

- Uncover all adjacent cells if the player selects a cell with no neighboring mines

- Determine whether the player has lost the game

- Determine whether the player has won the game

Task: Create a display for the minefield.
Logic: The game is played on a fixed-size grid of cells. Each cell must be able to display either a blank, a mine, or a number.
Solution: Create a control array of Label objects called **lblMines**. The code you will write to lay the cells out evenly in a grid uses the dynamic loading method first demonstrated in Chapter 5.

The technique involves creating the first element and placing it on the form during design time, then adding the remaining cells during the Form_Load event procedure at run time.

Task: Randomly lay mines throughout the minefield.
Logic: The game is played with a new arrangement of mines for every game. This is best done randomly.
Solution: In a loop that cycles through every cell in the minefield, generate a pseudorandom number using the Visual Basic function Rnd and compare its result to a fixed constant **conOdds** (set with a value of 10/64 for 10 mines per 64 cells). If the pseudorandom number is greater than the value of the ratio, place a mine in that cell. Continue until all cells are completed.

Task: Keep a record of the mine locations.
Logic: The visible minefield is a control array of labels. It would not be much of a game if the player could see where the mines are, but the program still needs to know their exact locations for the purpose of running the game.
Solution: Create an internal array named **blnMinesOn** that will be an internal representation of the minefield. When the game determines that a cell will contain a mine, it sets a value of True in the corresponding cell in this array.

Task: Compare the cell the player has marked with the actual placement of mines.
Logic: The player's main task in Minesweeper is uncovering cells. When the player uncovers a cell, the game must test to see whether the cell contains a mine.
Solution: When a player clicks a label in the minefield, the MouseDown event procedure executes. One of the parameters in this event procedure is the Index value of the label (cell) the player clicked. Using this Index value, compare the cell the player clicked with the internal array **blnMinesOn**, which stores the layout of the minefield. If the index value matches a cell where the game has placed a mine, the player loses and the game is over.

Task: Keep track of the cells the player has marked.
Logic: The player wins the game by correctly marking all of the mines in the minefield. Since marking the minefield is the objective of playing Minesweeper, the game must keep an internal record of this information.
Solution: Create a second internal array named **blnCellsMarked** that stores the player's marked cells. Even though the cells marked are visible to the player, it is easier for your code to examine this information in an internal array.

Task: When a cell is uncovered by the player, calculate and display the number of mines in neighboring cells.
Logic: Every cell has up to eight neighbors; cells on the boundary of the minefield will have fewer. If the player uncovers an empty cell (one without a mine), the game must look at each neighboring cell and count those that have mines.
Solution: Use two-dimensional arrays to simplify the task for determining neighbors. Increment a counter if a neighbor cell holds a mine. After all neighboring cells have been checked, change the caption of the cell the player has uncovered to display the number of neighboring mines.

Task: Keep track of elapsed time.
Logic: This game shows a constantly updated display of elapsed time.
Solution: Use a Timer control and its Timer event to increment a visible label showing elapsed time.

Task: Respond to the player's left and right mouse button clicks.
Logic: The game must support the player's moves, which include three distinct mouse actions: clicking the left mouse button, clicking the right mouse button, and holding down the right while clicking the left. This means that your code must distinguish a mouse down action (pressing) from a mouse up action (releasing).
Solution: Use MouseDown and MouseUp event procedures along with Boolean variables (flags) to indicate whether the player has pressed a button without releasing it.

Task: Uncover all adjacent cells if the player selects a cell with no neighboring mines.

Logic: When the player uncovers a cell with no adjacent mines, the game will then uncover each of its neighbors. The player could click each of these neighboring cells with no threat of losing the game, but the game is designed to do this automatically. You can implement this action using the same code that you have already designed for selecting a cell.

Solution: Use recursion; one function indirectly calling itself. This powerful facility is available in Visual Basic and some other programming languages. It is described in the next section.

Task: Determine whether the player has lost the game.

Logic: The player loses the game if he uncovers a cell containing a mine.

Solution: Each time a cell is uncovered, the game compares the cell locations with the locations of the mines, which are stored in the array **blnMinesOn**. If the player uncovers a cell containing a mine, the game is over and the player has lost.

Task: Determine whether the player has won the game.

Logic: The player wins the game if he uncovers all the cells and correctly flags all the mines.

Solution: The game keeps a running tally of the number of cells the player has uncovered and the number of cells flagged. If all cells have been uncovered, and the number of flagged cells equals the number of mines, the player has won the game.

◉ PREPARING TO PROGRAM

DATA REPRESENTATION

Minesweeper must keep track of three sets of data: the minefield that is visible to the player on the game form, the hidden location of mines, and the marks made by the player. You will need three data structures to represent these three sets of data: the visible minefield will be represented by a control array of labels, **lblMines**; the hidden locations of the mines with an internal array, **blnMinesOn**; and the player's markings with an internal array, **blnCellsMarked**.

Because of the calculations involving neighboring cells, it is advantageous to declare both **blnMinesOn** and **blnCellsMarked** as two-dimensional arrays. Keeping track of rows and columns is a classic application for a two-dimensional array, an array that assigns one dimension to rows and the other to columns. Visual Basic allows control arrays to have only one dimension—the minefield is represented by a control array. The solution is to develop procedures to convert back and forth between the one-dimensional control array of labels and the two-dimensional representation of the board information.

To declare a two-dimensional array, you use the familiar syntax for declaring an array, but include a second index (dimension). For example, the following code declares **blnMinesOn** and **blnCellsMarked** as two-dimensional arrays made up of eight rows of eight Boolean variables:

```
Dim blnMinesOn(1 To conSize, 1 To conSize) As Boolean
Dim blnCellsMarked(1 To conSize, 1 To conSize) As Boolean
```

conSize is a declared constant that represents the size of the minefield. In this version of Minesweeper, it is set to 8.

Processing two-dimensional arrays is usually done with nested For...Next loops. By programming convention, the first Index value is referenced by a variable named **i**, and the second Index value is referenced by a variable named **j**. Follow these conventions when processing two-dimensional arrays.

Figure 4 shows an example of a loop that resets all the elements in **blnMinesOn** to False. This code is used to erase the locations of any mines from a previous game.

Code that erases mines from previous games

Figure 4

```
For i = 1 To conSize
    For j = 1 To conSize
        blnMinesOn(i, j) = False
    Next j
Next i
```

It is quite common in programming for information the user (player) sees to be in a completely different form from what the program sees. For example: your Windows desktop has icons that can load programs. When you double-click these icons, the program begins execution. You see the icon, but what does the program see? The program (in this case, it is your operating system) sees a reference to a file on your hard drive that must be loaded into memory and executed. In Minesweeper, you will be performing a similar task. You will need to include code that converts the index specifying the label the player clicks that is part of **lblMines** into a reference, composed of two indices for the internal arrays **blnMinesOn** and **blnCellsMarked**.

To better understand this idea, look at the relationship between the one-dimensional numbering of the labels in the control array and the two-dimensional numbering of the internal arrays, as seen in the following tables. This game will require you, the programmer, to construct formulas that produce these numbers. Take a moment now and try to construct them yourself.

These are the indices for the control array of Label controls:

1	2	3	4	5	6	7	8
9	10	11	12	13	14	15	16
17	18	19	20	21	22	23	24
25	26	27	28	29	30	31	32
33	34	35	36	37	38	39	40
41	42	43	44	45	46	47	48
49	50	51	52	53	54	55	56
57	58	59	60	61	62	63	64

These are the two coordinates for the two-dimensional arrays:

1,1	1,2	1,3	1,4	1,5	1,6	1,7	1,8
2,1	2,2	2,3	2,4	2,5	2,6	2,7	2,8
3,1	3,2	3,3	3,4	3,5	3,6	3,7	3,8
4,1	4,2	4,3	4,4	4,5	4,6	4,7	4,8
5,1	5,2	5,3	5,4	5,5	5,6	5,7	5,8
6,1	6,2	6,3	6,4	6,5	6,6	6,7	6,8
7,1	7,2	7,3	7,4	7,5	7,6	7,7	7,8
8,1	8,2	8,3	8,4	8,5	8,6	8,7	8,8

You will need to code the following index conversion functions:

- **Function conindex(i As Integer, j As Integer) As Integer**
  This function will be passed two parameters representing the two index values and return the corresponding value for a one-dimensional index.

- **Function conind2i(Index As Integer) As Integer**
  This function calculates the i value for two-dimensional indices.

- **Function conind2j(Index As Integer) As Integer**
  This function calculates the j value for two-dimensional indices.

The **conindex** and **conind2i** functions are invoked by many of Minesweeper's event procedures and user-defined procedures to convert back and forth between one index and two.

USING NAMED CONSTANTS

It is important for the programmer to know how many rows and columns make up the minefield. For this version, the board is square with horizontal and vertical dimensions each equal to eight. This means that the code in Form_Load to set up the board is a nested For...Next loop, such as the one shown in Figure 5.

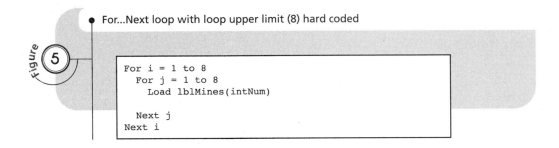

Figure 5

● For...Next loop with loop upper limit (8) hard coded

```
For i = 1 to 8
  For j = 1 to 8
    Load lblMines(intNum)

  Next j
Next i
```

Including the number 8 in the code to represent the number of rows and columns is poor programming style. You would have to change numerous places in your code if you decide to change the size or shape of the board. The literal number 1 would not have to be changed— 1 is generally the starting number. Visual Basic provides a construct for handling this: named constants declared in the **(General)** section. In this case, you enter the code:

```
Const conSize As Integer = 8
```

Then, in any code where you would have used the literal value 8, you would instead use **conSize**, as follows:

```
For 1 = 1 to conSize
```

Laying the Mines

You can use a named constant in the code that lays the mines. Each cell should have odds equal to 10/64 for containing a mine. This value loads approximately 10 mines in the 64 cells—a reasonable number for a board this size. However, this method of setting mines does not guarantee that exactly 10 will be placed. You will declare this ratio as a named constant:

```
Const conOdds = 10/64
```

How does this constant help with laying the mines? Recall how the function for pseudorandom numbers works. The Rnd function returns a fractional value between 0 and less than 1. Your strategy will be to call Rnd for each cell of the minefield. If the value returned by Rnd is less than the ratio set in **conOdds**, a mine is set in that cell.

IMPLEMENTING THE PLAYER'S MOVES

As explained previously, you must include logic in Minesweeper to distinguish among:

- A left mouse click to examine a cell

- A right mouse click to flag the cell as holding a mine

- A right mouse button down, left mouse button click to complete uncovering around an uncovered cell with all surrounding mines flagged

You cannot use the standard Click event procedure even though two of the three actions are simple clicks. Instead, you will use the MouseDown and MouseUp event procedures and a Boolean variable. These procedures each have parameters indicating which button the user clicked.

Your code will capture and recognize the mouse actions the player has performed. Then, each mouse procedure will call user-defined procedures to carry out the logic behind the player moves.

The three primary procedures are:

- **examine**: Your code will call this procedure if the player wants to examine a cell.

- **markflag**: Your code will call this procedure if the player wants to mark a cell with a flag.

- **complete**: Your code will call this procedure if the player wants to use the mouse button combination to uncover a group of cells.

You will also need to write code for these additional user-defined procedures:

- **countsurround**: This procedure counts and displays the number of neighboring mines.

- **fixbounds**: This is a utility function that calculates the bounds to be used when checking the neighbors of a given cell.

- **expand**: This procedure uncovers all the neighbors of a cell that has been examined and has no adjacent mines.

- **checkforwin**: After the player uncovers a cell, this procedure is called to determine whether the player has won the game.

- **gamelost**: If the game has determined the player has lost, this procedure uncovers all the remaining cells and displays the locations of all the hidden mines.

The code for each of these procedures is described in detail in "Algorithms for Event Procedures and User-Defined Procedures."

RECURSION IN PROGRAMMING

Recursion in programming occurs when a program or procedure calls itself. Recursion is used in Minesweeper when examining the neighbors of cells that have no surrounding mines.

> **TIP**
>
> **Some programming languages do not allow recursion, because the system cannot keep track of more than one invocation of the same procedure. The information necessary for the calling function to resume would be overridden by the information for the called procedure. So in some cases, recursion cannot be supported.**

A second consideration is independent of implementation in a particular programming language. If a procedure's definition requires calling the procedure again, how do you know that the process stops? There must be one category of inputs for which the function is not defined by calling itself. This category is called the **base case** or the **stopping case**. Each recursive solution must have a base case to work toward or it will cycle endlessly.

For Minesweeper, the arguments for the procedures involved in recursion are the cells in the minefield. Recursion is used in the user-defined procedure **examine** to test a cell the player has attempted to uncover. When the **examine** code uncovers a cell with no neighboring mines, the rules of the game call for the system to uncover all the neighboring cells. In the implementation suggested here, this means that a recursive call will be made. Actually, the situation is more complex than a procedure calling itself: the **countsurround** procedure calls **expand**, which then calls **countsurround**. How do you know that this won't lead to an infinite process? The answer is that the implementation is programmed not to re-examine cells that have already been uncovered. Given that a cell is never uncovered twice, the process is inherently finite: there are only a finite number of cells in the board.

PLAN FOR THE USER INTERFACE

Although Minesweeper is a complex game to program, the user interface is quite simple. The reason for this is that the game logic you code examines internal arrays that store information about the state of the game, very little of which is visible to the player during play. The player sees the minefield, a clock that displays the elapsed time since play began, a label that shows the number of mines hidden on the minefield, a button to restart the game (for subsequent play), and a button to exit.

FORM DESIGN

This is a description of all the objects contained on the final design for Minesweeper, which is shown in Figure 6. Follow this plan to place all the objects needed on your form or follow the layout of the game resident on your computer. The object names listed below are suggestions; you may rename them if desired (If you do, be sure to revise your code accordingly). Set the labels and captions as suggested. Placement of objects are suggestions—you may lay out your form differently, if you wish.

Labels

1. **lblMines(0)**: The first (model) element of the control array of labels that represents the minefield. It is used to indicate a win or a loss.

2. **Label1**: Static label "Number of Mines"

3. **Label2**: Static label "Number of Mines Flagged"

4. **Label3**: Static label "Elapsed Time"

5. **lblNumFlagged**: Holds the count of the cells flagged as mines by the player

6. **lblElapsed**: Displays the running time

7. **lblNumMines**: Displays the number of mines in the minefield

Command buttons

8. **cmdNew**: Starts a new game

9. **cmdRules**: Displays the rules of the game

10. **cmdExit**: Ends the game

Timer control

11. **tmrElapsed**: Used to update **lblElapsed**. Set its Interval property to 500 and Enabled property to False

Minesweeper form design elements

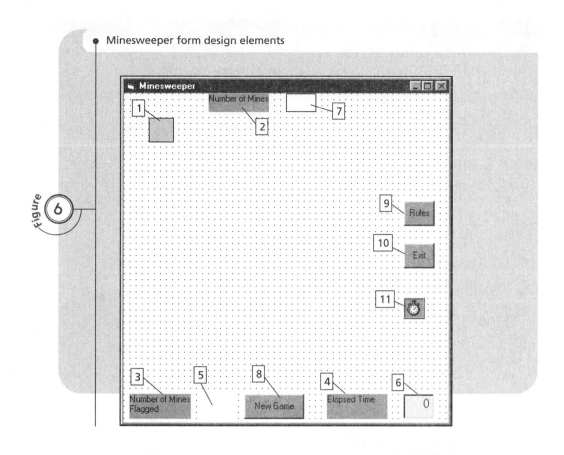

Figure 6

VARIABLES AND CONSTANTS DECLARED IN THE (General) SECTION

The following constants and variables are declared in the **(General)** section:

Element	Explanation
`Option Explicit`	Set this option, which requires a declaration of all variables
`Const conSize = 8`	Holds the length and width of a square minefield
`Const conOdds = 10/64`	Holds the odds of any one cell holding a mine, but does not guarantee 10 mines
`Dim blnMinesOn (1 to conSize,_` `    1 to conSize) As Boolean`	A two-dimensional array that stores the location of mines. If array element is True, it indicates the presence of a mine.
`Dim intCntr As Integer`	The total number of mines placed in the minefield by the game
`Dim blnCellsMarked (1 to conSize,_` `    1 to conSize) As Boolean`	A two-dimensional array that stores the marks made by the player during the game. If array element is True, it indicates that the cell has been flagged by the player.

Element	Explanation
`Dim intNumExamined As Integer`	Keeps count of cells examined by the player as the game progresses
`Dim blnRightFlag As Boolean`	The game sets this flag to True if the player is holding down the right mouse button. This is used to recognize when the right mouse button is held as the left mouse button is clicked.
`Dim blnGameoff As Boolean`	The game uses this flag to prevent responses to mouse actions if the game is not in play.

ALGORITHMS FOR EVENT PROCEDURES AND USER-DEFINED PROCEDURES

As you can tell, Minesweeper is a complex project with many different parts. The descriptions that follow divide the procedures you need to write into four categories:

- General event procedures

- Event procedures in response to mouse events

- User-defined conversion functions

- Other user-defined procedures

GENERAL EVENT PROCEDURES

This section explains the Visual Basic procedures you will need to code, such as the Form_Load event procedure and Click event procedures for the command buttons.

The Form_Load Event Procedure

You will program this event procedure to dynamically load the elements of the control array **lblMines** and position them to form a square grid to represent the minefield. The code you will write to position each element in the minefield will use the Width property and the Height property of the first element (**lblMines(0)**).

lblMines(0) will not be part of the minefield. Instead, after the grid has been laid out, your code will move **lblMines(0)** to the upper-left corner of the game board. By excluding **lblMines(0)**, the logic that keeps track of the player's actions will be greatly simplified. This version will use **lblMines(0)** to display the outcome of the game: the message "YOU WIN" or "YOU LOSE" appears in **lblMines(0)** when the game is over.

The Form_Load event procedure requires the following local variables:

Element	Explanation
`Dim intNum As Integer`	Serves as the index for the current element being dynamically loaded into **lblMines**
`Dim intTops As Integer`	This variable stores the Top property of **lblMines(0)**. It is used to position the array as a minefield.
`Dim intLefts As Integer`	This variable stores the Left property of **lblMines(0)**. It is used to position the array as a minefield.

Element	Explanation
`Dim intWidths As Integer`	This variable stores the Width property of `lblMines(0)`. It is used to position the array as a minefield.
`Dim intHeights As Integer`	This variable stores the Height property of `lblMines(0)`. It is used to position the array as a minefield.
`Dim i As Integer`	Used as a counter in the For...Next loop that lays out the minefield
`Dim j As Integer`	Used as a counter in the For...Next loop that lays out the minefield

You will place the first element (with an Index value of 0) of the array on the board during design time (see Figure 6). Include in this event procedure code that dynamically loads the rest of the elements in the array. This technique is similar to the way the alphabet was dynamically loaded for the Hangman game in Chapter 5.

One significant difference between Hangman and Minesweeper is the layout of the labels. In Hangman, the letters are lined up in one row. For Minesweeper, the code you will write must lay out the labels in eight rows of eight labels each. You will use three variables for indexing:

1. A variable that stores the total number of Label controls, **intNum**

2. A variable for rows, **i**

3. A variable for elements in a row (the number of columns), **j**

The code you will write for the Form_Load event procedure will carry out these tasks:

1. Store the Left, Top, Width, and Height properties of **lblMines(0)** in the local variables **intLefts**, **intTops**, **intWidths**, and **intHeights**. These values will be used to dynamically load the minefield and align it into eight rows and eight columns, as shown in Figure 7.

Code to initialize variables that will be used to dynamically lay out the minefield

```
intLefts = lblMines(0).Left
intWidths = lblMines(0).Width
intHeights = lblMines(0).Height
intTops = lblMines(0).Top
```

2. Initialize **intNum** to 1, as follows:

```
intNum = 1
```

This variable will serve as an index for loading new labels into **lblMines**.

3. In a nested For...Next loop using **i** to loop through the rows and **j** to loop through the columns, use the Load statement to create a new cell with an Index value equal to **intNum**. Then set its Top property to be equal to **intTops**, its Left property equal to **intLefts**, and its Visible property to True. Then add **intWidths** to the variable **intLefts** so that the next cell that is loaded into the array is placed one position to the right of the previous cell.

4. Increment **intNum** by 1

5. After the inner (**j**) loop ends, reset **intLefts** to be equal to **lblMines(0)** and **intTops** to be equal to **intTops** plus **intHeights**. This has the effect of moving down for the next row.

The code for tasks 3, 4, and 5 is shown in Figure 8.

Figure 8

● Nested For...Next loop that dynamically loads new elements of lblMines in rows of eight labels each

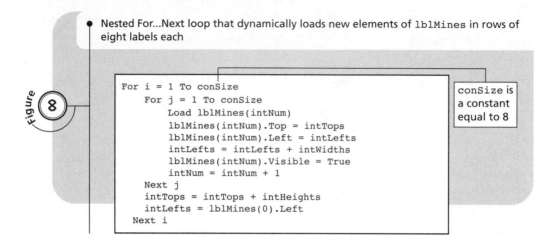

```
For i = 1 To conSize
    For j = 1 To conSize
        Load lblMines(intNum)
        lblMines(intNum).Top = intTops
        lblMines(intNum).Left = intLefts
        intLefts = intLefts + intWidths
        lblMines(intNum).Visible = True
        intNum = intNum + 1
    Next j
    intTops = intTops + intHeights
    intLefts = lblMines(0).Left
Next i
```

conSize is a constant equal to 8

6. Finally, move the 0th element away from the minefield (into the upper-left corner of the board) and call the user-defined procedure **startgame** to complete initialization and startup. The code to do this is shown in Figure 9.

Figure 9

● Code to initialize the Minesweeper game board

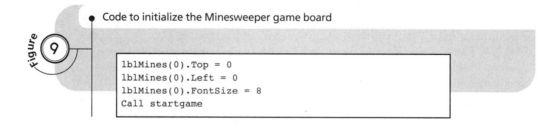

```
lblMines(0).Top = 0
lblMines(0).Left = 0
lblMines(0).FontSize = 8
Call startgame
```

The cmdNew_Click Event Procedure

There are no local variables required for this event procedure. To provide the initialization required for a player to begin a new game, insert the following line of code in this event procedure:

```
Call startgame
```

The tmrElapsed_Timer Event Procedure

You will need the following local variable for this event procedure:

Element	Explanation
Dim sngClock As Single	Used to update the elapsed time

The code you write here increments the elapsed time display. At design time, set the Interval property of **tmrElapsed** to one-half second (500 milliseconds). Each time this event occurs, the code in this event procedure will update the displayed time by adding one-half second, or .5.

Program this event procedure so that it completes the following tasks:

1. Use the Visual Basic function Val to store the numeric value of `lblElapsed.Caption` in the local variable **sngClock**

2. Add .5 to **sngClock**

3. Store the new elapsed time in `lblElapsed.Caption` by using the Visual Basic Format function

The code for the **tmrElapsed_Timer** event procedure is:

```
sngClock = Val(lblElapsed.Caption)
sngClock = sngClock + 0.5
lblElapsed.Caption = Format(sngClock, "###.#")
```

The cmdRules_Click Event Procedure

This event procedure requires the following local variable:

Element	Explanation
`Dim strMsg As String`	Used to construct a message explaining the rules of Minesweeper

Insert the code shown in Figure 10 in this event procedure.

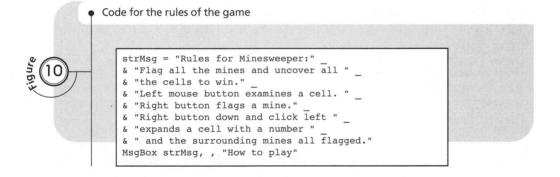

Code for the rules of the game

Figure 10

```
strMsg = "Rules for Minesweeper:" _
& "Flag all the mines and uncover all " _
& "the cells to win." _
& "Left mouse button examines a cell. " _
& "Right button flags a mine." _
& "Right button down and click left " _
& "expands a cell with a number " _
& " and the surrounding mines all flagged."
MsgBox strMsg, , "How to play"
```

The cmdExit_Click Event Procedure

This event procedure does not require any local variables. When the player clicks this button, the game ends. Insert this code in the **cmdExit_Click** event procedure:

```
End
```

EVENT PROCEDURES IN RESPONSE TO MOUSE EVENTS

You will write code for the MouseDown and MouseUp event procedures to respond to the player's moves. In these mouse event procedures, your code will call three user-defined procedures that you will create to finish the logic for these mouse actions:

- Right click: call **markflag** to flag a mine

- Left click: call **examine** to uncover a cell

- Combination: call **complete** to uncover all neighbors around a cell

The `lblMines_MouseDown` Event Procedure

This procedure receives the following parameters:

Element	Explanation
`Index As Integer`	Contains the Index value of the cell in `lblMines` that the player has clicked
`Button As Integer`	Indicates whether the player has clicked the left or right mouse button
`Shift As Integer`	Indicates whether the player is holding down the shift key. Not used in this event procedure.
`X As Single`	Indicates X position of mouse arrow. Not used in this event procedure.
`Y As Single`	Indicates Y position of mouse arrow. Not used in this event procedure.

Program the `lblMines_MouseDown` event procedure so that it carries out the following tasks:

1. If `blnGameOff` is set to True, then exit this procedure, since it means the game has ended. The code to exit the procedure is:

```
If blnGameoff Then Exit Sub
```

2. If the timer (`tmrElapsed`) is not enabled, set `tmrElapsed.Enabled` to True. This will turn on the timer when the player clicks a cell at the start of a new game, as follows:

```
If tmrElapsed.Enabled = False Then
    tmrElapsed.Enabled = True
End If
```

Next, you need to determine which mouse button the player has pressed. The parameter **Button** contains this information. The logic for determining which mouse button was pressed is as follows:

- If **Button** is equal to 1, the player has pressed the left mouse button, which means that either the player wants to examine a cell, or he is using the special combination of mouse buttons to uncover the remaining cells around a selected cell. To determine which of these two situations it is, test the variable `blnRightFlag`. If the variable is set to True, the player is using the special combination of mouse buttons, and you need to call the user-defined procedure `complete(Index)`, and then reset `blnRightFlag` to False. If `blnRightFlag` is False, the player wants to uncover a cell. In this case, call `examine(Index)`.

- If **Button** is equal to 2, the player has pressed the right mouse button. In this case, the only logic you need to carry out is to set `blnRightFlag` to True.

Figure 11 shows the code that determines which mouse button the player has pressed.

Code that determines which mouse action is occurring

Figure 11

```
If Button = 1 Then
        If blnRightFlag=False Then
            Call examine(Index)
        Else
            Call complete(Index)
            blnRightFlag = False
        End If
    Else  ' Button = 2, right button
        blnRightFlag = True
End If
```

The `lblMines_MouseUp` Event Procedure

This procedure receives the following parameters:

Element	Explanation
`Index As Integer`	Contains the **Index** value of the cell in **lblMines** that the player clicked
`Button As Integer`	Indicates whether the player clicked the left or right mouse button
`Shift As Integer`	Indicates whether the player is holding down the shift key. Not used in this event procedure.
`X As Single`	Indicates X position of mouse arrow. Not used in this event procedure.
`Y As Single`	Indicates Y position of mouse arrow. Not used in this event procedure.

This event is the second part of the Click event, which occurs when the player releases the mouse button. If **Button** is equal to 1, you don't need to program anything, because the logic for a left mouse click is handled in the MouseDown event procedure.

Program this event procedure so that if **Button** is equal to 2 and **blnRightFlag** is True, the user-defined procedure **markflag(Index)** is called to mark the cell.

The code for the **lblMines_MouseUp** event procedure is shown in Figure 12.

Code for processing the release of the mouse button

Figure 12

```
If Button = 2 And blnRightFlag Then
    Call markflag(Index)
    blnRightFlag = False
End If
```

USER-DEFINED CONVERSION FUNCTIONS

You will need to write index conversion routines because the control array on the form is one-dimensional, whereas the internal arrays that map the mine locations and record the state of the minefield are two-dimensional.

You must write three conversion functions. One function will convert a two-dimensional index into a one-dimensional index, and two functions will convert in the other direction: one to calculate the **i** value converted from a one-dimensional index and another to calculate the **j** value.

The `condindex(i As Integer, j As Integer) As Integer` Function

This conversion function is passed two parameters and returns a single value. You can use this function to translate the location of the selected cell in the two-dimensional array **blnMinesOn** into the location of that same cell in the one-dimensional control array **lblMines**.

This function is passed the following parameter values:

Element	Explanation
`i As Integer`	Represents the row where the cell is located
`j As Integer`	Represents the column where the cell is located

This function translates a pair of two-dimensional indices to a one-dimensional index. Remember: the **i** represents the number of rows and the **j** represents the number of columns. To convert from a pair of indices, first multiply the number of preceding rows (this is i - 1) by the size of each row (**conSize**), which results in the number of cells ahead of the current row. Then add the column index (**j**) corresponding to the element in the row. Figure 13 shows how this works.

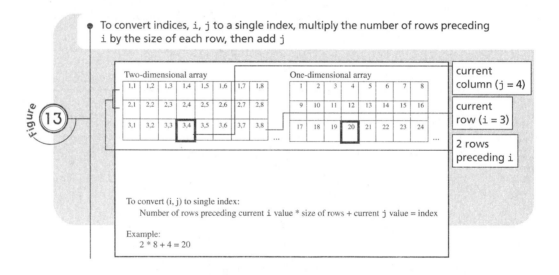

To convert indices, i, j to a single index, multiply the number of rows preceding i by the size of each row, then add j

Figure 13

To convert (i, j) to single index:
　Number of rows preceding current i value * size of rows + current j value = index

Example:
　2 * 8 + 4 = 20

The code for the **conIndex** function is:

```
conindex = j + conSize * (i - 1)
```

The `conind2i(Index As Integer) As Integer` Function

This conversion function is passed the parameter Index and returns the value indicating the row of a two-dimensional array. **conind2i** must be used along with the function **conind2j** (described next) to calculate a complete **i, j** value for a specified cell. You can use this function to translate a cell on the minefield in **lblMines** into a cell in the array **blnMinesOn**.

This function is passed one parameter:

Element	Explanation
`Index As Integer`	Represents the cell location in a one-dimensional array

Insert the following code into this function:

```
conind2i = 1 + Int((Index - 1) / conSize)
```

The `conind2j(Index As Integer) As Integer` Function

This conversion function is passed the parameter Index and returns the value indicating the column (j) of a two-dimensional array. `conind2j` must be used along with the function `conind2i` to calculate a complete **i, j** value for a specified cell. You can use this function to translate a cell on the minefield in **lblMines** into a cell in the array **blnMinesOn**.

This function is passed one parameter:

Element	Explanation
`Index As Integer`	Represents the cell location in a one-dimensional array

This function also requires one local variable:

Element	Explanation
`Dim j As Integer`	Used to calculate the column for this index

`conind2j` uses the Mod operator to determine the column into which this index converts. Insert the following code into the **conind2j** function:

```
j = Index Mod conSize
If j = 0 Then j = conSize
conind2j = j
```

OTHER USER-DEFINED PROCEDURES

The remaining logic for Minesweeper is carried out in a series of procedures that execute the main logic of the game. You can look ahead to the calling map in Figure 30 to see how these procedures are invoked. The procedures you will need to code are as follows:

- **startgame**: Provides initial setup of variables and captions

- **setmines**: Randomly lays the mines throughout the minefield

- **markflag**: Carries out the player's request to flag a cell as containing a mine

- **complete**: Carries out the player's request to complete the uncovering of cells using the special mouse button combination

- **examine**: Carries out the player's request to uncover a cell

- **countsurround**: Counts the number of mines adjacent to a specific cell

- **fixbounds**: Determines a specific cell's neighboring cells

- **expand**: Uncovers all of a cell's neighbors if the player uncovers a cell with no adjacent mines

- **checkforwin**: Tests to see if the player has won the game by uncovering or marking all the cells in the minefield

- **gamelost**: Carries out the logic if the player has lost; reveals the true layout of the minefield and indicates any mistakes by the player

The `startgame()` User-Defined Procedure

This procedure requires the following local variables:

Element	Explanation
`Dim i As Integer`	Used in a For...Next loop to reset the internal arrays **blnMinesOn** and **blnCellsMarked** to False
`Dim j As Integer`	Used in a For...Next loop to reset the internal arrays **blnMinesOn** and **blnCellsMarked** to False

Since this procedure is called after the completion of one game to set up a new game, it must execute code that initializes variables to reset the appearance of the minefield and reset all of the internal arrays that store relevant information.

Program this subroutine so that it completes the following tasks:

1. Set **lblElapsed.Caption** to "0"

2. Set **lblNumFlagged.Caption** to "0"

3. Set the global variable **intNumExamined** to 0

4. Set **blnGameoff** and **blnRightFlag** to False

5. Set the **lblMines(0)** label used to display "YOU WIN" or "YOU LOSE" to blank

6. Turn off the timer until the user clicks a cell (set **tmrElapsed.Enabled** to False)

The code for these six tasks is shown in Figure 14.

Figure 14

Code for the beginning of the `startgame` user-defined procedure

```
blnGameoff = False
blnRightFlag = False
lblElapsed.Caption = Format(0, "#0")
lblMines(0).Caption = ""
intNumExamined = 0
tmrElapsed.Enabled = False
lblNumFlagged.Caption = Format(0, "#0")
```

Next, the **startgame** code should:

1. Using a For...Next loop, loop through all the labels in the control array **lblMines**, set their caption to blanks, and set their ForeColor and BackColor properties to the values in **lblMines(0)**, as shown in Figure 15.

Figure 15

startgame code that clears the minefield

```
'clear the minefield
For i = 1 To (conSize * conSize)
    lblMines(i).Caption = ""
    lblMines(i).BackColor = lblMines(0).BackColor
    lblMines(i).ForeColor = lblMines(0).ForeColor
Next i
```

2. Using a nested For...Next loop, loop through the array **blnCellsMarked** and the array **blnMinesOn**, and set each element to False, as shown in Figure 16.

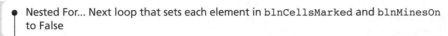

Nested For... Next loop that sets each element in blnCellsMarked and blnMinesOn to False

Figure 16

```
'clear all the internal arrays
For i = 1 To conSize
    For j = 1 To conSize
        blnCellsMarked(i, j) = False
        blnMinesOn(i, j) = False
    Next j
Next i
```

3. Call the user-defined procedure **setmines** to perform the major task of placing the mines around the minefield, using the code:

```
Call setmines
```

The setmines() User-Defined Procedure

Include the following local variables in this procedure:

Element	Explanation
Dim i As Integer	Used to control the outer For...Next statement to loop through all the cells in the minefield to randomly set mines
Dim j As Integer	Used to control the inner For...Next statement to loop through all the cells in the minefield to randomly set mines
Dim intNum As Integer	Used in optional code that makes the mines visible during debugging

This procedure sets the mines in the minefield by looping through all the cells in the minefield one at a time. For each cell, generate a random number. If the random number is less than the constant **conOdds** (less than 10/64), that cell will contain a mine. Using this technique means that the number of mines set will vary from game to game, as will their locations.

Recall that another internal array, **blnMinesOn(i,j)**, records the location of the mines. The mine laying is performed in a nested For...Next loop that iterates over the rows and columns of the minefield.

You can ease the chore of debugging your program by adding a line of code that sets the caption of the cell in question to "MINE" in the True case. You must remove or comment out this line when your project is fully debugged and operational.

Once the loop is done, you need to update the game board to display the number of mines, **lblNumMines**. The variable **intCntr** has been incremented by your code every time a new mine has been set, so convert this value to a string and then place it in the caption of **lblNumMines**.

Program the **setmines** procedure so that it completes the following tasks:

1. Call Randomize to initialize the random number generator

2. Set the global variable **intCntr** (declared in the **(General)** section) to 0. This variable counts the number of mines in the minefield.

3. Initialize **intNum** to 1. This variable is used to set the optional debugging information about the location of the mine.

The following code performs these three tasks:

```
Randomize
intNum = 1
intCntr = 0
```

Additional tasks performed by **setmines** are as follows:

- In a nested For...Next loop, perform the following test for each cell in the minefield: Compare the return value of the Visual Basic function Rnd to the constant **conOdds**. If the return value is less than the constant, lay a mine in the cell by setting the cell's **blnMinesOn** property to **True** and add 1 to **intCntr**. In the Else section (if the value returned by Rnd is greater than the constant), set the cell's **blnMinesOn** property to False.

The code to lay the mines is shown in Figure 17.

Figure 17

Code to place the mines in the minefield

```
For i = 1 To conSize
    For j = 1 To conSize
     If Rnd < conOdds Then
         blnMinesOn(i, j) = True
       ' lblMines(intNum).Caption = "MINE" for debugging
         intCntr + 1
     Else
         blnMinesOn(i, j) = False
     End If

     intNum = IntNum + 1
    Next j
Next i
```

- Finally, use the number in **intCntr** to display the number of mines set in **lblNumMines**, as follows:

```
lblNumMines.Caption = Format(intCntr, "#0")
```

The markflag(Index As Integer) User-Defined Procedure

This procedure receives the following parameter:

Element	Explanation
Index As Integer	Holds the location of the cell that the player clicked

This procedure requires the following local variables:

Element	Explanation
`Dim intOldf As Integer`	Used to increment `lblNumFlagged`
`Dim i As Integer`	Used as index for two-dimensional arrays
`Dim j As Integer`	Used as index for two-dimensional arrays

This procedure is called from the MouseUp event procedure if the player clicked the right mouse button to flag a mine. Usually this procedure is used to flag a mine, but it also must take care of unflagging a cell. Program the **markflag** procedure to perform the following tasks:

1. Convert the one-dimensional Index value into a pair of indices (**i, j**) using the conversion functions:

```
i = conind2i(Index)
j = conind2j(Index)
```

2. Test to determine whether **blnCellsMarked(i, j)** is False, which means this cell has not yet been marked. If so, set the caption to "F", increment the counter **intNumExamined**, and increase the number in **lblNumFlagged**. Call **checkforwin** to determine whether this latest action by the player of marking a flag means the game is over and the player has won.

3. If the cell was already flagged by the player, replace the "F" with a blank, decrement **intNumExamined**, and decrement the number displayed in **lblNumFlagged**.

Figure 18 shows the code that performs these tasks.

Figure 18 • Code for the markflag procedure

```
If blnCellsMarked(i, j) = False Then
    blnCellsMarked(i, j) = True
    lblMines(Index).BackColor = vbWhite
    lblMines(Index).Caption = "F"
    intNumExamined = intNumExamined + 1
    intOldf = Val(lblNumFlagged.Caption)
    lblNumFlagged.Caption = Format(1 + intOldf, "#0")
    Call checkforwin
Else 'take away flag
    If lblMines(Index).Caption = "F" Then
        lblMines(Index).Caption = ""
        lblMines(Index).BackColor = lblMines(0).BackColor
        lblMines(Index).ForeColor = lblMines(0).ForeColor
        blnCellsMarked(i, j) = False
        intNumExamined = intNumExamined - 1
        intOldf = Val(lblNumFlagged.Caption)
        lblNumFlagged.Caption = Format(intOldf - 1, "#0")
    End If
End If
```

The `complete(Index As Integer)` User-Defined Procedure

This procedure has the following parameter:

Element	Explanation
`Index As Integer`	Holds the location of the cell that the player clicked

This procedure requires the following local variables:

Element	Explanation
`Dim i As Integer`	Used to index two-dimensional arrays
`Dim j As Integer`	Used to index two-dimensional arrays
`Dim ii As Integer`	Used in a For...Next loop to loop through the neighbors of the cell represented by the parameter Index
`Dim jj As Integer`	Used in a For...Next loop to loop through the neighbors of the cell represented by the parameter Index
`Dim iL As Integer`	The lower-row boundary of the rectangle of neighboring cells
`Dim iH As Integer`	The upper-row boundary of the rectangle of neighboring cells
`Dim jL As Integer`	The lower-column boundary of the rectangle of neighboring cells
`Dim jH As Integer`	The upper-column boundary of the rectangle of neighboring cells
`Dim intSur As Integer`	Used by the code to count the number of surrounding mines
`Dim intSf As Integer`	Used by the code to count the number of cells flagged by the player
`Dim strCap As String`	Used by the code to compare the caption of a cell to "F"

This procedure is invoked when the player uses the special combination of mouse buttons. The player can only use this shortcut on uncovered cells with all surrounding mines flagged. If this is not the case, nothing happens when the player uses the shortcut.

If **Index** points to a marked cell, call the procedure **fixbounds** to determine the boundaries of the neighboring cells. This procedure requires six parameters, so you will need to declare variables to use as arguments for this procedure.

The procedure **fixbounds** returns four values that represent the boundaries of the neighbors of the selected cell. The next step for the code is to count the number of mines flagged by the player and see if that number matches the number of mines actually hidden around this cell. Do this by setting up a variable to act as a counter, then use a nested loop to loop through all of the selected cell's neighbors and count the number of flagged mines (those with a caption of F). Your code will compare the number of flagged mines with the number extracted from the selected cell's caption.

If the player has flagged the correct number of mines, execute a second set of nested loops that examines all of the selected cell's neighbors. For each cell that is not yet examined (its corresponding element in **blnCellsMarked** is False), call the procedure **examine**. This call to **examine** uncovers the cell and calculates and displays its count of surrounding mines.

Program the **complete** procedure to perform the following tasks:

1. Convert **Index** to an **i, j** pair using the conversion functions:

```
i = conind2i(Index)
j = conind2j(Index)
```

2. Test to see if the player has flagged the correct number of mines. The variable **intSf** is used to count the number of neighboring cells flagged by the player. Before that count begins, initialize **intSf** to 0:

```
intSf = 0
```

3. If the selected cell (referenced by **Index**) doesn't display an F or a blank, the procedure can continue.

4. Call **fixbounds** to determine which cells comprise the selected cell's neighboring rectangle.

5. Extract the number of neighboring mines stored in the caption of the selected cell and store that number in the variable **intSur** using the Visual Basic Val function.

6. In a nested loop, loop through the neighboring cells, adding 1 to **intSf** for each cell with a caption of F.

7. If **intSf** is equal to **intSur**, then the player has flagged the correct number of mines. The next step is then to once again loop through all the neighbors and call **examine** for any uncovered cells.

The code that executes this procedure's logic is shown in Figure 19.

Figure 19

Code for the complete procedure

```
If (lblMines(Index).Caption <> "F") Then
    If (lblMines(Index).Caption <> "") Then
        Call fixbounds(i, j, iL, iH, jL, jH)
        intSur = Val(lblMines(Index).Caption)
        For ii = iL To iH
            For jj = jL To jH
                strCap = lblMines(conindex(ii, jj)).Caption
                If strCap = "F" Then
                    intSf = intSf + 1
                End If
            Next jj
        Next ii
        If intSf = intSur Then 'flagged correct count
            For ii = iL To iH
                For jj = jL To jH
                    If blnCellsMarked(ii, jj) = False Then
                        Call examine(conindex(ii, jj))
                    End If
                Next jj
            Next ii
        End If
    End If
End If
```

The examine(Index As Integer) User-Defined Procedure

This procedure has the following parameter:

Element	Explanation
Index As Integer	Holds the location of the cell that the player clicked

This procedure has the following local variables:

Element	Explanation
Dim i As Integer	Used to index two-dimensional arrays
Dim j As Integer	Used to index two-dimensional arrays

This procedure lets the player examine, or uncover, a cell on the minefield. If the player uncovers a mine, the game is lost. If the cell does not contain a mine, then this procedure counts the number of surrounding cells and displays that number in the selected cell's caption.

Program this procedure to perform the following tasks:

1. Call the conversion routines to create two-dimensional indices, as follows:

```
i = conind2i(Index)
j = conind2j(Index)
```

2. Check for a mine in the corresponding array **blnMinesOn(i, j)**. If there is a mine in the array, call **gamelost**. If there is no mine, then the procedure should add 1 to **intNumExamined**, set **blnCellsMarked(i, j)** to True, and call **countsurround** and then **checkforwin**. Notice that the **countsurround** procedure places the appropriate value in the caption of this cell.

The code for the **examine** procedure is shown in Figure 20.

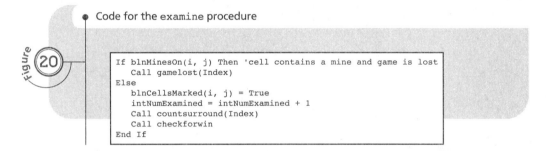

Code for the examine procedure

Figure 20

```
If blnMinesOn(i, j) Then 'cell contains a mine and game is lost
    Call gamelost(Index)
Else
    blnCellsMarked(i, j) = True
    intNumExamined = intNumExamined + 1
    Call countsurround(Index)
    Call checkforwin
End If
```

The countsurround(Index As Integer) User-Defined Procedure

This procedure has the following parameter:

Element	Explanation
Index As Integer	Counts the surrounding mines for the cell referenced by the value in Index

This procedure has the following local variables:

Element	Explanation
Dim i As Integer	Used to index two-dimensional arrays
Dim j As Integer	Used to index two-dimensional arrays
Dim ii As Integer	Used in a For...Next loop to loop through the neighbors of the cell represented by the parameter **Index**

Element	Explanation
`Dim jj As Integer`	Used in a For...Next loop to loop through the neighbors of the cell represented by the parameter **Index**
`Dim iL As Integer`	The lower-row boundary of the rectangle of neighboring cells
`Dim iH As Integer`	The upper-row boundary of the rectangle of neighboring cells
`Dim jL As Integer`	The lower-column boundary of the rectangle of neighboring cells
`Dim jH As Integer`	The upper-column boundary of the rectangle of neighboring cells
`Dim intSur As Integer`	Used to count the number of mines surrounding the selected cell

This procedure places the digit that represents the number of mines surrounding the selected cell in the caption of the cell referenced by **Index**. It first calls **fixbounds** to determine the bounding rectangle that defines the neighboring cells. Using the integer variable **intSur**, the code counts the surrounding mines using nested For...Next loops. The value in **intSur** is placed in the caption of the cell.

The procedure then uses a Select Case statement to test the value in **intSur**. If there are no mines, the ForeColor property of the cell is set to white. Notice that without special formatting, a zero will not appear in the cell and this label will be blank, which is the desired result. The other cases can be set to the following values:

- One mine: color is blue (**vbBlue**)

- Two mines: color is green (**vbGreen**)

- Three mines: color is red (**vbRed**)

- Four or more mines: color is magenta (**vbMagenta**)

The game then calls the **expand** procedure, which examines all the neighbors of the selected cell.

Program this procedure so that it performs the following tasks:

1. Convert **Index** into a two-dimensional **i, j** value, as follows:

```
i = conind2i(Index)
j = conind2j(Index)
```

2. Initialize **intSur** to 0:

```
intSur = 0
```

   This variable is used to count the number of neighboring mines.

3. Call **fixbounds** to determine the rectangle of neighboring cells, using the code:

```
Call fixbounds(i, j, iL, iH, jL, jH)
```

4. In a nested For...Next loop, loop through all the neighboring cells and add 1 to **intSur** for every cell that contains a mine (**blnMinesOn(ii,jj)** is True). This code is shown in Figure 21.

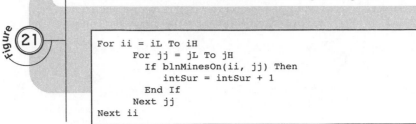

Figure 21

countsurround code that counts mines in neighboring cells

```
For ii = iL To iH
        For jj = jL To jH
            If blnMinesOn(ii, jj) Then
                intSur = intSur + 1
            End If
        Next jj
Next ii
```

5. Set the BackColor property of the cell to white and set the Caption property equal to the number of surrounding mines (**intSur**), using the following code:

```
lblMines(Index).BackColor = vbWhite
lblMines(Index).Caption = intSur
```

6. Using a Select Case statement, change the color of the number displayed (the new color depends on the number of surrounding mines). If a cell has no surrounding mines, call **expand** to uncover all that cell's neighbors. The code to change the number colors is shown in Figure 22.

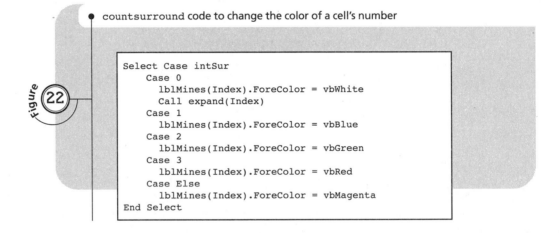

Figure 22

countsurround code to change the color of a cell's number

```
Select Case intSur
    Case 0
      lblMines(Index).ForeColor = vbWhite
      Call expand(Index)
    Case 1
      lblMines(Index).ForeColor = vbBlue
    Case 2
      lblMines(Index).ForeColor = vbGreen
    Case 3
      lblMines(Index).ForeColor = vbRed
    Case Else
      lblMines(Index).ForeColor = vbMagenta
End Select
```

The fixbounds (i As Integer, j As Integer, iL As Integer, iH As Integer, jL As Integer, jH As Integer) User-Defined Procedure

This procedure has the following parameters; the first two are set by the calling procedures and the last four are set in the **fixbounds** procedure:

Element	Explanation
i As Integer	Input parameter specifying row of two-dimensional arrays
j As Integer	Input parameter specifying column of two-dimensional arrays
iL As Integer	Output parameter: the lower-row boundary of the rectangle of neighboring cells
iH As Integer	Output parameter: the upper-row boundary of the rectangle of neighboring cells
jL As Integer	Output parameter: the lower-column boundary of the rectangle of neighboring cells

Element	Explanation
`jH As Integer`	Output parameter: the upper-column boundary of the rectangle of neighboring cells

This procedure defines the boundaries of a cell's neighbors. Think of the set of neighbors as a rectangular area with a hole in it—the hole being the original cell. Figure 23 shows a cell and its neighbors.

figure **23**

Determining a cell's neighbors

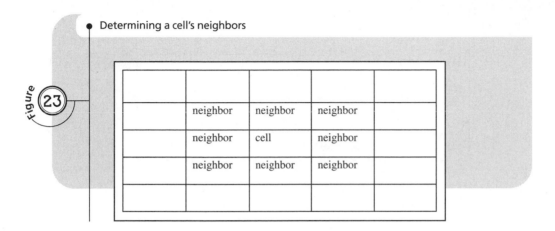

	neighbor	neighbor	neighbor	
	neighbor	cell	neighbor	
	neighbor	neighbor	neighbor	

Including the original cell in the code that defines its neighbors means that the checking can be done with nested For…Next loops. The **fixbounds** procedure calculates values (`iL`, `iH`, `jL`, and `jH`) that define the corners of the bounding rectangle for the cell referenced by `i, j`.

You can develop the logic for this procedure by noting that the bounds are generally one less and one more than the cell's index for each of the two dimensions, except for when the selected cell is at the edge of the board.

The logic here is straightforward, if somewhat tedious. To determine each bound, the code must determine whether either `i` or `j` is at a border, either the first or last row or column of the minefield. Figure 24 shows the first of four such checks.

figure **24**

Code that determines whether the selected cell is on the edge of the board

```
If i = 1 Then
        iL = 1
Else
        iL = i - 1
End If
```

You also need to determine whether `i` is equal to the last row of the grid (`i = size`), in which case `iH` = size, otherwise it equals `i + 1`. You also must perform similar logic for columns to determine whether `j` is equal to either 1 or `size`.

If the selected cell is not at a border, then the value of `iH` is one greater than `i` and `iL` is one less than `i`. The same logic applies to `j`. If `j` is not at a border, the value of `jH` is one up from `j` and `jL` is one down from `j`.

Figure 25 shows the complete code for the **fixbounds** procedure.

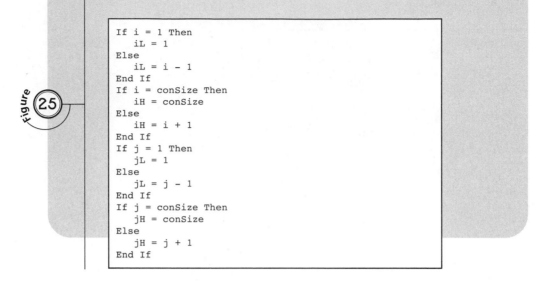

Figure 25

Code for the fixbounds procedure

```
If i = 1 Then
    iL = 1
Else
    iL = i - 1
End If
If i = conSize Then
    iH = conSize
Else
    iH = i + 1
End If
If j = 1 Then
    jL = 1
Else
    jL = j - 1
End If
If j = conSize Then
    jH = conSize
Else
    jH = j + 1
End If
```

The expand (Index As Integer) User-Defined Procedure

This procedure has the following parameter:

Element	Explanation
Index As Integer	The cell that is the starting point of the **expand** operation

This procedure has the following local variables:

Element	Explanation
Dim i As Integer	Used to index two-dimensional arrays
Dim j As Integer	Used to index two-dimensional arrays
Dim iL As Integer	The lower-row boundary of the rectangle of neighboring cells
Dim iH As Integer	The upper-row boundary of the rectangle of neighboring cells
Dim jL As Integer	The lower-column boundary of the rectangle of neighboring cells
Dim jH As Integer	The upper-column boundary of the rectangle of neighboring cells

This procedure uncovers the cells around the cell referenced by **Index**. Program this procedure so that it performs the following tasks:

1. Call the conversion routines to translate **Index** into two-dimensional indices

2. Call **fixbounds** to calculate the bounding rectangle of neighboring cells, as follows:

```
i = conind2i(Index)
j = conind2j(Index)
Call fixbounds(i, j, iL, iH, jL, jH)
```

3. Use a nested For...Next loop to test for cells that have not been flagged or examined (**blnCellsMarked(i,j) = False**). For these cells, call **countsurround** and set **blnCellsMarked(i,j)** to True, increment **intNumExamined**, and call checkforwin.

The code for the loop is shown in Figure 26.

Code that uncovers neighboring cells

Figure 26

```
For i = iL To iH
        For j = jL To jH
            If blnCellsMarked(i, j) = False Then
                blnCellsMarked(i, j) = True
                intNumExamined = intNumExamined + 1
                Call countsurround(conindex(i, j))
                Call checkforwin
            End If
        Next j
Next i
```

The checkforwin User-Defined Procedure

This procedure tests to determine if a win has occurred. A win occurs if **intNumExamined** is equal to the total number of cells on the board (**conSize * conSize**) and the number of cells flagged (in the variable **intCntr**) equals the number of mines (stored in **lblNumMines.Caption**).

This logic might seem too simple. What if the player flagged a cell incorrectly, and yet the right number of cells were flagged and all of the other cells had been examined? In fact, this situation couldn't happen, because it would mean that at some point, a cell containing a mine was examined—and once this happened, the player would lose.

Program the **checkforwin** procedure so that it performs the following tasks:

1. Test for a win by comparing **intNumExamined** to the number of cells in the minefield, using the formula **conSize * conSize**, and then click to determine whether the number of cells flagged equals the number of actual mines.

2. If there is a win, stop the timer by setting **Timer1.Enabled** to False. Also, place the string "YOU WIN" in **lblMines(0)**, then program a beep.

3. **Set blnGameOff** to True. This will disable play until the player presses the New Game button.

The code shown in Figure 27 performs these three tasks.

Code for the **checkwin** procedure

```
If intNumExamined = (conSize * conSize) Then
    If Val(lblNumFlagged.Caption) = intCntr Then
        Beep
        lblMines(0).Caption = "YOU WIN"
        tmrElapsed.Enabled = False
        blnGameoff = True
    End If
End If
```

Figure 27

The **gamelost(Index As Integer)** User-Defined Procedure

This procedure has the following parameter:

Element	Explanation
Index As Integer	Holds the location of the mine that ended the game

This procedure has the following local variables:

Element	Explanation
Dim i As Integer	Used to process two-dimensional arrays
Dim j As Integer	Used to process two-dimensional arrays

When this procedure is called, it means that the player revealed a mine and lost the game. Program this procedure so that it performs the following tasks:

1. Set **lblmines(0)** Caption to "YOU LOSE".

2. Disable the timer **tmrElapsed**.

3. Set **blnGameOff** to True. This will disable play until the player presses the New Game button.

4. Set the color of **lblMines(Index)** to **vbRed** and then program three beeps. The parameter **Index** refers to the cell containing the fatal mine.

Figure 28 shows the code that performs these four tasks.

gamelost code that changes game caption, disables the time, disables play, and makes the fatal cell red

Figure 28

```
tmrElapsed.Enabled = False
lblMines(0).Caption = "LOSE"
blnGameoff = True
lblMines(Index).BackColor = vbRed
Beep
Beep
Beep
```

The final action of the game is to uncover the entire minefield. All mines are displayed, and cells that the player incorrectly flagged as containing mines are indicated. These actions require nested For...Next loops that compare the True/False value for each element in **blnMinesOn** with the caption for each **lblMines** cell. If the cell is covered but has a mine, set its caption to "M". If the cell is incorrectly flagged, set the Caption to "X". The code to reveal and correct the mines is shown in Figure 29.

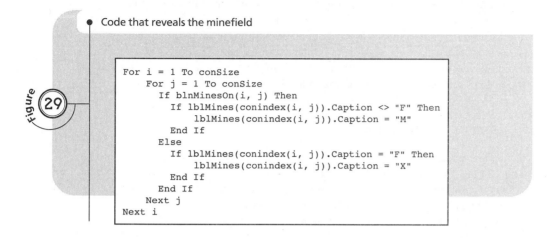

Code that reveals the minefield

```
For i = 1 To conSize
    For j = 1 To conSize
        If blnMinesOn(i, j) Then
            If lblMines(conindex(i, j)).Caption <> "F" Then
                lblMines(conindex(i, j)).Caption = "M"
            End If
        Else
            If lblMines(conindex(i, j)).Caption = "F" Then
                lblMines(conindex(i, j)).Caption = "X"
            End If
        End If
    Next j
Next i
```

figure 29

THE CALLING MAP

Defining procedures and functions is a good programming practice. Making several small tasks out of a few large ones makes your code more manageable; it is easier to debug and more modular. Figure 30 shows a calling map for the event procedures, user-defined functions, and user-defined procedures used in Minesweeper.

Calling map for Minesweeper

figure 30

Procedure	Invoked or called by	Invokes or calls
cmdRules	(action by player)	[not applicable]
Form_Load	(player loads game)	startgame
lblMines_MouseDown	(action by player)	examine, complete
lblMines_MouseUp	(action by player)	markflag
cmdNew	(action by player)	startgame
tmrElapsed_Timer	(system action)	[not applicable]
checkforwin	examine, expand, markflag	[not applicable]
complete	MouseDown	fixbounds, examine, conindex, conind2i, conin2j
conind2i	examine, markflag, complete, expand, countsurround	[not applicable]
conind2j	examine, markflag, complete, expand, countsurround	[not applicable]
conindex	complete, expand	[not applicable]
countsurround	examine, expand, gamelost	fixbounds, expand, conind2i
examine	MouseDown, complete	conind2i, conind2j, checkforwin, gamelost, countsurround
expand	countsurround	countsurround, checkforwin, fixbounds, conindex
fixbounds	expand, complete, countsurround	[not applicable]
gamelost	examine	conindex
markflag	MouseUp	checkforwin, conind2i, conind2j
setmines	startgame	[not applicable]
startgame	Form_Load, cmdNew	setmines

OPTIONAL ENHANCEMENTS

There are many ways you can customize your Minesweeper program. Following are some suggestions to get you started on adding original features and functionality.

1. In this version of Minesweeper, there is no guarantee that a fixed number of mines will be present. Develop a strategy that results in a consistent number of mines for each game. Make sure that your strategy does not automatically stop selecting mines when the desired number is reached; if that happened, it is likely that more mines would be placed at the top of the board, with fewer mines being placed in the lower cells.
2. Enhance the implementation with more sophisticated graphics and sound effects. In particular, making losing the game more dramatic.

DISCUSSION QUESTIONS

1. Minesweeper game programs typically feature three sizes of board. How would you change the system described here to use a different size board (it would still be square)? How would you change it to be a rectangular board? If you make the board bigger (in height, width, or both), at some point you will need to change the size of a cell. How and where is that done?
2. The implementation outlined here is only one of many ways to program the game and includes several choices that can be changed. Consider the following:
   * Design a different implementation in which the information is all on the board but covered up. In other words, construct two layers of labels.
   * Design a different implementation in which the internal data regarding the presence of mines and the cells being marked is kept as one-dimensional arrays corresponding to the control array of labels on display. What needs to be changed?

   After devoting some time to these ideas, decide which method is better and in which ways (you will need to explain your definition of "better"), and write a detailed explanation of your opinion.

CONSTRUCTION PLAN FOR
TIC TAC TOE

CONCEPTS, SKILLS, AND TOOLS

In this chapter, you will create a computer version of the well-known paper-and-pencil game Tic Tac Toe. As in earlier games, your code will display the player's moves and determine the outcome of the game. In addition, your code will select moves for the computer. In this game, the computer can make its move first or second, and can play at a variety of skill levels.

You will use the following general programming concepts in the Tic Tac Toe construction plan:

- Data representation, including structures with implicit relationships
- Replication of a familiar paper-and-pencil user interface
- Indexing
- Initialization and re-initialization of the game, including allowing the player and the computer to switch symbols
- Modularity and extensibility of programs
- Two-dimensional arrays
- Nested For...Next loops

The Visual Basic features used to construct this game include:
- Interaction of events
- Layered graphics
- Option buttons
- Change event procedure
- Control arrays
- Boolean variables
- Nested loops

DESCRIPTION OF THE GAME

Tic Tac Toe is a well-known children's game. It consists of a 3-x-3 grid of nine cells defined by two sets of parallel lines. One player uses X's, the other uses O's, and they take turns putting their symbols into unoccupied cells. The object is to place three symbols in a row (vertically, horizontally, or diagonally). By convention, X's go first; therefore; the X player has, at most, five turns to win while the O player has four.

HOW THIS VERSION OF TIC TAC TOE WORKS

Your challenge is to replicate the familiar Tic Tac Toe interface that you used when you first learned the game as a child. While the look of the game is simple, it can be challenging to develop code that implements a strategy. Furthermore, your version of the game should implement different levels of play for the computer. Experiment with the game by running the **tictactoe.exe** file located in your Ch9 folder.

SAMPLE SCREENS

Figure 1 shows the first screen of the computer version of the game that you will construct.

Initial screen for Tic Tac Toe

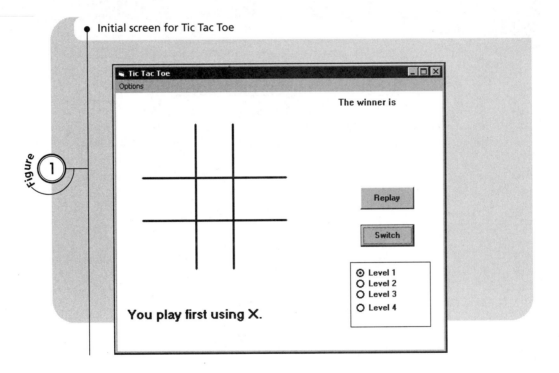

Figure 1

Figure 2 shows a win for the player. The player has marked the third X in a row and the game detects that this is a win. It indicates this by drawing a red line through the winning combination of symbols.

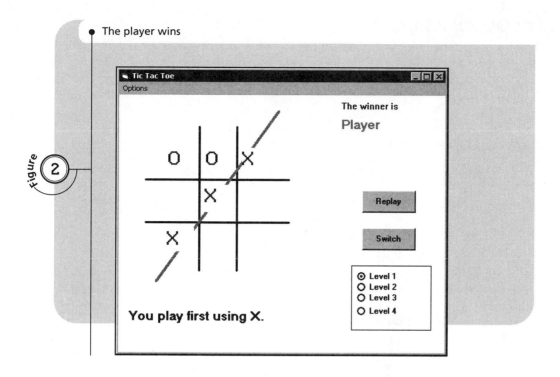

Figure 2

The player wins

It is possible for both players to have a perfect defense, in which case, the game ends in a tie. One version of Tic Tac Toe treats a tie as a special situation and refers to it as "the cat wins." In the case of a tie, a cat face is drawn around the playing board, as shown in Figure 3.

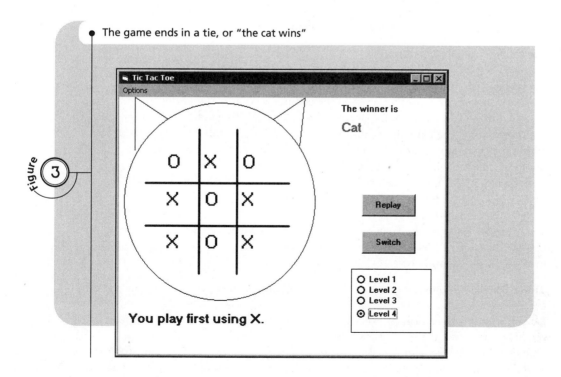

Figure 3

The game ends in a tie, or "the cat wins"

There are six critical design and programming tasks that you—the designer and programmer—must accomplish when creating the Tic Tac Toe game:

- Display the graphical elements of Tic Tac Toe

- Detect a player's move

- After every move by the player or the computer, determine whether the game has been won or tied

- Provide the flexibility of starting a new game and allowing the player and computer to take turns going first

- Design distinct strategies that allow the computer to play at different levels of difficulty

- Provide a mechanism for the player to use to choose the level of play

Task: Display the graphical elements of Tic Tac Toe.

Logic: The graphical elements of the game include elements that are always present and elements that appear only in certain situations. Elements always present include the four lines that define the game board (two horizontal and two vertical). Elements that only appear in certain situations are the lines drawn (by the code) on top of a winning row and the cat face drawn (by the code) in the case of a tie.

Solution: You will use the Visual Basic drawing objects to represent lines and circles. You create a line using the Line tool ▨ and a circle using the Shape tool ⬡. At design time, you will specify the position, length, width, and color of each graphical element. Your code will change the Visible property of controls when appropriate. For example, the parallel lines that define the boxes for the game are always visible, but this is not true for the lines marking wins. The line that indicates a winning combination of moves only appears in the case of that particular winning combination. Similarly, the cat face only appears after a tie. The cat face consists of five separate graphic elements, but your code will make them appear as one.

Task: Detect a player's move.

Logic: The player enters an X or an O into a specific place on the board, which consists of nine cells, outlined visually by the four lines. On paper, these lines are enough guidance for the player to place a move; however, in the computer version, the player makes a move by entering his symbol (X or O) into a control object, which triggers an event procedure. In that event procedure, the game recognizes the player's move and takes appropriate action. In addition to the game board lines, control objects must be placed on the form—the player will use these controls when making a move.

Solution: You will place nine text boxes—one for each cell in which the player might enter his symbol—on the form as a control array. Initially, they will each be empty (hold the empty string), and your code will refer to them by the indices 0 to 8. Each text box can hold an X, an O, or the empty string. Your code will use the Change event procedure to respond to a player's move. This event procedure executes whenever a player changes the contents of the text box by typing an X or an O.

Task: After every move by the player or the computer, determine whether the game has been won or tied.

Logic: This is a basic task for every computer game. For Tic Tac Toe, recognizing a win requires comparing the state of the game—the total of all moves—with a data structure that defines every possible winning combination. To do this, you will create data structures that store information on how to recognize a winning combination of moves and your code will refer to these to test whether the computer or the player has won. Your code will also recognize a tie when all the cells are occupied.

Solution: The state of the game is stored in the control array of text boxes that make up the game board. Your code (in the Form_Load event procedure) will also set up a two-dimensional array named **intWinCombos** that specifies the placement of X's and O's (indices in the control array of text boxes) that make up winning combinations. Each time a move is made (by either the player or the computer), the game compares the state of the game with the set of winning combinations. If a winning combination has been completed, the game draws the line over the winning symbols and the game is over. If the game is filled and there is no winning combination, the game ends in a tie.

Task: Provide the flexibility of starting a new game and allowing the player and computer to take turns going first.

Logic: In the tradition of Tic Tac Toe, the X symbol has the first move. When the game begins, the player has X by default. To allow the player to switch symbols and assign X to the computer, the code must provide a way to swap the player's symbol and the computer's symbol; this process must be under player control.

Solution: Your code will define variables for the player's symbol, the computer's symbol, the instructions for when the player goes first using X, and instructions for when the computer does. You will set up command button controls for replay and for switching symbols. Since switching symbols also signals a call for a new game, you will define a procedure to be called by the event procedures for both the switch and the replay buttons that will carry out the logic of restarting the game.

Task: Design distinct strategies that allow the computer to play at different levels of difficulty.

Logic: To make the game more interesting, you should develop not just one strategy for the computer's play, but at least four, ranging from simple to advanced.

Solution: The simplest strategy will instruct the computer to make a legal move; the most advanced strategy will make it unlikely for the player to beat the computer. For the more advanced levels of play, the strategy will check for the availability of a winning move or for a blocking move to prevent the player's win. The logic for the advanced strategy will analyze **intWinCombos**, the two-dimensional array that holds the winning combinations of moves. Since a complete winning move is three in a row, a potential winning move is when two out of three places contain the identical symbol with the third place empty, or blank. A blocking move can be recognized in a similar way. A blocking move is possible if two out of three places have the player's symbol with the third place blank.

Task: Provide a mechanism for the player to use to choose the level of play.

Logic: Option buttons, also called radio buttons, let a user click to select exactly one of a set of choices.

Solution: Visual Basic has a type of control called **option buttons**, which is a group of controls of which only one can be selected at a time. You will use option buttons to set the level of play.

⊚ PREPARING TO PROGRAM

GRAPHICAL ELEMENTS

The graphical elements required for Tic Tac Toe are simple: lines and circles. In Tic Tac Toe, your code uses lines to represent the static playing field and dynamic elements such as the indication of a win. Most of the lines and circles you will place on the form during design time are not visible at the start of the game; in fact, the only lines that remain visible throughout the game are those that define the playing board. Your code will make the other lines and shapes visible by changing their visible properties under the following circumstances: if the player or computer has won, a line is drawn through the cells that make up the winning combination; in the case of a tie, the cat's face is made visible.

DETECTING THE PLAYER'S MOVE AND PREVENTING ILLEGAL MOVES

You will place a control array of text boxes named **txtPlaces** on the form. The player and the computer will enter their X's and O's into this control array. The event procedure you will code to respond to the player's action is the Change event procedure, which executes whenever the contents of a text box (its Text property) are changed.

One potential problem here is that the computer also changes these text boxes. When the computer makes a move, it places an X or an O in the text box. When the computer, by executing code, changes a text box, the Change event procedure also executes. It is important to understand that the player's actions are not the only triggers for event procedures.

When the player's move and the computer's move trigger the same event procedure, you can end up with a situation known as a **cascading event**, which is a kind of endless loop. When using the Change event, you must plan carefully to avoid an endless loop that occurs when one automated change triggers the Change event, which then triggers another automated change, and so on until your computer locks up.

In Tic Tac Toe, the threat of a cascading event is caused by the procedure triggered by the player's move, **txtPlaces_Change**, making a move for the computer. The computer's move would also trigger the Change event. The standard practice for preventing cascading events is to use a Boolean variable to prevent a new change from being triggered until the current change is handled completely by code, and this is what you should do.

Another task you will handle in the Change event procedure is the insertion of the correct symbol in the text box, regardless of what symbol is typed in by the player. Your code should also lock any text box that already contains a symbol by setting its Locked property to True. This will prevent the player from reusing a place or changing symbols already on the board later in the game.

DETERMINING A WIN OR A TIE

A crucial task in any computer game is to include logic that can recognize a win. One approach is to define the set of all possible winning combinations, then test each after every move. This approach works well for Tic Tac Toe, because there are only eight possible winning combinations. You can easily store them in an array, which can then be searched for a match to determine a win.

Your code must also recognize a tie. Since the game can end before a win occurs, the program needs a variable to keep track of the cells used. When that variable, **intFilled**, reaches 9—the total number of cells—there is no win, and the game ends in a tie.

You will need to create a data structure that can store the winning combinations; for Tic Tac Toe, it should be a two-dimensional array—think of it as a list of lists—named **intWinCombos**. In Tic Tac Toe, **intWinCombos** is a list of eight lists—one for each winning combination.

Each individual winning combination is itself a list of three cells, indicated by the Index values that make up a winning combination. For example, the winning combination of all three cells across the top row is made up of Index values 0, 1, and 2.

The first step in constructing **intWinCombos** is to identify all the winning combinations. Using zero origin indexing, the text boxes representing the cells are laid out as shown in Figure 4.

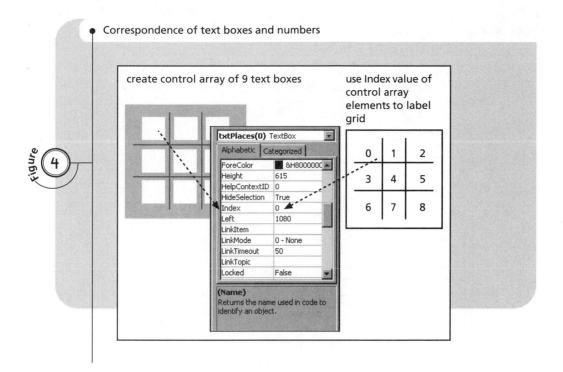

Figure 4

Correspondence of text boxes and numbers

Using the Index property of each text box, the set of all winning combinations can be documented: cells (0,1,2), (3,4,5), (6,7,8), (0,3,6), (1,4,7), (2,5,8), (0,4,8), and (2,4,6). These eight combinations of three cells are saved in the two-dimensional array **intWinCombos(8,3)**. Figure 5 shows the step-by-step process required to construct the complete set of winning combinations: label each cell (using their Index values), group winning combinations, then create a table of all possible winning combinations.

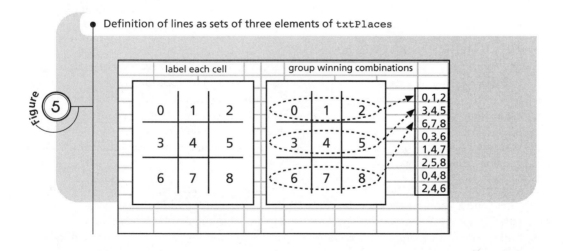

Figure 5

Definition of lines as sets of three elements of `txtPlaces`

Figure 6 shows the complete list (eight combinations multiplied by three cells per combination) of the 24 elements of the **intWinCombos** array. To understand how this array is used, you need to group elements in the list into eight sets of three. In the figure, the first column indicates the **i,j** Index values, and the second column is the value of the element in that position. These values are themselves Index values, namely references to elements in the text box control array **txtPlaces**.

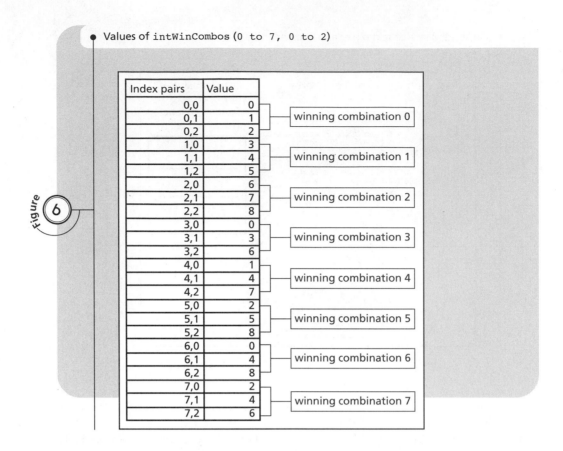

Values of intWinCombos (0 to 7, 0 to 2)

figure 6

DRAWING THE WINNING LINE

Once the game detects a win, the computer needs to draw a line on the form transecting the boxes that make up the winning combination. (Note that only this line is made visible.) To do this, you must have built into your game a way to create a direct connection between each winning combination and the line drawn to mark the win.

There is a simple way to link a winning combination with a winning line: use parallel structures, as you did in Chapters 2 and 4. You will create two arrays, **intWinCombos**—the internal array that stores sets of winning combinations—and **linWlines**—a control array of lines created with the Line tool. **intWinCombos** is an internal two-dimensional array that your code will create and initialize in Form_Load. **linWlines** is a control array, which by definition is an array you create by placing objects on the form. By carefully constructing these two arrays, you can make the connection between a winning combination and drawing a winning line.

The elements of **linWlines** are eight lines—one for each winning combination. You must make the connection between these two arrays by ensuring that the Index value of each line in **linWlines** is the same as the first dimension (i value) in the **intWinCombos** array. Do this by exactly following the instructions for placing the lines on the form as specified in the "Form Design" section.

Figure 7 shows one example of how a winning combination is connected to its winning line. While Figure 7 shows just one example, in your game you will have to connect eight winning combinations with eight lines. In Figure 7, the winning combination comprises the boxes in the left column. The Index values for these boxes are 0, 3, and 6. Make the connection between the indexes and the line by storing in **intWinCombos** values indicating that the 0, 3, 6 combination has an i value of 3 and its line has an Index value of 3.

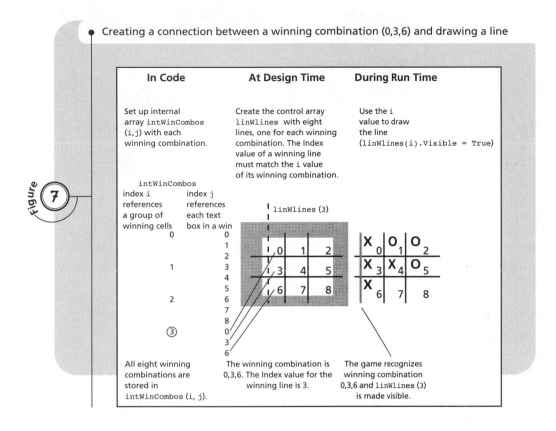

Creating a connection between a winning combination (0,3,6) and drawing a line

figure 7

In Code	At Design Time	During Run Time
Set up internal array intWinCombos (i,j) with each winning combination.	Create the control array linWlines with eight lines, one for each winning combination. The Index value of a winning line must match the i value of its winning combination.	Use the i value to draw the line (linWlines(i).Visible = True)

intWinCombos
index i references a group of winning cells
index j references each text box in a win

linWlines (3)

All eight winning combinations are stored in intWinCombos (i, j).

The winning combination is 0,3,6. The Index value for the winning line is 3.

The game recognizes winning combination 0,3,6 and linWlines (3) is made visible.

Providing Flexibility for the First Move and Starting a New Game

This version of Tic Tac Toe allows either the player or the computer to make the first move using the X symbol. Starting a new game and switching symbols are done using command buttons. You will need to use variables in the code to hold the symbols for the player and the computer. You will also use variables to hold instructions regarding whether the player or computer goes first. The event procedure for switching symbols swaps the variables holding the symbols and instructions. Switching symbols also starts a new game. You will define a procedure called **replay** to handle some of the initialization that is common to both situations; this includes erasing all winning lines, the cat, and symbols in the text boxes. You may wonder: why should you erase everything when at most, only one line or the cat was visible? The answer is that it is easier to set all Visible properties to False instead of determining which ones are True and need to be changed. The code in **replay** will also need to reset an internal array that keeps track of which places have been used.

Strategies for the Computer's Move

The biggest challenge in programming this game is to formulate the strategies for the computer's moves. Before reading on, we urge you to think about the strategy you use when you play Tic Tac Toe. You probably can play so that you almost always win or tie the game. But how do you do this? Can you articulate your strategy for winning? How do you assess the board? Try to write pseudocode to express your strategy.

After devising an expert strategy, try to devise strategies that are not so advanced.

This implementation of Tic Tac Toe has four levels of play; you are free to add more levels if you wish. Option 1 is the simplest: The computer picks the first available box. In Option 2, the computer tries to occupy the center square. In Option 3, the computer searches for a winning move and, if there is no winning move, the computer takes the next available move. In Option 4, the computer searches for a winning move. If there is no winning move, the computer checks to see if a blocking move is required.

Figure 8 shows the logic for the computer's moves at Option 4-level play.

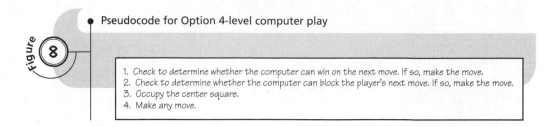

Figure 8

Pseudocode for Option 4-level computer play

1. Check to determine whether the computer can win on the next move. If so, make the move.
2. Check to determine whether the computer can block the player's next move. If so, make the move.
3. Occupy the center square.
4. Make any move.

To make a winning move, the computer has to identify a scenario where a win is possible on the next move. A potential winning move exists if any of the winning combinations has two text boxes containing the computer's symbol and one blank text box. A potential blocking move is quite similar: it exists if any of the winning combinations have two text boxes containing the player's symbol while the third text box is blank. The blank box becomes the blocking move, because the computer's symbol in that spot will block a win by the player.

SELECTING THE LEVEL OF COMPUTER PLAY

Many computer games let players select a level of difficulty, which can be done in Visual Basic using option buttons. These controls are grouped so that the user can select only one of several choices. You group option button controls by defining a **container**, which is a type of control used for grouping items, and placing the option buttons inside it. Container controls include frame controls, Picture Box controls, or forms. Figure 9 shows two option buttons placed in a container.

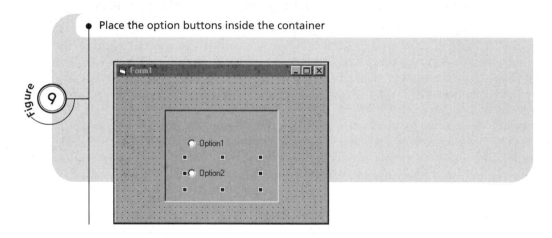

Figure 9

Place the option buttons inside the container

It is impossible for the player to set more than one option button at a time. The value of an option is its Value property. If the player has clicked to choose **Option1**, then **Option1.Value** will be True. Only one of a group of option buttons can have its Value set to True at a given time.

FORM DESIGN

This section describes all of the objects contained in the final design for Tic Tac Toe, which is shown in Figure 10. Keep in mind that many of these items are not visible when the game begins, and, for any one game, only some of the items appear. Follow this plan to place all the objects needed on your form. The object names listed below are suggestions; you may rename them if desired (if you do, be sure to revise your code accordingly. Set the labels and captions as suggested. Placement of objects are suggestions—you may lay out your form differently, if you wish.

TIP

For the game to draw the winning lines, you must create the lines at design time, add them to the form, then include code that will make one line visible if a win occurs. At design time, when you attempt to place a winning line over a text box, you will find that you cannot do it. The graphical controls reside in a different layer on the form; in this case, it is beneath the layer for text box controls. Look at Figure 2: The line is dashed instead of solid. This version of the Tic Tac Toe program accepts this dashed line effect; we challenge you to do better in your version of the game.

● Tic Tac Toe form design elements

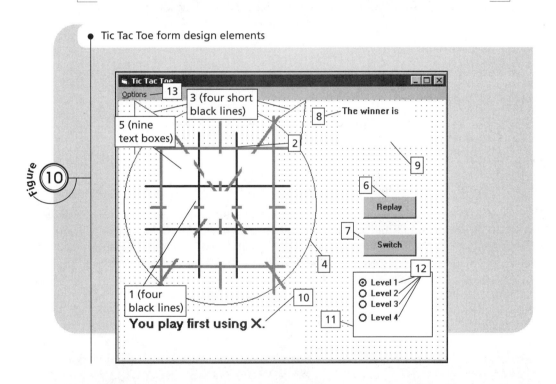

Figure 10

Lines

1. **Line1, Line2, Line3, Line4:** Lines representing the playing board, or grid. Always visible.

2. **linWlines:** Control array of eight winning lines. Set their BorderColor properties to red. Individual elements made visible by program.

3. **linRightear1, linRightear2, linLeftear1, linLeftear2:** Lines representing the cat ears. Made visible by the code following a tie.

Shapes

4. **shpCat**: Circle shape representing the cat face. Made visible by the code following a tie.

Control array of text boxes

5. **txtPlaces()**: Control array of nine text boxes: the nine cells for X's and O's. Modified by the player or code. Set the BorderStyle property to None to display the text boxes in plain style. When adding these text boxes to the form, be sure their Index values correspond to the pattern shown in Figure 5. The top row from left to right should be Index 0, 1, and 2; the middle row should be 3, 4, and 5; and the bottom row should be 6, 7, and 8.

Command buttons

6. **cmdReplay**: Starts a new game

7. **cmdSwitch**: Switches symbols for player and computer (allows player and computer to take turns going first)

Labels

8. **label1**: Static label "The winner is"

9. **lblWinner**: Label indicating winner

10. **lblDir**: Shows instructions to player (instructions change depending on whether the player is X or O)

Picture Box control

11. **Picture1**: Contains the option buttons

Option buttons

12. **Option1, Option2, Option3, Option4**: Used by player to choose level of play.

Menu

13. **&Options**: Pull-down menu caption that ends the game.

You will add a control array of lines named **linWlines** that contains all the lines that indicate a win. Remember: only one winning line will be drawn if there is a win. How will your code know which line to make visible? You need to carefully match the Index value of each winning line with its corresponding set of winning combinations in **intWinCombos**. To do this, you should add the lines to the array in the following order so that their Index properties match the winning combination.

Use this chart for reference:

linWlines index value	Winning combination	Description of winning combination
0	0,1,2	top row
1	3,4,5	middle row
2	6,7,8	bottom row
3	0,3,6	left column
4	1,4,7	middle column
5	2,5,8	right column

linWlines index value	Winning combination	Description of winning combination
6	0,4,8	diagonal from upper-left to lower-right
7	2,4,6	diagonal from upper-right to lower-left

VARIABLES AND CONSTANTS DECLARED IN THE (General) SECTION

In your Tic Tac Toe program, set the following variables and constants in the **(General)** section:

Element	Explanation
Option explicit	Set this option to require a declaration of all variables
Dim intWinCombos(8, 3) As Integer	Defines the winning combinations
Dim blnUsed(9) As Integer	Keeps track of which cells have been used (hold an X or an O)
Dim blnChangeoff As Boolean	Used for preventing cascading events
Dim intFilled As Integer	Keeps count of the number of cells filled
Dim strComputer As String	Holds the symbol used by the computer
Dim strPlayer As String	Holds the symbol used by the player
Dim strDircomputer As String	The directions indicating that the computer plays first
Dim strDirplayer As String	The directions indicating that the player plays first
Const nw = 7	Constant defining highest value for arrays. Used in For...Next loops to define upper limit of loops.

ALGORITHMS FOR EVENT PROCEDURES AND USER-DEFINED PROCEDURES

Program your Tic Tac Toe game in two stages to make debugging easier.

Stage 1: Define the play performed by the computer as the simplest strategy: putting its symbol in the next empty position. This stage allows you to make sure you can process and respond to the player's moves and detect when the game is over.

Stage 2: Define different levels of play for the computer.

Programming the game in two stages means that you defer setting up the options, have a simpler version of the user-defined procedure **makemove**, and can put off implementing the user-defined procedure **checkifclose**.

The following table outlines the tasks you must accomplish in each stage:

Stage	Work on these procedures	Preparation at design time	How to test your program
1	Form_Load cmdReplay_Click cmdSwitch_Click txtPlaces_Change replay do_win updatebox checkifwin mnuExit Stage 1 version of makemove	Place everything on the form except the option buttons and the Picture Box container	Play the game vs. the computer. To test, do not try to win each time. Use the Switch command button
2	Stage 2 version of makemove checkifclose	Place a Picture Box object as a container for the four option buttons and then place the four option buttons.	Play at each of the four levels of play. Play to win but also try to lose. Check whether the computer as player is doing what you have programmed.

STAGE 1: BASIC OPERATIONS OF THE GAME

In this stage, you program the logic for only the Option 1-level computer game strategy along with all of the form design elements.

Stage 1: The Form_Load Event Procedure

This procedure has just one local variable:

Element	Explanation
Dim i As Integer	Used in a For...Next loop

You typically place code that assigns initial values to variables in the **(General)** section as part of the Form_Load event. Program this event procedure so that it performs the following tasks:

1. Set **strDircomputer** and **strDirplayer** to display appropriate instructions, which will appear on the form depending on which player has which symbol. The code to set these strings is:

```
strDircomputer = "Computer plays first. You play O."
strDirplayer = "You play first using X."
```

2. Using a For...Next loop, set each element of the **blnUsed** array to False. The code to do this is:

```
For i = 0 To 8
    blnUsed(i) = False
Next i
```

3. Set **intFilled** to 0

4. Set **strPlayer** and **strComputer** to "X" and "O" respectively

5. Set **blnChangeoff** to False

You must also initialize the two-dimensional array **intWinCombos** with the values that represent the eight sets of winning combinations. This requires 24 assignment statements, because each of the eight sets of winning combinations has three locations in it. The code to do this is shown in Figure 11.

● Code that intitializes intWinCombos with the winning combinations

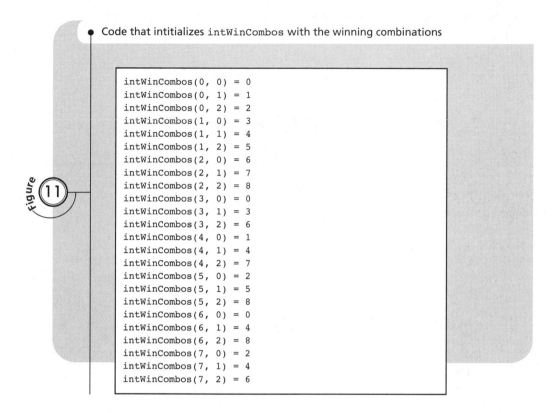

```
intWinCombos(0, 0) = 0
intWinCombos(0, 1) = 1
intWinCombos(0, 2) = 2
intWinCombos(1, 0) = 3
intWinCombos(1, 1) = 4
intWinCombos(1, 2) = 5
intWinCombos(2, 0) = 6
intWinCombos(2, 1) = 7
intWinCombos(2, 2) = 8
intWinCombos(3, 0) = 0
intWinCombos(3, 1) = 3
intWinCombos(3, 2) = 6
intWinCombos(4, 0) = 1
intWinCombos(4, 1) = 4
intWinCombos(4, 2) = 7
intWinCombos(5, 0) = 2
intWinCombos(5, 1) = 5
intWinCombos(5, 2) = 8
intWinCombos(6, 0) = 0
intWinCombos(6, 1) = 4
intWinCombos(6, 2) = 8
intWinCombos(7, 0) = 2
intWinCombos(7, 1) = 4
intWinCombos(7, 2) = 6
```

Figure 11

Stage 1: The cmdReplay_Click Event Procedure

This event procedure does not require any local variables. It executes when the player clicks the Replay button to start a new game. Program this event procedure so that it performs the following tasks:

1. Calls the user-defined procedure **replay**. This procedure will perform initialization tasks needed by both the **cmdReplay_Click** and **cmdSwitch_Click** event procedures. The specifications for **replay** are described below.

2. Determine whether the variable **strComputer** is the "X" symbol, and if so, set up and call the **makemove** procedure to make a move. Note: to **set up** means to set **blnChangeoff** to True and then reset it to False to prevent cascading events. The code for this event procedure is shown in Figure 12.

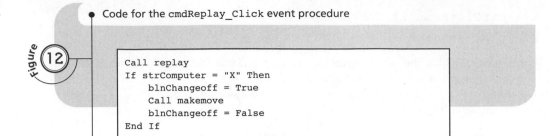

Code for the `cmdReplay_Click` event procedure

Figure 12

```
Call replay
If strComputer = "X" Then
    blnChangeoff = True
    Call makemove
    blnChangeoff = False
End If
```

Stage 1: The `cmdSwitch_Click` Event Procedure

This procedure requires one local variable:

Element	Explanation
`Dim strSym As String`	Used for swapping symbols for player and computer

This event procedure executes when the player clicks the **cmdSwitch** button. This action by the player indicates that he wants to switch symbols (either change from X to O or from O to X). Notice that you cannot assume that switching symbols means the player becomes O. It also could be true that the player, through an earlier switch, already is playing O and wants to switch back to X.

Program this event procedure as follows:

1. Swap the symbols of the computer and the player, which are stored in the global variables **strPlayer** and **strComputer**. Recall that you learned how to swap values in Chapter 4. When you want two variables to swap values, you must use a third variable to temporarily hold one of the values before you can reassign the first two. The code to perform this swap is:

   ```
   strSym = strPlayer
   strPlayer = strComputer
   strComputer = strSym
   ```

2. Call the user-defined procedure **replay** to initialize the game for replay.

3. Change the instructions by setting **lblDir.Caption** to the appropriate string (**strDircomputer** or **strDirplayer**). The code to perform this task is shown in Figure 13.

Code that changes the visible instructions

Figure 13

```
If strComputer = "X" Then
    lblDir.Caption = strDircomputer
Else
    lblDir.Caption = strDirplayer
End If
```

4. If the computer is now X, generate a move for the computer. Using the same logic as was included in **cmdReplay_Click**, the steps your code will need to perform are to set **blnChangeoff** to True, call **makemove**, then set

blnChangeoff to False. The code to perform these tasks is shown in Figure 14.

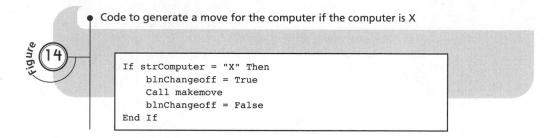

Code to generate a move for the computer if the computer is X

Figure 14

```
If strComputer = "X" Then
    blnChangeoff = True
    Call makemove
    blnChangeoff = False
End If
```

Stage 1: The txtPlaces_Change(Index As Integer) Event Procedure

This event procedure has one parameter:

Element	Explanation
Index As Integer	**Index** refers to the specific text box on the game board that was changed

This event procedure executes when the contents of any text box in the control array **txtPlaces** are changed. As explained earlier, this event procedure executes no matter what action—either a move by the player or the computer—causes the contents to change. Therefore, when the game generates a move for the computer and places a value in one of the text boxes, **txtPlaces_Change** executes. To prevent cascading events from occurring, use the Boolean variable **blnChangeoff** to control the execution of this event procedure. If **blnChangeoff** is True, it means that **txtPlaces_Change** is still processing a move by the player, and the routine should be immediately exited. If it is False, then this event procedure is *about* to process a player's move, so the code must set **blnChangeoff** to True. Finally, after the player makes his move, the computer makes a move, the game tests for a win or a tie, and **blnChangeoff** is set to False.

Program this event procedure as follows:

1. If **blnChangeoff** is True, then exit this event procedure using the following code:

   If blnChangeoff Then Exit Sub

2. Set **blnChangeoff** to True so subsequent changes do not cause a cascading event.

3. Call the user-defined procedure **updatebox** and pass in the value from Index and the symbol in **strPlayer**. The code to perform these two steps is:

   blnChangeoff = True
   Call updatebox(Index, strPlayer)

4. Call the user-defined function **checkifwin** to determine whether the player has won on his move. This function returns the empty string ("") if there is no winner at this time, or returns the player's symbol if the player has won the game. If the player has won, call the user-defined procedure **do_win**. If the game is not over, then your code needs to generate a move for the computer. Do this by calling the user-defined procedure **makemove**. The code to perform these tasks is shown in Figure 15.

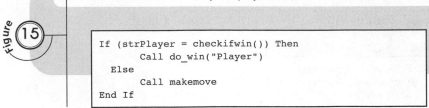

Code that tests for a win by the player

Figure 15

```
If (strPlayer = checkifwin()) Then
        Call do_win("Player")
  Else
        Call makemove
End If
```

Note that the **Makemove** procedure, which generates a move for the computer, will also call **checkifwin**, to determine whether the computer has won the game. At this point, there are three possibilities: the game has been won by the player, the game has been won by the computer, or the game has not been won. In the last case, you need to determine whether the game is over. To determine whether it is the no-winner case, you compare **lblWinner.Caption** to the empty string. If the caption is equal to the empty string, then the game has not been won.

If the game has not been won, test for a tie, which occurs when the entire board is filled with symbols. Your code recognizes this condition by testing the variable **intFilled**, which is incremented any time a move is made by either the computer or the player. If **intFilled** equals 9, the game has ended in a tie. Your code must then draw the cat by making the five parts of the cat visible, and put the word "Cat" in **lblWinner.Caption**. Program a beep to signal the end of the game.

Finally, your code should set **blnChangeoff** back to False.

The code to perform these three tasks is shown in Figure 16.

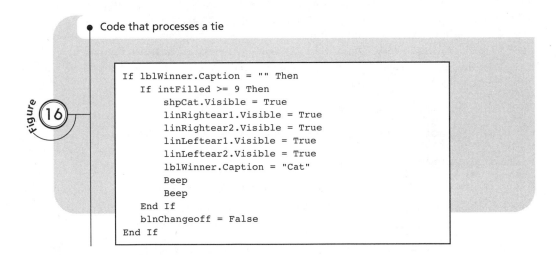

Code that processes a tie

Figure 16

```
If lblWinner.Caption = "" Then
    If intFilled >= 9 Then
        shpCat.Visible = True
        linRightear1.Visible = True
        linRightear2.Visible = True
        linLeftear1.Visible = True
        linLeftear2.Visible = True
        lblWinner.Caption = "Cat"
        Beep
        Beep
    End If
    blnChangeoff = False
End If
```

Stage 1: The `replay` User-Defined Procedure

This procedure requires one local variable:

Element	Explanation
`Dim i As Integer`	Used in two For...Next loops

This user-defined procedure performs initialization tasks to set up for a new game. Program this procedure to perform the following tasks:

1. Set **intFilled** to 0

2. Set **blnChangeoff** to True

3. Using a For...Next loop from 0 to 8, set the Text property of the **txtPlaces** text boxes to blank, set the Locked property to False to allow user input, and set all the components of the **blnUsed** array to False. The code to perform these tasks is shown in Figure 17.

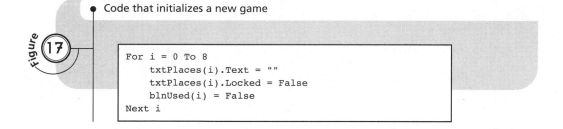

Figure 17 Code that initializes a new game

```
For i = 0 To 8
    txtPlaces(i).Text = ""
    txtPlaces(i).Locked = False
    blnUsed(i) = False
Next i
```

4. In a For...Next loop from 0 to **nw** (a constant representing the number of winning lines), set all the **linWlines** to be invisible, using the following code:

```
For i = 0 To nw
  linWlines(i).Visible = False
Next i
```

5. Make all the parts of the cat drawing invisible using the code shown in Figure 18

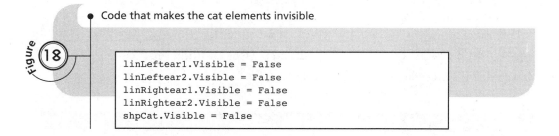

Figure 18 Code that makes the cat elements invisible

```
linLeftear1.Visible = False
linLeftear2.Visible = False
linRightear1.Visible = False
linRightear2.Visible = False
shpCat.Visible = False
```

6. Set **lblWinner.Caption** to blank ("")

7. Set **blnChangeoff** back to False

Stage 1: The makemove User-Defined Procedure

This user-defined procedure requires the following variables:

Element	Explanation
Dim intPlace As Integer	Holds the reference to the **txtPlaces** control array for the computer move
Dim i As Integer	Used in a For...Next loop

Program this user-defined procedure to select a move for the computer. In this simple version for Stage 1, write code that selects a move for the computer by finding the first unfilled place (starting at **txtPlaces(0)** and going in order through to **txtPlaces(8)**) and entering into this place the computer's symbol. After the computer's move has been selected, your code must determine whether this move resulted in a win for the computer and, if so, perform the necessary logic.

Program this user-defined procedure so that it performs the following tasks:

1. Find the first unused place on the grid. As soon as it is found, your code should exit the For loop. The code for this step is shown in Figure 19.

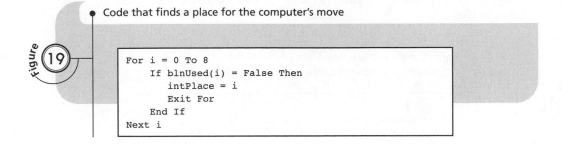

● Code that finds a place for the computer's move

Figure 19

```
For i = 0 To 8
    If blnUsed(i) = False Then
        intPlace = i
        Exit For
    End If
Next i
```

2. Call the user-defined procedure **updatebox** with the first parameter indicating the first available cell and the second parameter indicating the computer's symbol, using the following code:

```
Call updatebox(intPlace, strComputer)
```

3. Test to determine whether the move was a winning move for the computer by calling the user-defined function **checkifwin**. If **checkifwin** returns the computer's symbol, call the **do_win** procedure with a parameter equal to "Computer", like this:

```
If strComputer = checkifwin() Then
    Call do_win("Computer")
End If
```

Stage 1: The do_win (strSym As String) User-Defined Procedure

This user-defined procedure has one parameter:

Element	Explanation
strSym As String	Indicates who has won the game

This user-defined procedure indicates who has won the game. Program this procedure to perform the following tasks:

1. Set **lblWinner.Caption** equal to the parameter **strSym**

2. Signal that the game is over by programming a beep

Stage 1: The updatebox(index As Integer, strSym As String) User-Defined Procedure

This user-defined procedure receives two parameters:

Element	Explanation
index As Integer	References the element in **txtPlaces** to be updated
strSym As String	Contains the symbol that is placed in the element being updated

This procedure carries out the logic needed to record a move. Program this event procedure so that it performs the following tasks:

1. Set the **index** element in the **blnUsed** array to True, like this:

   ```
   blnUsed(index) = True
   ```

2. Set the **index** element of the **txtPlaces** array to **strSym**, like this:

   ```
   txtPlaces(index).Text = strSym
   ```

3. Set the **Locked** property of the **index** element to True, like this:

   ```
   txtPlaces(index).Locked = True
   ```

4. Increment **intFilled** by 1, like this:

   ```
   intFilled = intFilled + 1
   ```

Stage 1: The checkifwin() As Integer User-Defined Function

This user-defined function has two local variables:

Element	Explanation
`Dim i As Integer`	Used in a For...Next loop
`Dim strSym As String`	Used to hold the symbol found in the first element of a row

This user-defined function determines whether the game has been won by determining whether the same symbol occupies all the cells in any winning combination. It returns the symbol of the winner if there is a winner, or returns a blank ("") if a win has not occurred. Notice that this check is independent of the player or the computer winning. The procedures calling this function, **makemove** and **txtPlaces_Change**, determine whether a win has occurred when the function returns either the winning symbol or the empty string.

To determine a win, the code needs to compare the state of the board with the collections of winning combinations stored in the **intWinCombos** array.

The entire task of determining a win is done in one For...Next loop. The loop iterates from **0** to **nw** (equal to **7** for this game), which examines the eight defined winning combinations. First, the variable, **strSym**, is set to the value of the first cell of the **i**th row of the game board grid. If the first cell contains either the player's symbol or the computer's symbol, then the next If statement determines whether the first cell is equal to the values of both of the remaining cells. When the contents of all three cells are equal, the code recognizes that a win has occurred. To return the winning symbol to the calling procedure, your code will set **checkifwin** equal to **strSym**.

The last step your code must perform is to draw the winning line. Remember: at design time, the **linWlines** control array is configured in such a way that there is a match between the **i** value of a winning combination in **intWinCombos** and the Index property of the line in **linWlines**. Draw the winning line by setting the Visible property of **linWlines(i)** to True.

The code for **checkifwin** is shown in Figure 20.

Figure 20

● Code for the `checkifwin` procedure

```
For i = 0 To nw
    strSym = txtPlaces(intWinCombos(i, 0)).Text
    If strSym = strPlayer Or strSym = strComputer Then
        If strSym = txtPlaces(intWinCombos(i, 1)).Text And _
                    strSym = txtPlaces(intWinCombos(i, 2)).Text Then
                    checkifwin = strSym
                    linWlines(i).Visible = True
        End If
    End If
Next i
```

Stage 1: The `mnuExit` Procedure

This procedure ends the game using the code:

> **End**

When the user clicks the pull-down menu labeled "Options," then selects the Exit Game option, the game ends.

STAGE 2: ADDING LEVELS OF PLAY

Stage 2: Form Design

The only addition you need to make to the form is to add option buttons to allow the player to choose the level of play. First, use the Picture Box control ▣ here to add an object to the form to act as a container. Then, place four option buttons inside the container and set their Caption properties to "Level 1", "Level 2", "Level 3", and "Level 4".

Stage 2: The `makemove( )` Procedure

Erase the **makemove** procedure you wrote in Stage 1 and start from scratch. The Stage 2 version will include some of your original code, but it is easier to rewrite the procedure. Include the following local variables in your Stage 2 version of this procedure:

Element	Explanation
`Dim blnMademove As Boolean`	Set when the procedure determines a move for the computer
`Dim i As Integer`	Used in the For...Next loop that loops through **txtPlaces** array
`Dim intPlace As Integer`	Holds the move calculated for the computer (the index in **txtPlaces**)

In Stage 2, you will handle the more complex task of programming different skill levels for the computer. Your code will recognize the computer's level by determining which option button the player selected.

Following is a summary of the four skill levels for the computer:

Option 1: Your code selects the first available cell for the computer's move. You have already implemented this strategy in Stage 1.

Option 2: The computer attempts to occupy the center square (Index value is 4). If it is not blank, the next available place is selected.

Option 3: The computer searches for a winning move, that is, a move that completes a winning combination. If a winning move is not available, it chooses the next open place.

Option 4: First, the computer searches for a winning move. If none is available, it will attempt to block a potential win by the player. If a blocking move is not available, then the computer selects the next available cell.

To fully implement this four-level strategy, the code attempts to calculate a move for the computer by determining what options are set and examining the board. A sequence of tests is made to determine a move. Once a move is found, no further tests should be made. To control this, **blnMadeMove** is initialized to False, and set to True if a move is found. Every subsequent test first looks at **blnMadeMove** and does nothing if it is True. Add the following logic to the **makemove** procedure:

1. Initialize **blnMademove** to False. After the code selects a move for the computer, **blnMademove** is set to True.

2. If the player selected Options 3 or 4, the code must determine whether the computer can win with its move. You do this by calling the user-defined function **checkifclose**. This function will return -1 if no winning move is available; if a winning move is available, it will return the Index value of the winning move. The code to process the Option 3 or Option 4 logic is shown in Figure 21.

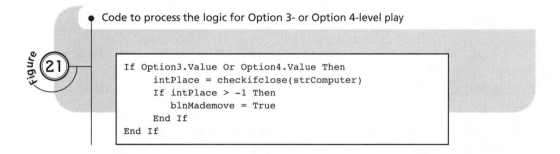

Code to process the logic for Option 3- or Option 4-level play

Figure 21

```
If Option3.Value Or Option4.Value Then
    intPlace = checkifclose(strComputer)
    If intPlace > -1 Then
        blnMademove = True
    End If
End If
```

3. If the prior code did not calculate a move (**blnMademove = False**) and the option in effect is Option 4, the code will try to make a blocking move. Your code again calls the user-defined function **checkifclose**, but this time **checkifclose** uses the player's symbol as the parameter. Notice that you are reusing **checkifclose** for a different purpose. By passing in the player's symbol, **checkifclose** can determine whether the player will win on the next move. If the game can recognize this condition, it can block the player's win by placing the computer's symbol in the winning cell spot. The code for a blocking move by the computer is shown in Figure 22. Notice the nesting of three **If** statements.

Figure 22

Option 4-level code to block a win by the player

```
If blnMademove = False Then
        'check to determine whether the computer needs to block
            If Option4.Value Then
                intPlace = checkifclose(strPlayer)
                        If intPlace > -1 Then
                blnMademove = True
                End If
            End If
End If
```

It is still possible that a move for the computer has not been calculated. If the level of play is set to Options 2, 3, or 4, then your code must determine whether the center cell of the grid is taken. If the center cell is available, the computer should take it. This is one of the rare occasions where you use a number in code rather than a variable. The code to capture the center cell is shown in Figure 23.

Figure 23

Code for the computer to capture the center cell

```
If blnMademove = False Then
    If Option4.Value Or Option3.Value Or Option2.Value Then
        If blnUsed(4) = False Then
            intPlace = 4
            blnMademove = True
        End If
    End If
End If
```

If a move for the computer is still not determined (**blnMademove** equals False), then your code should find the first unfilled position and make that the move. This is essentially the code from Stage 1 (see Figure 20), with the addition of the check of **blnMademove** and the setting of **blnMademove**. The code for the computer to take the next available space is shown in Figure 24.

Figure 24

Code for the computer to take the next available cell

```
If blnMademove = False Then
    For i = 0 To 8
        If blnUsed(i) = False Then
            intPlace = i
            blnMademove = True
            Exit For
        End If
    Next i
End If
```

Once the move is determined, the code makes the move for the computer by calling **updatebox**. It then checks for a win by calling **checkifwin**, and, if there is a win, it calls the **do_win** procedure. The code for this step is shown in Figure 25.

Figure 25

● Code that precesses the computer's move

```
If blnMademove Then
    Call updatebox(intPlace, strComputer)
    'now test for win
    If strComputer = checkifwin() Then
        Call do_win("Computer")
    End If
End If
```

Stage 2: The `checkifclose(strSym As String) As Integer` User-Defined Function

This user-defined function has the following parameter:

Element	Explanation
`strSym As String`	Stores the symbol to be used in the test

This function requires the following local variables:

Element	Explanation
`Dim i As Integer`	Used in outer For...Next loop iterating over `intWinCombos` array
`Dim j As Integer`	Used in inner For...Next loop iterating over places in a winning combination
`Dim intPlace As Integer`	Holds potential winning position or win-blocking position
`Dim intCnt As Integer`	Counts number of filled cells

This function determines whether any winning combination is nearly complete, meaning it has two out of three cells containing the symbol that is passed as the parameter. If this situation exists, then **checkifclose** returns the location of the (available) cell that would complete the win. If the situation doesn't exist, **checkifclose** returns -1 to indicate that no such line was found.

TIP It is a common convention in programming for a function to return an out-of-bounds value (such as -1) to indicate that the condition being searched for doesn't exist.

The **checkifclose** function is used for two purposes: to determine whether the computer can make a winning move or whether the computer must block the player from completing a line. The calling procedure in both cases is the **makemove** procedure. In the first case, the parameter will be the computer's symbol, and in the second case, the parameter will be the player's.

Program this function to perform the following tasks:

1. Use an outer For...Next loop to iterate through all the winning combinations and an inner For...Next loop to examine the three cells in each line. For the start of the outer loop, use the following code to set a counter variable, **intCnt**, to 0:

```
For i = 0 To nw
intCnt = 0
```

2. For the start of the inner loop, use a Select Case statement to examine the element of **txtPlaces** indexed by the value in **intWinCombos(i, j)**, like this:

```
For j = 0 To 2
Select Case txtPlaces(intWinCombos(i, j)).Text
```

3. Each text box can have three possible values: the symbol in **strSym**, the opposite symbol, or blank (""). You can determine the contents of each text box by placing a Select Case statement inside a For…Next loop, as shown in Figure 26. If one text box has a blank (""), then its index is saved in **intPlace**.

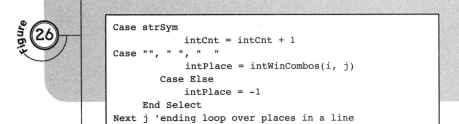

● Code that determines a text box's contents

Figure 26

```
Case strSym
          intCnt = intCnt + 1
Case "", " ", "  "
          intPlace = intWinCombos(i, j)
      Case Else
          intPlace = -1
    End Select
Next j 'ending loop over places in a line
```

4. After the inner loop finishes iterating, your code determines whether the critical condition has been met: is this a combination with exactly two cells holding **strSym** and the other cell blank (holding an empty string)? If this condition is true, **intCnt** is equal to 2 and **intPlace** has a value (other than -1), that points to the blank cell. The **intPlace** value is assigned to **checkifclose** and the function is ended. This means that **intPlace**—the blank position in the line where a blocking or a winning move can be made—will be returned to one of two possible places in the **makemove** procedure. Figure 27 shows the code that determines whether a winning or blocking move can be made.

● Code that determines whether the computer can perform a winning or blocking move

Figure 27

```
If intCnt = 2 And intPlace > -1 Then
   checkifclose = intPlace
   Exit Function
End If
Next i 'ending outer loop over all lines
```

5. If the next line of code is reached, it means this function has not exited in the case of a positive result. In other words, either there was no combination with two occurrences of **strSym** or, if there was, the third cell was filled with the other symbol. In this case, the function returns -1, like this:

```
checkifclose = -1
```

THE TIC TAC TOE CALLING MAP

Figure 28 shows the calling map for event procedures, user-defined procedures, and functions used in Tic Tac Toe.

Calling map for Tic Tac Toe

Figure 28

Procedure	Invoked/called by	Invokes /calls
Form_Load	(player loads game)	[not applicable]
cmdReplay_Click	(player action)	replay, makemove
cmdSwitch_Click	(player action)	replay, makemove
txtPlaces_Change	(player action)	updatebox, checkifwin, makemove, do_win
replay	cmdReplay_Click, cmdSwitch_Click	[not applicable]
makemove	txtPlaces_Change, cmdReplay_Click, cmdSwitch_Click	checkifclose (two calls), updatebox, checkifwin, do_win
do_win	txtPlaces_Change, makemove	[not applicable]
updatebox	txtPlaces_Change, makemove	[not applicable]
checkifwin	txtPlaces_Change, makemove	[not applicable]
checkifclose	makemove	[not applicable]

OPTIONAL ENHANCEMENTS

There are many ways you can customize your Tic Tac Toe program. Following are some suggestions to get you started on adding original features and functionality.

1. To simplify the game, when a player has won, change the color of the text boxes that make up a winning combination rather than drawing a line.
2. Improve the look and feel of the game. Add images and sound to signal a win, loss, and tie. Make the program dynamically draw a line through the winning set of cells, perhaps in one color for the player and another for the computer.
3. As it is described in this chapter, the game makes a correction when the player tries to enter something other than X or O onto the game board. The game makes this correction using its knowledge of who is to play next. What other action could be taken? Decide the best course of action and implement it.
4. Expand the game to a larger board: 4×4, 5×5, or $n \times n$.
5. Put pressure on the player by requiring a move within a fixed number of seconds. Make play more challenging for the user by combining increasing time pressure with raising the skill level of the computer.

◎ DISCUSSION QUESTIONS

1. How could your program allow for switching symbols without restarting play?
2. Devise strategies that improve the quality or sophistication of the computer's play. Could you devise a better—or at least a different—way to define levels of play?
3. Using the Change event to handle a player's move runs the risk of cascading events. Explore what other events can be used to handle this logic without such a risk. (*Hint*: Look at the mouse functions.)

10

THE BEST SCORES FEATURE

CONCEPTS, SKILLS, AND TOOLS

In this chapter, you will learn how to construct a program, called Best Scores, that maintains a list of the top sets of scores and names of the players who achieved those scores. This chapter does not describe a separate game. Instead, it describes a feature you can add to games with scores, such as Quiz or Minesweeper.

As part of this Best Scores project, you will build a testing interface—called a **driver program**—to serve as a prototype for the best score facility. This interface is the part of the program that you will use to check the functionality of the program logic. The driver part of the Best Scores program is not included in a best scores facility for a real game.

You will use the following general programming concepts in the Best Scores program:

- Setting up a test for a specific feature
- General file concepts

The Visual Basic features used to construct this facility include:

- File handling
- Type definitions
- String variables of a fixed length
- The InputBox command for reading user input
- Exit statements out of For...Next loops
- Manipulation of arrays

DESCRIPTION OF THE PROJECT

HOW THIS BEST SCORES PROGRAM WORKS

A best scores feature is common on many computer and arcade games and could be added to several of the games included in this text, such as Quiz from Chapter 7. In Quiz, a best scores feature would store names and scores of the players with the highest point totals. If you chose to add a best scores feature to Minesweeper, you could store the times and names for the players who took the shortest amount of time to win the game. Experiment with a best scores feature by running the bestscores.exe file, which is located in the Ch10 folder.

In general, the best scores feature works like this: If your score is among the best ever recorded for the game, the program prompts you for your name (or nickname or "handle") so it can be added to a list for all future players to see. For the purposes of this chapter, the program assumes that "best" means highest. You will need to change this definition for games in which lower scores are better, such as Minesweeper.

To implement this feature, your code will store the score information in a data file that is external to the program. By doing this, the information is preserved even when the game is ended and the computer is turned off.

Since this project can apply to several games, this chapter will describe a general solution that you must adapt to install in a particular game. This chapter represents the best scores facility using a generic interface into which players insert their scores. These scores are then compared to a list of pre-existing best scores maintained in the external data file.

The testing method described in this chapter is used frequently when software is developed. Testing a piece of code is referred to as a **unit test**. After the individual parts are tested, you put the pieces together for a **system test**. This chapter describes the unit test for the best scores facility. Some of the code for the unit test is throwaway code; it is only used for this demonstration project and is not included in a real game's best scores feature.

SAMPLE SCREENS

The interface for the Best Scores testing program is a screen with a text box and three buttons, as shown in Figure 1.

Figure 1

Test interface for a best scores feature

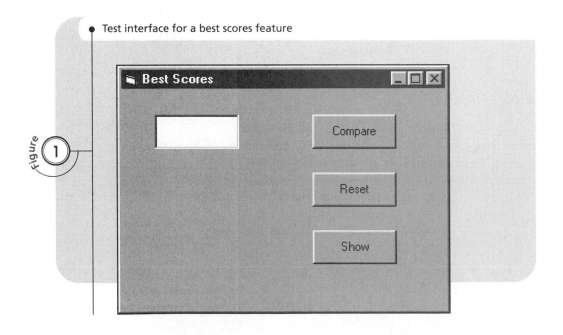

The interface prompts you, the programmer/tester/player, to enter numbers into the text box. These numbers serve as a collection of sample values that you can use to test Best Score's functionality. As you enter the scores into the text box, the program stores the values in an external data file—not in the Visual Basic program. Figures 2 and 3 demonstrate what happens when a player named Jeanine enters "89" as a best score. After Jeanine enters "89" into the text box shown in Figure 1 and presses the Compare button, if the program determines that 89 is one of the best scores, the computer displays a dialog box requesting her name. She types in her name, then clicks the OK button. Figure 2 shows the dialog box that requests the user's name.

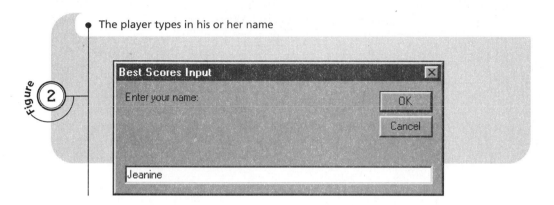

Figure 2

• The player types in his or her name

After she enters her name, the program displays the current set of best scores and the associated player names, as shown in Figure 3.

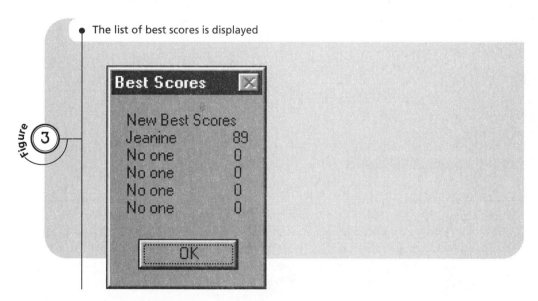

Figure 3

• The list of best scores is displayed

Games with a best scores facility maintain a list containing a fixed number of best scores—for example, the top 10. The Best Scores program described in this chapter displays the top five scores. To maintain this list, your code compares the number entered into the text box by the player with the pre-existing scores already on file. When a new number qualifies as one of the best five scores—that is, better than at least one of the top scores recorded—your code then requests the player's name. The score and the name are incorporated into the list of best scores. To include this feature in a game and compare the new score with the best score on file, you must insert the best scores code at the point in the game program at which a score is calculated.

To store data on a file, you will need to create a record. As you learned in Chapter 7, a **record** is a compound data construct that is used to group different items together. Your address is an example of a record—it groups your name, street address, state, city, and ZIP code. In this project, you will create a record that combines a score with its associated name.

In this chapter, the file you will be using, **best.dat**, is made up of a series of records. You can find a copy of this file in your Ch10 folder. Each record represents one entry in the best scores list; since the best scores list has five entries, the **best.dat** file has five records.

You must also write code that modifies the list of best scores—extracted from the records stored in the **best.dat** data file—whenever a player achieves a new, higher score. Since you will be adding new best scores and deleting older scores that are no longer high enough to stay on the list, your Best Scores program will perform Input, Output, and other types of file access. Notice that the insertion of a new best score can change the ranking for more than one record. For example, if the new score is better than the third-best score on record, the new record becomes the new third record on file; the old third record becomes the new fourth record; and the old fourth record becomes the new fifth record.

This chapter describes how to work with external (non-Visual Basic) files and Visual Basic types to add a best scores feature to a game. The Visual Basic type construct has many uses beyond setting up data to work with files. Similarly, files are important parts of many applications.

KEY DESIGN ISSUES

There is only one key design task that you—the designer and programmer—must accomplish when creating your Best Scores program.

Task: Organize and maintain information between one round of a game and the next.
Logic: Your Best Scores program needs to keep track of the game's best scores over time and not just in one game session. The program must compare these scores to the final score of every new game that is played.
Solution: This is an application for files, specifically, a file holding the list of best scores. Visual Basic supports creating, reading, writing, and updating of external data files. Because the amount of data is small, just a number and a name, this application does not require a database.

PREPARING TO PROGRAM

FILES AND TYPES

Programmers use files to save data between executions of a program. The terms **flat file** or **raw data file** are used to distinguish these general data storage files from files that are organized into databases using one of the commercial database management systems such as Access. Visual Basic provides many ways of handling files; some of these methods provide consistency with older versions of Visual Basic and QBasic.

In this chapter, you will use commands that allow for input to and output from the file in order to append and update the records. These commands allow your Best Scores program to retrieve the score records by record number. This is similar to playing a single song on a CD using its track number.

You have used Visual Basic built-in types in every chapter of this book. Type examples include **Integer**, a type that stores whole numbers, and **String**, a type that holds character data. Visual Basic allows you to construct your own user-defined type. User-defined types allow you to group together parts made up of different data types. The individual components are referenced by name. The user-defined type **bestdata** that you will use for the Best Scores program is defined as follows:

```
Private Type bestdata
   strBname As String * 20
   intBscore As Integer
End Type
```

The user-defined type **bestdata** consists of two components: the first component is a string, **strBname**, fixed at 20 characters, and the second is an integer, **intBscore**. The size of **strBname** is fixed to ensure that the records in the file will each be the same size. It is much easier to manage fixed-size records in a file.

You will insert the type definition for **bestdata** in the **(General)** section, which allows you to create records based on this type, for example:

```
Dim oldbest as bestdata
Dim newbest as bestdata
```

These two statements set up two records of the type **bestdata**. To access each part of the record, your code must use dot notation. Following is an example of the syntax for referencing a **bestdata** variable with dot notation:

```
If newbest.intBscore > oldbest.intBscore Then ...
```

You can interpret this syntax as "if the **intBscore** part of **newbest** is greater than the **intBscore** part of **oldbest**, then carry out the code that follows."

Opening a File

Next, you will learn how to use a file with a Visual Basic program. When you want to make a connection with a file, you use the command Open, which will be described shortly. However, before you invoke this command, you must first calculate the size of the data you are reading from the file. In this case, you will use the variable **intLen** to store the size of a record of user-defined type **bestdata**. Give **intLen** the correct value prior to the Open statement with the following code:

```
intLen = Len(newbest)
```

Len calculates the size of the record, **newbest**, which contains the data that is sent back and forth between the **best.dat** file and Visual Basic.

Prior to reading data into or writing data out of a file, Visual Basic needs to communicate with the operating system to identify the file and to allocate space in RAM (called a **buffer** or **buffer space**) for the data. This step is done using the Open statement, as follows:

```
Open "best.dat" For Random As intBest Len = intLen
```

This statement includes four arguments that are specified by the programmer: **"best.dat"**, **Random**, **intBest**, and **intLen**.

The Open statement establishes Random as the access mode for the file. Other choices for access are Input, Output, Append, and Binary. The Input choice tells that system that the records will be read from the file; while the Output choice indicates that new records will be written to the file. Append indicates that new records will be written at the end of the file as additions to existing data. The Binary access mode is used when programmers want to handle data in individual bytes, not structured into records.

The Random keyword specifies that the Best Scores program can use **best.dat** for both the input and output of data, including appending new records. It also specifies that records can be inserted in the middle—not just at the end—of the **best.dat** file.

> This use of the term "Random" has no connection with the Randomize and Rnd functions.

Visual Basic requires you to assign an integer, called a **file number**, to serve as a numeric reference to the file. You will need to use this file number to refer to the data file (in this project, `best.dat`) in program statements. For this project, your code will use the built-in Visual Basic function FreeFile, which obtains from the operating system the next available file number. Store this file number in the integer variable `intBest`, like this:

```
intBest = FreeFile
```

The variable `intBest` must be set by FreeFile prior to the Open statement.

> If you know that your code only uses one file, you can replace `intBest` with the constant 1 in the Open statement.

The Open statement performs initialization necessary for file input and output by:

- Specifying the file name
- Specifying the access method
- Setting the file number, in this case stored in the variable `intBest`
- Defining the size of the records in this file

Writing Records to a File

Think about what is necessary to specify in the code to write data to a file: the name of the file that you want to use, the location where you'll be adding data, and which specific record will contain such information. The **Put** command specifies the information that Visual Basic needs to access the correct information in the correct file. Following is an example of the Put command:

```
Put #intBest, 3, newbest
```

The first argument—`intBest`—is the file number. The pound or number (#) sign is a required part of the syntax for the command and always precedes the file number. The second argument—3—indicates which record in the file will be written. The third argument—`newbest`—indicates the name of the record that will be written to the file. This Put statement takes the contents of the variable `newbest` and writes it out as the third element of the file opened and assigned the file number stored in `intBest`.

Reading Records from a File

Reading from a file is the opposite of writing to a file. You will still need to specify the name of the file, which file record you will be reading, and where the data read from the file should be stored. The command for reading records from a file is **Get**. Its syntax is similar to that of Put, as shown in the following code:

```
Get #intBest, i, oldbest
```

As in the Put statement, the first argument—`intBest`—is the file number, the second argument—`i`—is the record number to be read in, and the third argument—`oldBest`—is the variable that will store the record read in from the file. In the previous code example, the variable **i** is used for the record number. Use the Get command to assign the contents of the **i**th record, which in your code will be set to a valid value, into the record **oldbest**.

Closing Files

After you finish using a file, you must close the file using the Close command, as follows:

```
Close #intBest
```

This command sends a message to the operating system indicating that your code is done with this file (represented by the **intBest** file number). This releases the Visual Basic resources needed to manage the program's connection to the file. Notice once again that when you refer to a file, the argument is in the form of a file number.

INSERTING A NEW BEST SCORE INTO THE LIST

You will write code that will create a new best score record, determine its position relative to the existing best scores, and insert the new best score while maintaining the correct order of scores. This requires a tricky manipulation of the records, because it is likely the records on file may need to change position. To do this rearranging, you will use two arrays: one for the score portion of the record and one for the name portion of the record. Your code does the insertion by moving down entries in the array following the insertion point to make room for the new score.

To understand how this insertion will work, assume that your code has already determined the point of insertion (the complete code for this is shown in the "Algorithms for Event Procedures and User-Defined Procedures" section). Let's assume that the existing set of best scores consists of 190, 130, 89, 54, and 30. The number 110, held in the variable **today**, will be inserted in the third position, with 89 becoming the new fourth entry and 54, the new fifth entry. The old fifth score is discarded because it is no longer among the best scores. We will now explain how the values are changed for this example.

Figure 4 illustrates the **shuffling**, or motion of the values, in the best score list as the loop cycles.

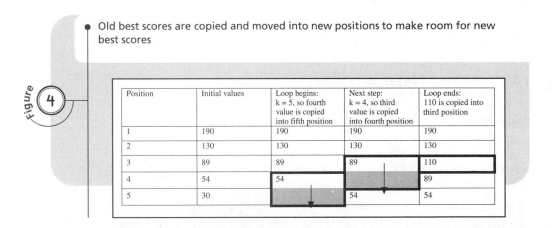

● Old best scores are copied and moved into new positions to make room for new best scores

Figure 4

Position	Initial values	Loop begins: k = 5, so fourth value is copied into fifth position	Next step: k = 4, so third value is copied into fourth position	Loop ends: 110 is copied into third position
1	190	190	190	190
2	130	130	130	130
3	89	89	89	110
4	54	54		89
5	30		54	54

In the example shown in Figure 4, the For...Next loop is executed twice (for **k = 5** and **k = 4**). In the first cycle, the 54 gets copied into the fifth position, and the 30 is overwritten. In the second cycle, the 89 gets written into the fourth position. After the loop ends, the new best score, 110, is then inserted into the third (the **i**th) position.

It is important to realize that the shuffling of scores proceeds backward. For this example, you must move the 54 before the 89 can take its new position. The location of the new best score (in variable **i**) will tell you which old scores you need to move with your code. The code to do this is a For...Next loop with **k** as the loop control variable that goes backwards from

5 and stops at **i + 1**, which is **4** in the example. The reason **k** stops at **i + 1** is that **i** is the insertion point, and you want to move what was in that insertion point position down into the **i + 1** position. Once the value in the **i** position has been copied—freeing up a space for the new best score—this loop has done its job and can end.

The For statement header indicates that the loop control variable **k** begins at **5** and steps backward (the **Step** value is **−1**) until it reaches the value **i + 1**. Each iteration of the For…Next loop copies a score from the **k − 1** position to the **k** position. This has the effect of writing over the fifth score, which is acceptable, because it is no longer among the best

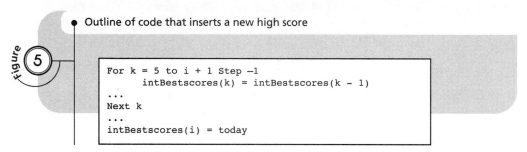

Outline of code that inserts a new high score

figure 5

```
For k = 5 to i + 1 Step −1
        intBestscores(k) = intBestscores(k - 1)
...
Next k
...
intBestscores(i) = today
```

scores. Finally, the loop ends and the new best score can be copied into the appropriate position. Figure 5 shows the code for the loop and the final insertion.

◎ OBTAINING INPUT FROM PLAYER

When the program determines that a score is a best score, you need to find out the player's name. The Visual Basic InputBox command provides the mechanism for displaying a dialog box, with a title and a prompt and even a default value, and then collecting input from the player. For this application, the code would be:

```
strNname = InputBox("Enter your name",_
    "Best Score Input", "anonymous")
```

After the player enters his name and hits enter, the name entered is assigned to the variable **strNname**.

◎ PLAN FOR THE USER INTERFACE

Remember that the focus in this chapter is not on a complete game, but on developing and testing a set of procedures that must be adapted in order to work in a game.

The required procedures include:

• A mechanism to reset the collection of saved best scores. The Click event procedure for a command button will be used to erase any stored scores.

• A mechanism to display the current best scores. Your Best Scores program will use the Click event procedure for another command button to display the best scores.

• A mechanism to compare the score achieved in the most recent round of the game with the collection of best scores. One way of implementing this is as a procedure with a single parameter, the latest score. The parameter you will use in this chapter is named **today**.

TESTING YOUR PROCEDURES

After you have written these procedures, you will need to test them. Since you are writing procedures that ultimately will be added to other projects, you will need a stand-in for those games to test your code. This is where the driver program comes in. A driver, sometimes called a **stem program**, is meant for testing part of a larger program. Once your driver program verifies that a particular section of code is working as expected, that code is placed in the larger project and the driver program is discarded.

To create a useful driver program, you must determine how to anticipate and replicate all possible scenarios for your Best Scores program.

Although major system development efforts often use a whole team of people developing the test suite of possibilities, the scope of this project is small enough that you can easily handle the testing of it on your own. To test Best Scores, you must construct the driver program and then plan and perform the testing. Your driver program should include a form that has a text box for entering a score and a command button to call the comparison procedure, as shown in Figure 1. The program will compare the old best scores to the value of the contents of the text box, which is the new score. You will insert code into the game program that makes a call to the **comparetobest** procedure at the point that the game calculates a score.

FORM DESIGN

This section describes all of the objects contained in the final design for your Best Scores driver program, as shown in Figure 6. Follow this plan to place all the objects needed on your form. The object names listed below are suggestions; you may rename them if desired (if you do, be sure to revise your code accordingly). Set captions for command buttons as suggested. Placement of objects are suggestions—you may lay out your form differently, if you wish.

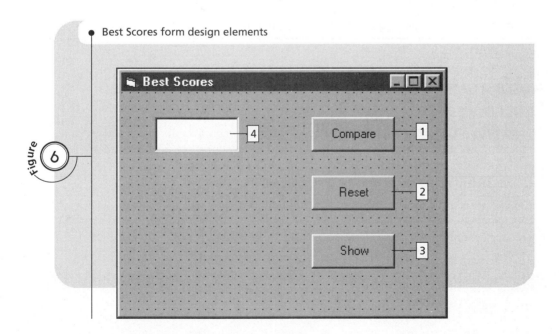

Best Scores form design elements

Figure 6

Command buttons

1. **cmdCompare**: Used to evaluate the current score and determine whether it is a best score

2. **cmdReset**: Clears the record of best scores

3. **cmdShowBest**: Shows the current list of best scores

Text box

4. **txtScore**: The location where the tester enters scores for evaluation (this feature is not included in a real game—it is one of the "throwaway" code elements that is used only in the testing or demonstration of the project)

VARIABLES AND CONSTANTS DECLARED IN THE (General) SECTION

The **(General)** section includes the Type definition, as shown in Figure 7.

● Code for the Type definition

Figure **7**

```
PrivateType bestdata
    strBname As String * 20
    intBscore As Integer
End Type
```

The other variables in the **(General)** section are:

Element	Explanation
`Option Explicit`	Set this option, which requires declaration of all variables
`Dim intBest As Integer`	Used in file statements to refer to the file
`Dim intLen As Integer`	Holds length of the record of type **bestdata**

ALGORITHMS FOR EVENT PROCEDURES AND USER-DEFINED PROCEDURES

The **cmdReset_Click** and **cmdShowBest_Click** event procedures will use variables belonging to the **bestdata** data type. Both of these procedures use the **best.dat** file.

THE cmdReset_Click EVENT PROCEDURE

This Click event procedure carries out the action of resetting the file to its initial values, removing all the scores and player information. This Click event procedure requires the following local variable:

Element	Explanation
`Dim best1data1 As bestdata`	Used to hold a record from the file
`Dim i As Integer`	Used to control a For...Next loop

This procedure determines the length of the records for the file, uses the Visual Basic function FreeFile to obtain the next available file number, then opens the **best.dat** file using the Open command. This code also uses App.Path to specify the folder for this file. The code to perform these tasks is:

```
intLen = Len(bestdata1)
intBest = FreeFile
Open App.Path & "\" & "best.dat" For_
   Random As intBest Len = intLen
```

Next, your code must write dummy records to **best.dat** using the Put command. A For...Next loop, controlled by the loop variable **i**, sets the two components (name and score) of the record. The choice of the phrase "No one" to represent player names for the initial (dummy) scores is arbitrary; you could also leave these labels blank using an empty string, or you could use another phrase such as "No score," "Initial score," and so on. Since zero is an appropriate initial value for these dummy scores, your code should use 0 as the initial starting score value. Your code must ensure that valid scores are better than these initial values. The code to reset the file by writing five dummy records to the file is shown in Figure 8.

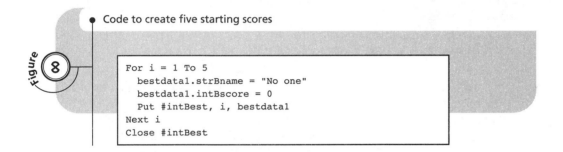

● Code to create five starting scores

Figure 8

```
For i = 1 To 5
  bestdata1.strBname = "No one"
  bestdata1.intBscore = 0
  Put #intBest, i, bestdata1
Next i
Close #intBest
```

THE cmdShowBest_Click EVENT PROCEDURE

The player clicks the Show button to display the current list of best scores, which is constructed from the records stored in the file. This event procedure must read in all the records from the data source file, then display them.

The **cmdShowBest_Click** event procedure uses the following variables:

Element	Explanation
`Dim bestdata1 As bestdata`	Placeholder for a record in the file
`Dim strMessages As String`	Used to hold list of best scores
`Dim i As Integer`	Used to control a For...Next loop

The **cmdShowBest_Click** event procedure begins by opening the file, as follows:

```
intLen = Len(bestdata1)
intBest = FreeFile
Open App.Path & "\" & "best.dat" For_
   Random As intBest Len = intLen
```

Use a message box to display the best scores. Your code should call the command **MsgBox** with an argument, the variable **strMessages**. Your code loads **strMessages** with the score information from the file. Start constructing the best scores message with the following code:

```
strMessages = "Best Scores" & Chr(13)
```

Chr(13) is the ASCII code for a carriage return. The text that follows Chr(13) appears on a new line.

Use a For...Next loop to add the name and score information to **strMessages**, as shown in Figure 9.

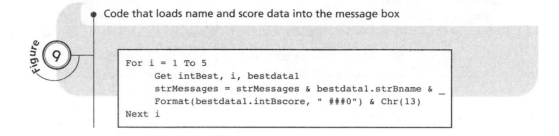

Code that loads name and score data into the message box

Figure 9

```
For i = 1 To 5
    Get intBest, i, bestdata1
    strMessages = strMessages & bestdata1.strBname & _
    Format(bestdata1.intBscore, " ###0") & Chr(13)
Next i
```

Finally, the procedure should display the message and close the file, as follows:

```
MsgBox strMessages, "Best Scores"
Close #intBest
```

THE cmdCompare_Click EVENT PROCEDURE

This procedure simulates a whole game. The code converts the value that the user enters into the text box into a number, then calls a user-defined procedure, **comparetobest**. If you are implementing a best scores feature into a real game, you would not include the **cmdCompare** button and its Click event procedure; however, a real game implementation would require the **comparetobest** procedure. Insert the following code into the **cmdCompare_Click** procedure:

```
Call comparetobest(Val(txtScore.Text))
```

THE comparetobest (today As Integer) USER-DEFINED PROCEDURE

This user-defined procedure has one parameter:

Element	Explanation
today As Integer	Contains the new game score achieved by the player, to be compared with previous high scores

This user-defined procedure requires the following local variables:

Element	Explanation
Dim strMessages As String	Used to display best scores
Dim strNname As String * 20	Used to hold names
Dim strBestplayers(1 To 5) As String	An array that holds the five names that are part of the best scores list

Element	Explanation
`Dim intBestscores(1 To 5) As Integer`	An array that holds the five scores that are part of the best scores list
`Dim bestdata1 As bestdata`	Each record from the data file is read into this variable
`Dim i As Integer`	Variable for indexing
`Dim k As Integer`	Variable for indexing

The procedure for comparing a new score with the set of best scores is the most complex part of the code. The first part of the procedure, shown in Figure 10, reads the data from the file into two parallel arrays: one holds the scores and one holds the names of the players who made those scores.

Figure 10

Code that reads data from the data file

```
intLen = Len(bestdata1)
intBest = FreeFile
Open App.Path & "\" & "best.dat" For Random As intBest Len = intLen
For i = 1 To 5
  Get intBest, i, bestdata1
  strBestplayers(i) = bestdata1.strBname
  intBestscores(i) = bestdata1.intBscore
Next i
```

The **comparetobest** code continues with the task of determining whether the new score, held in the variable **today**, needs to be inserted into the set of best scores. This situation calls for a For...Next loop, as follows:

```
For i = 1 To 5
  If today >= intBestscores(i) Then Exit For
Next i
```

The Exit For statement means that this loop ends early only if the new value is a high score that should be inserted into the best scores list, which then means that the value of **i** is the position *after* the new insertion. If the For...Next loop does not end early, the value of **i** is greater than 5. To determine which situation it is, use an If statement (without an Else clause) to determine whether **i** is less than or equal to five.

If an insertion is to be made, the first step is to obtain the player's name, which is done using the **InputBox** function, as follows:

```
strNname = InputBox("Enter your name", "Best_
    Scores Input", "anonymous")
```

Next, you must write code to perform the insertion of the new name and score into the list of best scores. The code differs somewhat from the insertion logic presented in "Preparing to Program," because you need to manipulate two arrays. Your code will only use the array of scores to determine the insertion point, but both arrays—the scores and the associated names—need to be modified to make the insertion. Use a For...Next loop that starts with **k** and iterates by **−1** to just before the insertion point, moving the scores below the insertion point down to make room for the new record. The code that processes the insertion of a new score and value into the best scores list is shown in Figure 11.

Figure 11

Code to move down the existing best scores

```
For k = 5 To i + 1 Step -1
    strBestplayers(k) = strBestplayers(k - 1)
    intBestscores(k) = intBestscores(k - 1)
Next k
```

The code makes the insertion as follows:

```
strBestplayers(i) = strNname
intBestscores(i) = today
```

The last step is to display the new best scores. Your code should construct a string, with line breaks (Chr(13)), that holds a title ("New Best Scores") and all the best scores. The code to create the title is as follows:

```
strMessages = "New Best Scores " & Chr(13)
```

To display the scores, use a For...Next loop iterating from 1 to 5. Your code will do two things at each iteration:

1. Add the data from a best scores record to a string (**strMessages**) that displays the best scores

2. Construct and then write a record to the file using the code shown in Figure 12

Figure 12

Code that writes a new record to the best.dat file

```
For k = 1 to 5
    strMessages = strMessages & strBestplayers(k) & _
        Format(intBestscores(k), " ###0") & Chr(13)
    Bestdata1.strBname = strBestplayers(k)
    Bestdata1.intBscore = intBestscores(k)
    Put #intBest, k, bestdata1
Next k
```

Finally, use the following code to display all the scores:

```
MsgBox strMessages
```

TESTING BEST SCORES

To test the program, you should first click the Reset button to set up a file with five dummy entries. You should also (in a subsequent test) start the program without doing this. In this case, the program creates a file with no records.

Test the logic of the program's compare operation by entering test scores into the text box. First fill up the **best.dat** file: the first five scores that you enter will be the highest scores. When you do your testing, be sure to test more than five scores. Although the file will only save five records, you must test your program with more than five records to confirm that the program logic is handling the insertion correctly. Also be sure to enter a number larger than the current highest score as well as one that is larger than the lowest score. End the program by using the End button on the toolbar or the Close button ☒ on the form window. Restart the program and see if your score updates were saved. Enter some additional scores. End the

THE BEST SCORES FEATURE

program again and exit Visual Basic completely. You should also shut down your computer. Then restart your computer, launch Visual Basic, and run Best Scores to see if the set of best scores remains.

HOW TO ADD A BEST SCORES FEATURE TO A GAME

To add a best scores feature to a real game, do the following:

1. In the game program, add the **cmdReset** button to the game form to reset the list of scores. Add the **cmdShowBest** button to the game form to display the list of scores. Copy and paste the event procedures for the Click events for these two command buttons into the game program.

2. Copy and paste the **comparetobest** procedure into the code of your game. If your game rates lower scores better than higher scores (as in Minesweeper), you will need to change the expression

   ```
   If today >= intBestscores(i) Then Exit For
   ```
   to
   ```
   If today <= intBestscores(i) Then Exit For
   ```

   You will also need to change the initial value (now 0) in **cmdReset_Click** to an appropriate value.

3. In your game code, find the code that calculates the final score for a player. At this point, insert a call to **comparetobest** using the variable holding the score as the argument.

   You do not need the text box (**txtScore**), the **cmdCompare** button, or its Click event procedure to add a best scores feature to a game. This is the previously mentioned throwaway code that is only required for the demonstration of the best scores feature.

OPTIONAL ENHANCEMENTS

There are many ways you can customize your Best Scores program. Following are some suggestions to get you started on adding original features and functionality.

1. Improve the formatting of the best scores display. Use Visual Basic Help to learn how the Format function can be used with character strings.
2. The size of the best scores set is fixed at five records in this program. Change the code by using a named constant and give that constant a value other than 5: try 3 and 6.
3. Change the format of the records to include the date on which the score was achieved. You will need to use the Date function to obtain the current date from the operating system and change the definition of the **bestdata** type. You will also need to manipulate three arrays to handle the insertion.
4. Add a score-keeping feature to one of the games described so far in the text, if it does not have one (Chance or Cannonball are good choices), then add a best scores feature. You will need to determine where in the game program to add the call to the **comparetobest** procedure.
5. Change the code in Best Scores to handle the case of low scores being better than high scores. Then change the code in the **comparetobest** routine to include one more parameter, set to 1 or -1, indicating the direction for comparison.
6. Change the code in Best Scores to handle scores that contain decimals. Change the code so that the scores represent dollars and cents or some other currency (as in the Quiz game).

1. The project as described here works if the user clicks the Show button or the Compare button before any scores have been entered; when clicked, these buttons create a new, empty file. If the Reset button is clicked, the program creates a file with the player name "No one" and the score "0" repeated for five entries. Is this action appropriate for an actual game? If not, what approach should you take?

2. The project described here handles a best score tie by inserting it above the best scores with the same value. Is this action appropriate for an actual game? How else might Best Scores handle a tie?

3. Once you have created a user-defined type, you may use it just as you do the built-in types. You may define an array of records and perform the insertions with this array. What are the advantages and disadvantages of this approach?

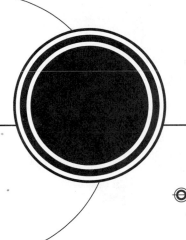

INDEX

INDEX